THE
BOSSES

THE
BOSSES

THE GROWTH INDUSTRIES
OF THE FUTURE
AND THE MEN WHO
LEAD THEM

WILLIAM KAY

PIATKUS

First published in 1994 by
Judy Piatkus (Publishers) Ltd of
5 Windmill Street, London W1P 1HF

**The moral right of the author
has been asserted**

*A catalogue record for this book is
available from the British Library*

ISBN 0-7499-1358-4

Designed by Paul Saunders

Set in Linotron Times by
Computerset, Harmondsworth, Middlesex
Printed and bound in Great Britain by
Bookcraft Ltd, Midsomer Norton, Avon

To Lynne, without whose patience and forbearance this book would have been infinitely the poorer.

ACKNOWLEDGEMENTS

My main thanks must go to the businessmen who gave so generously of their time in providing the material for this book through my interviews with them – in some cases two or even three times – and in helping me to ensure that the errors were minimised.

I am also indebted to Gill Cormode and Judy Piatkus of Piatkus Books, who talked me through the several forms this book took before it finally emerged, and to my agent, John Pawsey, who kept me on the straight and narrow.

However, for all their efforts, all errors and omissions are my own.

CONTENTS

Introduction

THE RECESSION of the early 1990s etched a deep scar into Britain's business landscape. Big names toppled, from Robert Maxwell to Sir Ralph Halpern. The effect was very like living through a war. No bombs fell, but factories and offices closed, companies and individuals disappeared, just as surely as if they had been flattened by enemy air raids. People who seemed permanent fixtures suddenly retired, fled abroad or, in Maxwell's case, dramatically died. This created a 'here today – gone tomorrow' atmosphere that had strangely debilitating effects on business life. Horizons were shortened, because it had become futile to look very far ahead. The emphasis in business moved away from relationships to concentrate on the transaction, with all the impact on morale and business morality that such an attitude implies.

But many business leaders have for some time been looking beyond the recession. They have already put their anti-recession survival drills into practice, cut costs, chased debtors and organised as much protection as possible against the commercial blizzard. That has enabled them, cautiously but with growing confidence, to scan the horizon for the sort of opportunities that are going to become available in the later 1990s and into the new century.

This vital period of reassessment could not come at a better time. For it coincides with a period when a fresh generation of managers is taking control of British industry. They have grown up in the environment of the welfare state, nationalisation, the rise and fall of union power, privatisation and the Thatcher years. They tend to be from grammar schools, rather than public schools or comprehensives. Their style is laid-back but focused, easygoing most of the time but ruthless when they have to be. A few days after Greg Hutchings of Tomkins bid for RHM in October 1992, he was photographed playing his regular game of hockey. Greg Dyke and Michael Grade are fond of five-a-side football. Jim Slater or Sir Jimmy Goldsmith, Hutchings and Dyke's counterparts in the 1960s and 1970s, would have been more likely to be found at the chess or backgammon board. The generation before that would probably have taken to the grouse moors. Yet the new breed is probably quicker than any of their predecessors to sack surplus labour. Tony Greener of Guinness summed it up when he told me:

> 'The one thing that is going to be less stable in the 1990s is the market and the environment in which we're living, so businesses which themselves are in a state of chaos through change are going to be much less able to cope than the ones that are finely-tuned, well-adjusted and focused on the market place.'

At the same time, the contrast between industry and the financial sector is becoming starker. The City of London's banks and securities houses know how to use the new breed of meritocrats to make money for themselves, without ever entirely accepting them. They embraced Margaret Thatcher and John Major in the same spirit. But the old boy public school network still prevails, and so do its conservative attitudes. In some respects, this exclusiveness has left the City twenty years behind industry. The recession was traumatic. Financiers were subjected to the most remarkable strains. New ideas were turned away because the odds were that they would merely add to the problems, certainly in the short run. Loan officers were torn between pulling the plug on corporate clients in order to salvage what money could be raised from a fire sale, and sweating it out with them in the hope that the corner would be reached, turned, and the road to solvency open out before them. But, now that recovery is under way, even in the City the scene is changing. Newcomers to the top table like Derek Wanless of National Westminster Bank, Peter Ellwood of TSB Group and, despite his Etonian pedigree, Martin Taylor at Barclays – may be closing the gap. One reported: 'When a lot of senior executives returned from their holidays in September 1992, they were horrified by what they saw happening to sales and costs. If the pound had not been devalued and interest rates begun to come down, a large proportion of companies quoted on the London stock market would have gone bust.' As it was, many industrial managers fended off their creditors by redoing their sums and announcing another wave of redundancies.

Such experiences have marked the likely survivors of the recession in the same way that previous lows in the business cycle have. They are imbued with qualities – caution, an emphasis on cash, a refusal to take too much for granted – that will come to be scorned by the next generation. But they are also toughened by an education that no money could buy.

The central question for potential investors, employees, suppliers and even customers is to spot those managers who can combine survival drills with the flair necessary to produce blueprints that will take their companies out of recession and on to a new growth track. It is significant that for a long period it was fashionable to talk of the 'no-growth nineties', as if the rest of the decade is going to be characterised by gloom. That view rests on the assumption that consumers are going to spend a sizeable chunk of their adult lives rejecting the chance to better themselves through spending, even in a more discriminating way than in the now-derided 1980s. It also assumes that young people growing up into adulthood in the 1990s are obediently going to ape their elders in reining back their own spending. I find neither of these beliefs convincing.

Although the recession was prolonged by a communal desire to cut debt and build savings, inspired as much as anything by fear of unemployment, the fact is that people do want to better themselves and the most tangible way of doing that is to spend. What is characterising the early years of regeneration is a perfectly logical and understandable wish to obtain value for money. As Peter Jarvis of Whitbread admitted to me, people in Britain have for the first time this century got used to the idea of haggling over anything from a restaurant meal upwards. We are more aware of how business works, including the invaluable realisation that prices are not fixed by some unreachable deity, but by other human beings – often the person on the other side of the counter. Two, it follows, can play at that game. From this has flowed a more questioning attitude by consumers, a determination not to be ripped off, and a near-obsession with getting the best value. Liam Strong of Sears points out that this may not mean trading down. Despite the recession, standards of living are high enough for consumers still to aspire to the best. The difference is that they are not going to pay through the nose for the privilege. They will, of course, once memories fade. But for several years to come this generation is going to count its pennies.

That is no easy matter for the businesses which seek to satisfy such discriminating demand, and the companies which supply those businesses, and so on back down the industrial chain. Past recessions have shown that most bankruptcies and liquidations occur during the recovery phase, when it is so easy to make a wrong bet about the size and direction of demand. It is also a period when lenders are at their most nervous, patience is liable to wear thin and there are still no prizes for sticking your neck out. No one has an infallible answer to these problems, which are based on people's fragile ability to predict after several years in which the most doughty forecaster has suffered setbacks. Such difficulties are going to require an extra layer of skills on top of survival before flair can blossom. They represent a set of hurdles which will be one test too many for some managerial reputations.

But a few businessmen are ideally placed to take advantage of the lessons from the recession. They have been talented enough to reach high rank before or during the downturn, yet they are young enough to be able to apply those lessons to corporate strategies that are likely to endure into the first decade of the next century. Many of those who are older will be content to slot a suitable successor into place before making what they hope will be a graceful exit. Younger entrepreneurs may be quicker to spot new opportunities, but their innocence makes it likely that many will either falter or fall prey to a takeover by the recession-beaters. But those who have survived the worst the economic misery of the past few years can throw at them have a perspective which should give them a special strength. They can empathise with the desire for value, and lead their employees with conviction. Understanding the customer is going to become the single most important quality for successful business people in the 1990s. Those who fondly think they are insulated because they supply only other professionals, other companies, are in for a rude jolt. For the value-for-money mood is quickly being passed down the line from the high street or out-of-town mall. Relationships are being reassessed and reputations reviewed against the new criteria.

These trends make the companies featured in this book a good starting point for building an investment portfolio, as well as a guide to the people who are probably going to be shaping our lives for the rest of the 1990s and beyond. Some will become giants. Others, having got this far, will still be unlucky enough to step on a business landmine and self-destruct. Greg Dyke has not quite done that, but in March 1994 his company, LWT (Holdings), was taken over by Granada Group whose chief executive is another subject of this book, Gerry Robinson. But they all have proven ability. So it is illuminating to learn how they see business in general, and their industries in particular, developing in the years that lie ahead. Some have a vision beyond their present predicaments towards great transformations. Others are mired in today's troubles. But that in itself is no litmus test. Much depends on how accurately they assess their company's position and prospects. Are the pessimists merely being realistic? Are the optimists simply making a valid logical deduction from the facts as they see them? Only time will tell, but the insights they offer here should give clues to their likely form.

THE
BOSSES

CHAPTER 1

SIR BRYAN CARSBERG

Director General of the Office of Fair Trading

SIR BRYAN CARSBERG is the emollient crusader. While the companies he regulates rail against him from time to time, he is all smoothness and sweet reasonableness. 'I do see competition as a very important weapon,' he admits, sitting donnishly in his spartan office, as if conducting a tutorial. 'Making markets work effectively is far and away the best thing that I can do for customers.' That is why Sir Bryan Carsberg is one of the most influential people in British business today: his moral values set the tone for the strategies of many of the businessmen featured in this book. Of course, 'making markets work effectively' implies that they were ineffective before, and that one or more companies in an industry were either keeping others out or twisting consumers' arms up their backs. It almost never means that there are too many suppliers tearing one another to bits, because that usually sorts itself out via the law of the jungle.

So Sir Bryan, the diminutive son of an accountant who himself became professor of accounting at the London School of Economics without taking a degree course, is avowedly on the side of the small man against the big battalions. He insists that he is not anti-business, claiming that as a result of his eight years as director general of the Office of Telecommunications – Oftel – the cold blast of competition has made British Telecom a world-class player. BT does not see his time at Oftel in quite the same rosy light. Sir Iain Vallance, the chairman, says: 'Oftel has shown little grasp of the kind of telecommunications environment it believes it will bring to pass, and has abandoned its earlier correct stance that the regulator is a surrogate for competition, not a manager of the industry.'

Nevertheless, Sir Bryan steadily chipped away at BT's UK telephone

monopoly, giving Mercury the room to establish itself as a viable competitor. 'I still go hot and cold when I think that I almost didn't take that job,' he recalls, 'because at first the government didn't offer a high enough salary. In 1984, you have to remember, this was a very controversial matter. People said the privatisation of BT wouldn't get through the House of Commons, and if it did it would be thrown out in the Lords anyway. Even if it got through, it was an undoable job, introducing competition to an industry like telecommunications. Now everyone thinks that it's a splendid idea, and all round the world countries are following suit.'

Sir Bryan was born on January 3, 1939. He quit Berkhamsted School, Hertfordshire at 16 and qualified as a chartered accountant. 'I left school because I was debarred from taking mathematics in the sixth form,' he relates with a lingering bitterness. Instead he won the top accountancy prize in his year. He inherited his father's practice, but it was not a broad enough canvas for him. So he wrote to a contact he had met at the accountants' prize-giving, to ask about the chances of a university teaching post – which some would say was slightly cheeky, given that he had no degree. 'The fact that I had done well in my own exams encouraged that kind of thought,' he argues.

Carsberg was sent to Professor Harold Edey at LSE, which prides itself on embracing unorthodox but talented people. The pair found a mutual interest in astronomy and Edey offered the young man a lectureship. One appointment followed another. Carsberg went to America in 1968 as a visiting lecturer at Chicago University's Graduate School of Business. While there, the University of Manchester appointed him to its chair of accounting. Nine years later he was invited back to America by their Financial Accounting Standards Board, which writes the rules for US accounting.

'The FASB had to come up with something on inflation accounting, or the Securities and Exchange Commission was going to take it out of their hands,' Sir Bryan explains. 'But people couldn't agree, and gradually I got more and more involved. To cut a long story short, I ended up heading the team and taking the project over. We met our targets and got off the SEC hook, and I stayed with them until the summer of 1981.'

He had returned to America thinking that he might not come back. Britain's economy in the early 1980s went through a mild version of the recession which hit it a decade later. Given Carsberg's preference for competition and free markets, he thought that America might be more congenial than the UK. But, sure enough, along came another job offer to disturb his plans. He was invited to be the first Arthur Andersen professor of

Sir Bryan Victor Carsberg

BORN: 3 January, 1939

EDUCATED: Berkhamsted School, London School of Economics and Political Science

MARRIED: Margaret Graham, 1960. Two daughters

CAREER:

1960 Chartered Accountant

1962 Began sole practice as an accountant

1964 Lecturer in Accounting, LSE

1968 Visiting lecturer, Graduate School of Business, Chicago University

1969 Professor of Accounting, Manchester University

1981 Arthur Andersen Professor of Accounting, LSE

1981 Director of Resources, Institute of Chartered Accountants

1984 Director General of Telecommunications

1992 Director General of Fair Trading

OTHER INTERESTS: Member of the Accounting Standards Board

OFFICE OF FAIR TRADING

HEAD OFFICE: Field House, Bream's Buildings, London EC4A 1PR
Tel: 071-242 2858

ACTIVITIES: The OFT is a non-ministerial government department. Its aim is to protect the consumer by encouraging competition amongst businesses, and by making sure that trading practices are as fair as possible.

accounting, a new chair at the LSE. 'By that time the Thatcher administration had come in and things had begun to turn around here,' he points out. 'I was also asked to become the first director of research at the Institute of Chartered Accountants on a part-time basis, so they really offered me a package deal to do both jobs. It was the opportunity to do that that was very special and made me feel that coming back to the UK was the right thing to do at that stage.'

Sir Bryan first came into direct contact with the privatisation crusade in 1982, when the then Department of Industry asked him to join a three-person panel to advise the secretary of state on the liberalisation of telecommunications, with a consumer and a telecoms technologist. The panel advised on some of the early issues, refereeing the beauty contest for who should have the first private sector license for mobile telephones, which went to Racal Vodaphone. That whetted Carsberg's interest in telecommunications, so when the government decided to privatise British Telecom and set up Oftel they asked him to put his name in the ring for the position of director-general. The first he knew that he was a serious candidate was when his wife spotted a *Times* story headlined 'Don tipped as phones watchdog'. After some polite haggling over the pay, Sir Bryan accepted. He has no doubt that he did the right thing.

'In a sense,' he says, 'it was a leap but I believed it could work, and that was the key thing. This was very much the politics that are the right politics. In principle, they could have been better, but some of those privatisations and, more importantly, the introduction of competition, are among the most important economic changes in the UK that have been made in our lifetime. From that point of view, looking back, it went reasonably well. It takes a long time to see the benefits and it won't be for another five or ten years that we will see the full extent of what has been achieved, but I think the contrast with what we had before will be enormous. From that point of view it was a very special thing to be the first regulator of that industry.'

There was a touch of cat-and-mouse about the early relationship between Carsberg and BT. Things didn't go all that well with the quality of the telephone service in the first three years. BT unsportingly decided to stop publishing quality of service indicators when it was privatised, on the dubious grounds that other private companies did not publish such indicators. There was no regulation available that Carsberg could use immediately to force the group to change its policy back, so Carsberg waited. Toward the end of 1986 he brought matters to a head by threatening to go to the Monopolies and Mergers Commission. BT reluctantly agreed, but just in case there was another change of heart, Carsberg issued a press statement to say that the company had agreed – and that he had BT's agreement to say so. Then in 1987 there was a telecom engineers' strike and BT was running late with modernising the network and introducing new exchanges. 'The old exchanges were past their sell-by date,' says Sir Bryan, 'and were starting to perform rather badly so, for that reason alone, service was deteriorating. Complaints were starting to well up. We were getting some very bad cases where BT had given estimated dates for installing new exchange lines for businesses which planned on the basis of that, then the line wasn't there on the date or a month or two months later. BT was regularly missing its installation dates that year: one company ordered many, many lines over the course of the year and BT hadn't met its target date on one of them. One had the impression that these weren't taken very seriously. And there were problems with fault repair. Some people had to wait weeks to have their telephone put back into working order.'

None of this encouraged BT to resume publication of statistics, so in the middle of 1987 Carsberg published his own, based on information which BT had to give him under the terms of its licence. That miraculously broke the log jam and BT resumed publication. But by then the service problems were getting more serious, so Carsberg turned up the heat by pressing BT to introduce compensation for customers.

'I really wanted to get this delay in repairing faults down and the date for installing new services more reliable,' he recalls. 'I remember in one of my speeches, I got a very strong reaction from the audience by saying that it doesn't matter waiting a bit for your telephone line so long as you can rely on the date you're given. That was clearly what they thought too. I then worked on the idea that BT must give a guarantee in quotation marks of installation dates and fault repair times and came up with the suggestion that it should give a firm date for new installations with a two-day period of grace for installations and repairing faults. If they didn't do the job within that two-day period, then BT would pay compensation to its customers. Five pounds a day was what I asked for as a minimum, and larger sums if a customer could demonstrate financial loss. That was a very radical development. As far as I'm aware, no telephone company did this then, or to my knowledge, does so today and it had always been a kind of linchpin of BT's position that it could not guarantee things of that kind. But I insisted and, when it came to it, BT didn't resist the principle all that strongly.' The figures show a huge improvement in performance after compensation became payable in 1989, and it became symbolic of a change in the public image of BT – and, of course, in the relationship between the telecoms giant and Oftel, in the shape of Sir Bryan. The key was to create conditions by which it was in the interests of the privatised business to do what the regulator wanted. That set the tone for the other regulators, who by 1989 also covered gas and were being extended to water and electricity.

The calm and effective way in which Sir Bryan made the most of the legal framework at his disposal to lay down the basis of regulation helped to earn him the much wider role of director-general of the Office of Fair Trading, which oversees trading questions and has the power to refer problems to the Monopolies and Mergers Commission and the secretary of state for trade and industry. He moved to the OFT after the retirement of the first DG, Sir Gordon Borrie, setting the precedent that the privatised industry regulators should be at least nominally on the short list for the post whenever it falls vacant.

'I thought of my move here from Oftel as much more of a case of continuity and extension rather than a turning point,' Sir Bryan explains. 'I think, to some extent, the government saw the merits of having a system where a career of regulation started to develop. In that context, it was natural that one should move on from a regulator like Oftel and go to a rather more general regulatory kind of job such as I have here. The policies and the issues are very much the same – a mixture of helping customers to get value for money by making markets and competitions work better, and combining them with more direct kinds of regulation in cases where the market has defects. In Oftel, the kind of thing I was talking about was the quality of service, regulation and pricing control, and handling complaints from customers. Here the biggest example is consumer credit regulations.'

But although Sir Bryan's scope is wider, the rules of the game are considerably more complex. Instead of dealing with one industry by reference to a licence, the OFT is part of a chain of decision-making, with interlocking checks and balances. If a big industrial merger is on the cards, Sir Bryan is likely to be advising the secretary of state on whether or not a reference to the MMC is required. If so, the MMC will then investigate and publish a report, at which point Sir Bryan comes back into play, advising the secretary of state what to do about its recommendations – at least if they point to a veto.

Sir Bryan adds: 'In the case of monopolies situations or restrictive practices, which are sometimes mixed up together, I generally initiate the regulator action but the MMC has a crucial role and you can't take the matter very far without its support, or the restrictive practices court in the case of restrictive practices. Again it finishes up on the secretary of state's desk if the MMC thinks something should be done, and again I advise at that point. One is constantly interacting with the secretary of state and the MMC, sometimes other bodies. One wasn't so conscious of doing that at Oftel, where technological change was a so much bigger factor. I do try and, I hope, succeed in taking an interest in similar technological points here at the OFT, and I think it's a very important dimension of competition policy to think of the potential for innovation. It was a particularly marked feature in telecom because it was going through such a rapid period of change.'

The trickier area in fair trading policy lies in deciding how far to tame the animals in the business jungle. Let them roam too wild, and consumers are liable to be savaged. Knock the stuffing out of them completely, and industries will cease to innovate and may even atrophy. Apart from merger policy, which always contains a strong whiff of politics, Sir Bryan is principally concerned with fair distribution of goods and services, exploitation of the monopoly power of copyright and companies' failure to come clean about what their products can and cannot do.

'The sort of objectives one can sign up to unhesitatingly,' he says, 'are the obvious kind of things of improving value for money for customers. I find as time goes on that I am frequently attracted by cases where there are stickinesses in the market. At present, there seems to be some friction and it seems to me that you find this in no end of places — certainly in the UK, and probably in other countries. You almost get to the point where you wonder if there are any markets that are free from some kind of impediment or another. Of course, there are and one tends to see some of the worst cases. It's understandable, because people who are actually there have an interest in making it difficult for other people to get in. The first reference I made to the MMC was about newspaper distribution and that was a "refusal to supply" case. My concern was that that kind of thing inhibits innovation and retailing practice. One can think of all sorts of ways in which the retailing of information could be restricted. They are strong cases for investigation, and one could say that I have the objective of freeing markets from restraints.'

In 1993 he picked up on the way in which life insurance companies ration the information they let would-be customers see, especially the commission paid to sales people. 'We have the opportunity to make a step change in the quality of information made available to consumers in the marketing and sale of life insurance products,' he says.

While that particular fight promises to be a long and arduous one, Sir Bryan has shown that much of the stickiness which markets spontaneously produce can be melted simply by asking 'Why not?' It is a question that captains of industry are becoming accustomed to having to answer, and sets a standard for the regulation of the privatised industries.

CHAPTER **2**

JOHN CLARE

of Dixons Group

JOHN CLARE has what should be one of the most enviable jobs in British retailing. He presides over a constant stream of new gadgets that his mentor, Stanley Kalms, has memorably described as 'toys for adults' – watches, cameras, camcorders, VCRs, PCs, phones of every stripe from mobile to Mickey Mouse, and TVs small enough to strap on your wrist or big enough to rival the local cinema screen. But while this mad inventor's torrent shows no sign of abating, Dixons faces problems of success from customer complaints to ram raiding. And while it has nailed its colours to the home computer market with its PC World chain, its Currys offshoot has been caught by the freeze in the housing market.

All this adds up to a daunting challenge for Clare, a former Mars Bar salesman from Great Yarmouth. He worked an early aptitude for arithmetic into a degree in applied mathematics, oceanography and fluid dynamics at Edinburgh University. Clare joined Mars because they offered him £50 a year more than other would-be employers, and the US group sent him off round the country with a Hillman Estate car filled with stock to sell for cash.

'I would always recommend starting in sales,' he says. 'That's where the business is won or lost. The sharp end.'

Before long he was running a team of ten salesmen in Glasgow. Then one day he got a call telling him to be in Switzerland by Friday. That marked the start of a hectic round of continental postings, somewhere in the midst of which he married a Scots lass he had met at university. He left Mars in 1982 after eleven years, wearied by the travelling. 'I had a young family and didn't want to have a career with every other year in another country,'

John Charles Clare

BORN:	2 August, 1950
EDUCATED:	Great Yarmouth Grammar School, Edinburgh University
MARRIED:	Anne Ross, 1974. Two sons

CAREER:

1972	Sales and marketing, Mars
1982	Group Business Development Director and Marketing Director of the Racing Division, Ladbroke Group
1985	Marketing Director, Dixons Group
1988	Managing Director, Dixons Stores
1992	Managing Director, Dixons Group
1994	Chief executive, Dixons Group

DIXONS GROUP

HEAD OFFICE:	29 Farm Street, London W1X 7RD Tel: 071-499 3494
ACTIVITIES:	Electrical retailing
MAIN BRANDS:	Dixons, Currys, PC World

Clare recalls. 'It's a very attractive lifestyle for some people, but the top people at Mars had no family.'

He went to Ladbroke Group, which at that stage was entirely in the UK – though not for long. 'I got caught up in Ladbroke's submission on cable TV,' says Clare. 'We put the submission in for Ealing and got it. Then the guy who had been offered the marketing job in racing left and I was asked to do that as well. It was a very enjoyable time. We bought our first race-track in the States and went into retail betting in Belgium and Holland. I was trying to get into other European markets. In the UK there was the build-up to allowing live TV in betting shops, provision of drinks and snacks. For a year I was very heavily involved in that.'

Next, Ladbroke wanted to post Clare to Brussels. But the Monday before he was due to take a reluctant family back across the Channel he got a phone call from a headhunter asking if he would be interested in talking to Dixons about a job as marketing director. 'I met the personnel and managing directors on the Tuesday, Stanley Kalms and his deputy, Mark Souhami, on the Wednesday and an industrial psychologist on the Thursday. On Friday morning they offered me the job and I accepted.'

Clare is the chosen successor to Kalms, the founder and guiding light of Dixons, who is eighteen years older than his protégé and has become famous in the business world for his one-liners. 'If you want space, go for a walk in the park,' he once said, referring to the busy atmosphere in Dixons branches. Clare is inevitably quieter, more of a manager, but he may be destined to run Dixons at its most critical stage.

'You eventually run out of things you can do in terms of selling products that communicate to your hearing, vision and maybe even feeling in time,' Clare points out. 'I would describe what is happening in the 1990s as much more about improving the quality of the product through new technology, than generating brand new product groups. It's clearly generating new products, but not new groups in the way that microwaves appeared from nowhere. Improvement in quality is primarily coming from digital technology. Everyone knows the compact disc is digital, but the basic technology underpinning a lot of our products, which has been basically magnetic in the past, is becoming digital. That is hitting not only sound but vision in a big way.'

Clare sees that development coming through in the emergence of PCs as a multimedia home electrical product using CD to store data. Out of that will emerge not only games and business information, but also films.

'All of that is being driven by the improvement that digital gives,' Clare adds. 'It's quicker, faster, cheaper, smaller if you want compactness, bigger if you want High Definition TV. The quality is much, much better. That will lead to waves of new products through the 1990s and into the next century. Virtual reality will come, depending on your definition. The concept of closing off your sensors and wrapping yourself into the game itself, through the graphics and the noise, isn't very far away.

'Interactive CD will be a winner in a few years, as a home entertainment and education system. It's a CD that plays through the TV as well as the hi-fi system, with digital sound and picture quality. You can go to any track very rapidly, giving manufacturers the opportunity to make software that is exciting and very different. You can store an encyclopaedia and access it with any name you choose, giving you sound, pictures and film. You can ask it about a country and back will come the story of that country, its development, way of life. It can be a cookbook: one disc will store 70,000 recipes. Not only will it tell you how to make them, it will show you. It will take people through GCSEs, A Levels, degrees and language courses. In entertainment, it's a wonderful vehicle for video games, which will become that much more sophisticated.'

Apart from PC World, Dixons in Britain has two distinct identities, Dixons and Currys. Dixons concentrates only on what the trade calls brown goods (which include PCs, even though they are normally greyish) while Currys carries the bigger brown goods such as TVs and the full range of so-called white goods – fridges, freezers, washing machines, dishwashers, microwaves, kettles, toasters and vacuum cleaners.

'The white sector had a rough ride through the recession,' Clare admits. 'It's much more closely linked to housing transactions. When people buy a new house they frequently have the money with which to fit it out, increasing the mortgage to do so. During the recession, the functional aspect of the electrical market was hit fairly hard, and so there should be a lot of growth in that sector as we emerge from recession. But the new products will tend to come into the brown goods area. That's where a lot of the research is done, where the Japanese have invested very heavily in research and development. They are already working on the fundamental technology to come after digital.

'Evolution carries on at a pace. By the turn of the century we will have HDTV, or as good as, and I think that will be a major, major improvement in the quality of the pictures we watch in the home. Relatively speaking, in a TV today you're looking at quality that is twenty years old. The difference between today's CD and the old Dansette record player is the sort of change we're going to see in vision. It's just a very different viewing experience. That'll take some years and will require satellite transmission and a certain amount of politics to be resolved to achieve standard formats across Europe. But it will happen.'

Although supermarketeers and managers of everything from DIY sheds to fashion boutiques would fall over themselves for such a glittering array of new products with which to delight the eye and make people reach for their wallets, Dixons is dogged by the problems of success. Its public has become first knowledgeable, then sated, now cynical and even crooked. Dixons has been the principal victim of the horrendous trend towards ram-raiding, rocketing its costs of insurance and protection. So bad has the problem become that Kalms caused a stir in 1993 by arguing: 'We need to legitimise the meaning of vigilantism. It is an honourable word and must be seen to be so.'

Says Clare: 'The customer for electrical products buys functional and entertainment goods in a very different way. Something being bought as a functional product for the home - that can be a TV or hi-fi system but is certainly true of all the major white goods – is a planned purchase and a major cost. It leads to a destination shopping experience. You know in advance you are going to buy it, and you go to where you think there will be the best range, best choice or best deal. And invariably when it's being bought for the home it's being bought by husbands and wives together, or even sometimes a family together, because it's going to be shared by the family. Even if it's the washing machine that's principally used by the housewife, the husband will help buy it. The wife thinks it's got a bit of technology in it, and therefore she needs some help. The washing machines are deliberately not that exciting to look at, there's not that many buttons on them, because if you do put lots of flashing lights on them you're as likely as not to put people off.'

That, of course, is fairly controllable from Dixons' point of view. Currys' windows concentrate more on price than pizzazz, more on sober functions than jazzy extras. That may be why there have not been so many cases of thieves ram-raiding branches of Currys. The fun and personal electronics items in which Dixons specialises are, however, another matter.

'These are products that you wish to enjoy,' Clare explains. 'You either enjoy the end product or you enjoy the technology, or you enjoy all the buttons and the features, depending on the sort of person you are. You will very, very frequently buy these products on impulse, even though they're quite expensive. You'd be amazed at the number of individuals that will buy even something as expensive as a camcorder when it was sort of in their mind that they would like a camcorder, but that particular morning they did not set out to go to a shop to buy one. They were there, they were wandering around, they saw the product, were tempted, got into a chat with the salesman and bought a camcorder.

'What we have tried to do, therefore, is to identify our own customers. I think we're unique in running retail chains covering different parts of the market. We've tried to identify customers from their attitude to the shopping experience rather than any other way because we find that the same person will buy a washing machine or fridge in a very different way than they'll buy a TV. They can buy a washing machine in Currys on a Saturday and a personal CD in Dixons on a Wednesday and their approach is very, very different. But demographically they're the same person. So we can't say Currys has this profile and Dixons has that profile. It's rather that in Currys people are making planned purchases and destination shopping. Increasingly therefore we're moving the stores to out-of-town locations, which give us the advantage of longer opening hours, parking, bigger stores, wider ranges and selection. We believe that with these products and that attitude to the purchase, service is very important, particularly aftersales service. They want confidence in the retailer, they want the retailer to be reliable and that includes the backup service.'

Dixons, on the other hand, tends to be in smaller high-street locations where there are a lot of people walking up and down outside, mainly men. There is a tendency for Dixons customers to be male, and for Dixons to sell to the individual rather to a family or a husband and wife together. The stores are designed to appeal to the impulsive side of men's nature and get passers-by walking into the stores. They're trying to do so by catching people who will respond to that sort of appeal – not necessarily society's masterminds and not perhaps the most scrupulous chaps that you ever bumped into. Therefore the windows of Dixons are very important, like fashion retailers in the high street. Indeed, they are trying to exert very much the same appeal to men that boutiques do to women.

'We're trying to generate stores that are exciting, modern, have a lot in them so it's very difficult to walk past the store if you have any interest in Dixons products at all,' admits Clare. 'You may not be planning to buy a camera, camcorder or CD player that day, but if you're interested in technology you will find it impossible for one reason or another to walk past. That's a combination of product displays and the excitement of the products themselves, and also promotion. Unlike his counterpart in Currys, a Dixons customer is as likely as not to want to know what all the buttons do, and to be interested in what they do. He may or may not finish up using them, but he is interested in the technology. If you are selling computers, he is going to want to know what the interface ports are, what they can plug into, what the speed of this is and the time of that. So there is a lot of product knowledge required to service that customer.'

But along with that increase in product knowledge there has arisen a demand for better service which Clare sees as spilling over into a downright impatience, particularly at the till, and a greater readiness to use complaints to con the retailer.

Says Clare: 'It's a fact of life that in the two weeks running up to Christmas, Dixons stores are going to be very busy and there will be queues. We can't actually put enough staff in the stores and operate the tills and the systems fast enough to avoid queues. But two or three times last Christmas I saw people get very unreasonable and out of hand because they were being asked to queue to make a purchase. It isn't that they put the product down and said "I'm not going to buy, I'll go somewhere else." They stamped and screamed and yelled and kicked up an enormous fuss in the store, which just absorbs managers' and staff time in sorting them out. To draw attention to themselves, to try and bypass the queue, to try and get to the front, by being unreasonable they thought they could get what they wanted before anyone else. It may work on occasion. If I was the manager of a store, it would be difficult to know what to do to handle some of these people.'

Some critics may answer that perhaps Dixons should take out some of the space it devotes to displaying goods in order to put in an extra till and so shorten high-season queues. But such incidents say much about the type of clientele the group is attracting – as does their attitude to alleged breakdowns.

'It's a fact of life that you cannot make 100 per cent perfect products all of the time,' insists Clare. 'At least you can't at the moment and it's unlikely for many years. So we have to build into our retail structure an aftersales service and repair operation that keeps those products working, keeps the customer satisfied. But we're also dealing with customers who increasingly believe that if something doesn't work it should be replaced. That is fine: we have replacement guarantees, they cover the first period of a product's life, but we have customers who think that a TV should be replaced with a brand new one if it breaks down after seven years. And kick up an enormous fuss, even sue – they don't succeed in getting away with anything, we try and put them off, but we have to handle them. I don't know how long they think electrical products are going to last, but they want them to last forever. We have customers that bring back products that have apparently broken down, want them replaced with a brand new product. When we look at the products they've damaged them. We've had camcorders coming back, two weeks old, because they don't work and they've been dropped in a swimming pool. Or they've been dropped on the beach and if you take the back off they're full of sand. Customers are trying to rip us off. Consumerism can only go so far before it becomes unreasonable.'

Naturally, such customer attitudes make staff recruitment and training all the more important. And here Dixons hits another snag: the sort of youngsters who want to demonstrate video games all day long do not always look like professional salespeople, treat customers politely or are as patient with older customers as the management would like.

'They do have to go through regular training programmes and know the products,' says Clare, 'because new products are coming in all the time. So there's a fair amount of effort required on the part of the staff to want to do that. Some people are interested in some products and not in others. That can work in a very large store, all other things being equal. But if you've got a smaller Dixons store being operated by only seven or eight full-time staff, then they have to be prepared to learn about a wide range of products. People of seventeen or eighteen, who come into our store and only want to sell electronic games because that's what they like, are not likely to be any use.

'How on earth can you expect to be a salesman when you won't go up to somebody and say, "Good morning, can I help you? I see you're interested in this TV set, is there anything I can tell you about it?" These issues are pushing us towards a minority of people, especially part-timers: we need staff for when customers are there. It's much too expensive to have staff for when customers aren't there, and customers' shopping patterns are polarising. We're seeing an increasing percentage of our business being done on Saturdays, almost year by year. Out of town, Sundays are increasingly important, and so is the period between six and eight at night because husbands and wives go together when they can. We run special training programmes for people leaving the armed forces and for mums who want to get back to work.'

While youthful aggression continues to be honed by unemployment and other stimulants, Dixons may have to consider what would otherwise be the heretical notion of making its shops and the 'toys' they stock less attractive. The shops are becoming too much like a battleground for comfort, and that could eventually become bad enough to make the cost of theft, fraud and customer hassle outweigh the profits, if only by deterring less troublesome customers from visiting during the key Christmas selling season. We are some way off that yet, which is presumably why Clare is soldiering on with present policies. But meanwhile Dixons is turning into a grim barometer of many social ills.

CHAPTER 3

PETER DAVIS

of Reed Elsevier

THE UNILEVER of publishing: that is how Peter Davis sees Reed Elsevier which, like its giant soap-to-foods counterpart, is a true Anglo-Dutch partnership. It operates as one entity, owned fifty-fifty by London-based Reed International and Elsevier (pronounced El-suh-veer) in Amsterdam. The new group did not start with quite Unilever's clout at the time of the merger in 1992, but underneath his amiable exterior Davis' ambition is boundless. The only question is whether he really wants to take on the likes of Time-Warner or News International in a head-to-head battle. Reed Elsevier's chosen route is more likely to lead it along the equivalent of leafy country lanes than the media motorways which promise to become uncomfortably crowded as the 21st century unfolds.

'It's in the non-sexy areas of the industry, and that's not a bad thing,' says Neil Blackley, media analyst at the Goldman Sachs securities house, 'because they can achieve profit margins of thirty per cent or more in scientific, medical, professional and business publishing. The volumes are much smaller than in consumer publishing, but price sensitivity is nowhere near as great.'

None of the group's operations illustrates this better than Pergamon Press, which Elsevier bought from the notorious Robert Maxwell only six months before his controversial death in 1991. Pergamon had for many years been Maxwell's main profits engine: he liked to boast how he charged subscriptions of thousands of pounds a year for some of Pergamon's more obscure scientific journals – and then charged the academics for writing the articles. Universities and, in some cases, industrial companies had to have the journals, while academics needed space in them so they would get full credit for their discoveries. Pergamon's financial numbers are no longer published

Peter John Davis

BORN: 23 December, 1941

EDUCATED: Shrewsbury School

MARRIED: Susan Hillman 1968. Two sons, one daughter

CAREER:

1959	Management Trainee, Ditchburn Organisation
1965	General Foods, marketing
1973	Marketing Director, Key Markets
1977	Marketing Director, J. Sainsbury
1979	Assistant Managing Director, J. Sainsbury
1986	Chief Executive, Reed International
1990	Chairman, Reed International
1993	Chairman, Reed Elsevier

OTHER INTERESTS: Non-executive Director of The Boots Company. Member of the Supervisory Board of Aegon NV. Chairman of the Adult Literacy and Basic Skills Unit. Deputy Chairman of Business in the Community.

REED ELSEVIER (UK) LTD

HEAD OFFICE: 6 Chesterfield Gardens, London W1A 1EJ
Tel: 071-499 4020

ACTIVITIES: Publishing, managing exhibitions

MAIN BRANDS: *The Lancet, Tetrahedron Letters, The Journal of Chromatography, Halsbury's Laws of England, Martindale-Hubbell Law Directory, Who's Who in America, The American Journal of Medicine, Official Airline Guides, Kompass, World Travel Market, Hotel & Travel Index, Variety, Estates Gazette, Country Life, Woman, Woman's Own, Modern Bride, What's on TV, Marie Claire, Hugh Johnson's Pocket Wine Book.*

separately, but it is part of the group's Scientific and Medical division which in the mid-1990s was displaying the thirty per cent-plus profit margins that caught Blackley's eye. At the other end of the spectrum, the Consumer division's margins were less than half as good.

'In the next five or ten years I'd expect Reed Elsevier to be more international, more electronic, probably not a lot larger,' predicts Davis, 'but I think you will see some change in the makeup of the businesses we're in, particularly because of developments in business and professional information. You'll see more electronic databases and electronic distribution of material and people using it electronically. I think you might see some of that information being tied into transactions, because it's all very well giving people the information but they then want to do something with it, to add value to it. We're technology-neutral, in that we're not committed to one solution or one route or one partner. Our material is already available on a huge number of services. You can look up a lot of stuff that's in *Variety*, the American showbusiness paper, on Reuters. You can look up Profile, the *Financial Times* newspaper database, and find lots of things from our publications. So in that way we've been neutral, but whether that's a long-term position and whether at some point we're going to have to make some choices, or whether we should get involved with one or other of the distribution networks... I think it's unlikely at the moment, but you shouldn't rule anything out.'

Reed Elsevier claims to have as much data of various kinds as anyone else around the world, from *Halsbury's Laws of England* to *The Lancet* and their equivalents in other countries. The group is making that data machine-readable and switchable between different formats, whilst putting more and more value round it to make it more necessary. 'We'll be moving the portfolio more up that "need to know" line,' Davis explains, 'because we think that's one of the best protections against unexpected distribution developments. We've invested a lot of money to get those sorts of databases and that sort of work done in most of our businesses now. So if the market moves, we're ready, and in some of the markets it's going to move faster than in others. I wish I knew which ones they all were, but I suspect that we and the machine people will be able to deliver a service before most customers want it.'

Some take longer than others to get used to pressing a keyboard instead of turning a page. Streetwise City dealers leapt onto Reuters foreign exchange and money market screens as soon as they became available in the 1980s. At about the same time Butterworths, a group subsidiary that is Britain's largest legal and tax publisher, became agent for the Lexis on-line legal database. But, thanks to lawyers' inbred love of loose-leaf hard copy, it took virtually a decade to take off. 'It's a question of moving from getting information "just in case" to "just in time",' says Blackley. 'Companies don't want to pay for a lot of stuff that doesn't get looked at. Increasingly, they'd rather pay more for what their people actually want – and the same is becoming true of academics as well.'

In a sense, Davis has always been in packaging, whether it is information, juke boxes or pounds of butter. He personally exemplifies Reed Elsevier, because his cotton trader father was British and his mother Dutch. He was reared on Merseyside and there was enough money in the family to send him to Shrewsbury public school, but after national service he plunged straight into work. His first employer was the Ditchburn Organisation, an engineering group run by an entrepreneur called Norman Ditchburn who made an eclectic range of gadgetry from office equipment to vending machines and juke boxes. After a spell as a storeman Davis was earmarked for marketing. He studied the subject at night school and won a scholarship to travel round America, talking shop with the big advertising agencies over there. That gave him a taste for the big US corporation, so when he returned to England he joined General Foods, the Bird's Custard group. He helped launch Bird's Angel Delight with the slogan 'Tastes like strawberries and cream'. 'I'm not sure it was like either of them,' Davis remembers, 'but we won a bevy of awards for the test launch.'

Married by then, Davis realised that American companies like to move their executives around the world, which did not suit him. He shifted to the Key Markets supermarket chain as marketing and then managing director. But after a few years the parent company, Fitch Lovell, decided to quit retailing, so he wrote to J. Sainsbury and a year later was on the board. He became managing director there, but yet again a snag loomed: in those days you did not get to run the show unless your name was Sainsbury. By this time, 1986, Davis was a big enough wheel to put himself on a headhunter's list and the chief executive's job at Reed came up. 'I think you should decide what you want to do and go for it,' he believes. 'My own career has lurched in different directions, and I have often taken a reduction in salary and position to move in a new direction.'

It is a career path which suggests an unwillingness to put up with the status quo if he does not feel it is right for him. Happily, Davis had virtually carte blanche at Reed. He inherited a crumbling empire of forests, paper mills, shower fittings, wallpaper, squeezy bottles and cardboard boxes, printing and packaging, as well as book and magazine publishing.

Management morale was still bruised by the clumsy way in which they had been steamrollered a couple of years earlier into offloading Mirror Group Newspapers onto Robert Maxwell for what soon became clear to the world was a ludicrously low price.

'When I took over I was having to think in one day about titanium oxide, glue plants in the US, paper mills in Canada and should we launch a new magazine in the UK,' Davis recalls. 'It was crazy. It's hard to master all the strands we have now, but it was impossible to master all that.'

So he went for publishing, raising around £1.5 billion from selling the rest and reinvesting most of it in Octopus Books, *TV Times*, Travel Information Group and Martindale-Hubbell, the US equivalent of Butterworths. But all the time Reed, even before Davis joined them, coveted Elsevier. Their relationship has all the ingredients of the sort of pulp fiction bestseller that the group would love to publish. They tried and failed to get together twice before, and in between Elsevier was wooed by Maxwell, other European publishers and Pearson, the aristocratic conglomerate that owns the *Financial Times* and Penguin Books. Pearson and Elsevier got as far as exchanging shares in one another, but the two chairmen – Pierre Vinken and Lord Blakenham – did not get on.

Says Davis: 'It isn't surprising, in trying to put two successful companies together on a fifty-fifty basis, that you don't expect everything to go entirely smoothly. It's much more difficult to be successful in a merger than a takeover. You need balance, agreement, you need to be fair and you need to be seen to be fair. It's more difficult to achieve change by consensus than it is by banging heads together in an acquisition. If there's been any pressure since our merger, it's been at the top or at the centre because the operating businesses have had quite clear instructions as to who does what. At the centre, we've been trying to establish a sort of pan-European way of working with an executive committee that has two from Reed and two from Elsevier on it, in the style of the Unilever special committee and the Royal Dutch-Shell committee of managing directors.'

Davis spends a minimum of a day every two weeks in Holland. The amount of time he spends in Reed's imposing Mayfair head office depends on the time of year and whether the top management are compiling budgets and holding strategy meetings. The routine meeting of the executive committee is alternated between the two countries, but full board meetings are largely in London, because the operating companies are a PLC and the group has more companies in the UK than in Holland.

'Moving, in the case of Elsevier, from a smaller company to a very much bigger group inevitably caused some change and some pressure,' Davis points out. 'In the case of Reed, moving from a classic Anglo-Saxon chairmanship to the continental executive committee style required a change of gears and that has taken a little longer, so it isn't surprising that it has produced one or two lively debates. In Reed we've made over a hundred acquisitions in the publishing world and we're used to acting in a particular way – putting systems in and getting on with it. So have Elsevier. But this is not that. This is the bringing together of two ships to sort of run alongside, bolted together, and not to make one bigger ship. Pierre Vinken, my co-chairman, has a phrase that what we're trying to do is bring together two fishing fleets to fish together, and when you think about publishing and the individual operating companies running from books to magazines to newspapers to databases, we're in very different businesses.'

It is a size and complexity of group that, unlike Robin Miller at Emap, (Chapter 12) no one person can run in a hands-on fashion. But that suits Davis, whose career has made him a manager who could perform well in any industry that had a strong marketing element. 'I'm a great believer in getting out,' he says. 'Much of the central head office function can be devolved to the individual business units. It's unrealistic to think that we will know more about how to price a magazine in Chicago than the man in Chicago, but that is how a lot of businesses used to be run. So we still make the strategic decisions, while the local people are closer to their local market. We have got to be more laid back, because someone is not going to make the same decisions that you are, and sometimes they will get it wrong. But they and the people working for them will find it more satisfying. It's partly a basis of making decisions. You may be too close to the market, you may be missing the developing trends because people are too close, but in strategic terms you have got to keep some strong input from the centre to see what the local manager may be missing.'

That makes Davis' lack of previous publishing experience less important than it might be in a smaller company, but also makes him and the rest of the executive committee more reliant on the specialists one or two tiers below them.

'On a day-to-day basis, we talk regularly,' says Davis. 'We meet once a week as a group of four plus the finance director. We talk and decide what we want to do as a group. It's not very different from how any other company works. Reed before had a central group of three – myself, Ian Irvine and Nigel Stapleton – and then we had a wider group of six executive directors, which was the management board if you like, and then we had the non-executives forming the whole board. Everyone accepted that the three of us would take any day-to-day decisions that needed to be taken before we went up to the bigger board. We're doing exactly the same now, except that in the Reed days there was a clear pecking order amongst the three. Amongst the four of us there is a less clear pecking order. That sort of set-up is common on the Continent and less common in the UK and America, and it has taken a bit of getting used to. But there's no problem with getting a quick decision. In the old days one of the operating directors would phone either Pierre or myself, depending on which company they were in, and except on something very routine I would always have said to either Nigel or Ian: "They want to make a bid for this, what do you think? They want to get a letter in tonight because there's a bidding war tomorrow." Now instead of walking down that corridor to see Ian and Nigel, I'll walk into a different office, or if they're in Amsterdam, I'll pick up the phone or write a fax – it's not very complicated. I think a company needs a clear focus and clear leadership, but I think the myth of the chief executive is very much overstated because very few chief executives work in isolation: they work as a team with a more clearly differentiated leader, perhaps. I'm sure much of the success of the executive committee system depends on the selection of the four-man team. The other thing is not to rush at it. Unilever and Shell have been doing it for fifty years. It'll be interesting to see over a longer time which is the better system.'

The immediate impact of the merger has been felt in three areas of the combined business: business magazines in the US, science journals and the medical group, which was pulled out of both companies and put in a new free-standing unit. The physical merging of operations into one or more sites has been limited, mainly because of building restrictions or the amount of space available. Only units in the same country have been physically combined. Many of the scientific journals have been put in the old Pergamon offices in the grounds of Headington Hill Hall, Oxford. However, the medical journals are published in a dozen different countries and are managed from Princeton, New Jersey. The legal journals are run from England.

Aside from the scientific, medical, professional and business operations, the group has a major consumer publishing division which accounts for nearly a third of total sales. It owns two Dutch national newspapers, four regional paid-for papers including the *Lancashire Evening Telegraph*, a collection of freesheets and a magazine stable which takes in *Marie Claire, Woman, Woman's Own, Horse and Hound, Country Life, TV Times* and *What's On TV*. On the face of it, these should be sold so that time and resources can be concentrated on the high-margin end of the business. But in terms of return on capital they are second only to the forty per cent-plus earned by the Scientific and Medical division, so they earn their keep.

'We have two national newspapers in Holland,' says Davis, 'but I'd be surprised if it made sense for us to go back into national newspapers in the UK. It's very much a question of where you start from. The Dutch newspapers are successful and have been invested with new printing plant. If we were starting from scratch we probably wouldn't include national newspapers in the picture. But as we have two very successful ones that make good money, there's no reason why we would want to do other than keep them. The Dutch national newspaper market has a very significant difference from the British, in that they are sold on subscription, so the cash flow is good, the sales are less volatile and they are less sensational because they are less dependent on day-to-day newsstand sales. It's closer to the cash-flow characteristics of a science journal or an exhibition. Reed's interest in the UK is to build up local advertising through local newspapers, and not to be in the grip of the unions as they were in the days of the *Mirror*, where it had become very difficult to manage. I think that we would see better returns from investing now in other kinds of publishing than a national newspaper.'

There are plenty of gaps in the ideal portfolio that Davis would like to assemble. Some business and consumer magazine and newspaper infill acquisitions would make sense, but his main emphasis is on professional and database information publishing and trade exhibitions. Every day of the year on average, the group is running an exhibition somewhere in the world, particularly the US, UK and Asia Pacific. More scientific and legal publishing acquisitions are also on the cards. In 1993 the group bought Editions Techniques, the largest French-language law publisher. That was the first acquisition by either Reed or Elsevier in continental Europe, outside their home countries, but it was unlikely to be the last. Later that same year the group bought Official Airline Guides from the joint administrators of Maxwell Communication Corporation. OAG is a major publisher of US airline schedules, and fitted in well with the group's existing ABC World Airways Guide.

Those guides plug Reed Elsevier straight into the boom in air travel, particularly by business executives. Says Davis: 'The world is moving faster and faster. My chairman in my first company, Norman Ditchburn, drove himself fairly hard, but he used to go to the US only once a year in the late 1950s and early 1960s. He used to go over there by ship to get used to the time change, and return by ship to ensure he was fresh when he returned. But

I've been to New York for lunch and back, because it was particularly important, and I think nothing of going over there for a couple of days. And the fax has changed things so much. It demands instant response. As a result, business has become much more international. When my deputy is in Australia we fax papers to him tonight, for him to reply to by tomorrow. That simply wouldn't have been possible ten years ago.'

By the mid-1990s, Davis is more likely to be flying or faxing east than west, as he strives to build more significant businesses in Asia's emerging markets. The group has a company in southern China called Mandarin, which is one of the world's biggest print brokers and is responsible for producing 40 million books a year. Working from sales offices in London, New York, Washington, Sydney and Paris, it offers a package service of production, paper-buying, print, delivery and distribution to people, so they can just give Mandarin a manuscript and art work and get it produced. It takes orders from within Reed Elsevier, but also from hundreds of other publishers.

'We're doing a lot of sourcing of print product in China,' says Davis, 'and it's very high-quality stuff. It used to be in Hong Kong, but a lot of it has swung now into China. Nearly fifty per cent of our total print production in books is now coming out of China.' These are mainly the large illustrated books that adorn so many coffee tables: novels and textbooks tend to be produced nearer to where they are going to be sold.

The moot point is how much longer the world is going to be content to turn pages instead of gazing at electronic screens. Davis thinks that print still has a long way to run before it is finally abandoned – if ever.

He predicts: 'I think in the consumer businesses – books, magazines and local newspapers – I would be surprised if many of them were being received in non-printed form by the majority of people, even in ten years. A lot of that electronic impact has already happened: it is called television. Although there will obviously be developments of personalised newspapers or magazines or books on Nintendo games or TV Walkmans, the technology will be able to deliver a product much sooner than the customer is wanting it in many of those markets. I still think you'll be taking a paperback to read by the pool on holiday in ten years' time, rather than plugging yourself into a handheld little screen.

'In the case of one of our American businesses, Books in Print, we have a service that when the library or bookseller has found the book that they're looking for, they can then transmit an order, either to their regular supplier or one that we nominate locally, who can then execute that order for him. It doesn't mean we're in the business of becoming wholesalers or retailers, but transmitters of orders and providers of business. If you can get a small turn on that, you're taking it through to its logical conclusion. It's the same in hotel bookings or airline seats – there are defined transactions that are important to the people transacting them, but in the overall scheme of things it's not huge and they're used to paying commissions in those areas.'

CHAPTER **4**

GREG DYKE

AFTER THE current franchise period ends in 2003, British television will never be the same again. Indeed, according to Greg Dyke, former chief executive of LWT (Holdings), parent of London Weekend Television, it will be unrecognisable. He should know. In March 1994 he became one of the most prominent victims of that remodelling process, when LWT was taken over by Granada Group. He explains: 'There will be a massive number of channels. The ownership of delivery systems itself, what the franchise companies paid for through the last auction, will not be a major factor. There will be so many delivery systems that I don't think there will anything for the government to sell in 2003. There'll be satellite, there'll be cable, there'll be other methods of distribution, so television transmitters will be seen as an old-fashioned way of getting a signal on the air and LWT will be long forgotten, if it is still only the holder of the London weekend franchise by then. The government will realise that they can't make people pay for something that is not a scarce resource, and all indications are that it won't be a scarce resource by then. I don't see people paying £30 million or £40 million a year for the right to broadcast in the south of England if they can rent space on a satellite that covers the whole country for about £3 million a year. The price will go up a bit, but there are competing satellites that won't allow the price to go up wholly unrealistically.'

Set against such a prospect, 1993's battle over moving *News at Ten* seems small beer. More significant was BSkyB's coup in snatching the rights to Premiership football off the ITV companies, rubbing in the agony by sharing a few crumbs with the BBC. That hurt Dyke, not least because he was leading the negotiations, and showed the way market muscle was moving. 'I

wasn't really worried about my reputation – I mean, does the person once named as Roland Rat's Dad really have a reputation to lose?' he joked. 'But I feel strongly for people like my dad, who died in 1990, who was a devoted football fan and who would never have bought a dish and who wouldn't be able to see the game any more. I resent that. I also resent the fact that LWT, which was a low bidder in the franchise auction, will pay the government some £22 million a year for its licence, that the ITV network overall will pay £300 million or so, and we were outbid for the football by a company that is barely regulated, has no requirements for certain quotas of programmes and doesn't have to pay the government anything. Competition has come quicker than anyone expected.'

Dyke's account of the football episode shows him as a millionaire who likes to put his arm round his humble roots, with a sense of humour that prevents him from getting too emotional about television, yet at the same time a sharp businessman who is quick to cut the candyfloss and get to the core of an argument. He is able to relish capitalism with one breath and despise it with the next.

'The trouble is that populism has got a bad name,' he explains. 'Everyone thinks it means cheap game shows and Roland Rat, who I might say was quite a clever idea, actually. In fact, the television audience is increasingly sophisticated. It spots what's good and what isn't. People watch *Poirot*, for instance. The stories in *Poirot* are so thin it's absurd, but they watch it because it's good. ITV in the 1990s, so long as it keeps up the spending on programmes, will be strong, with a middle-brow, commercial schedule. And all I ever said about current affairs on ITV is that they don't need to play in peak time. There's no difference between playing them at 8.30pm and 10.30pm. I would defend to the death the need to spend proper money on something like *World in Action*. And I would defend to the death the right of ITV's current affairs to make difficult and challenging programmes. You shouldn't confuse journalistic integrity and funding with where current affairs is played in the schedule. *World in Action* is the best-known current affairs show in this country: *The South Bank Show* is the best-known arts programme. These are part of ITV's branding. But if you keep them in peak-time and you lose revenue, there's no point in defending them to the death when two years later you can't afford them anyway.'

This almost split-personality approach owes much to Dyke's origins. 'I'm an old-fashioned sixties liberal who happened to find himself running a business,' he says, 'and I try to use that position to do the things that I believe in. I'm going to end up rich which is odd, because I think I'm one of the few

Gregory Dyke

BORN: 20 May, 1947

EDUCATED: Hayes Grammar School, York University, Harvard Business School

CAREER:

1965 Trainee, Marks & Spencer
1966 Local newspaper journalist
1975 Community worker
1977 Reporter, LWT's *The London Programme*
1978 Producer, *Weekend World*
1979 Deputy Editor, *The London Programme*
1981 Editor, *The Six o'Clock Show*
1983 Editor in Chief, TV-AM
1984 Director of Programmes, TVS
1987 Director of Programmes, London Weekend Television
1989 Deputy managing director, LWT (Holdings)
1990 Group Chief Executive, LWT (Holdings)

OTHER INTERESTS: Director of Channel Four Television, ITV Association, *Good Morning Television*

people in television who really doesn't worry about being rich. The one advantage of being rich is that it's fuck-off money. If you don't like it, you can walk away.' As he did after the Granada takeover.

As those remarks indicate, Dyke did not start rich. Born in 1947 in Hayes, one of that splurge of suburbs that now escort the M40 west out of London, his father was an insurance salesman and Greg did just well enough in the eleven-plus exam to get to grammar school. Armed with an A level in maths, he was taken on as a trainee by Marks & Spencer, but gave that up after three months to try local-paper journalism. Then he decided to catch up on university education by going to York as a mature politics student. That admirably equipped him for a career in social work, to say nothing of standing unsuccessfully for Labour in Putney at elections to the then Greater London Council. But the journalistic instinct reasserted itself – he would be a more than useful newspaper executive today – and in 1977 he landed a job as a researcher with LWT on *The London Programme*. Promotion was swift. A year later he was a producer on *Weekend World*, the prestige-drenched Sunday showcase for Peter Jay. By 1979 he was back as deputy editor of *The London Programme*. In 1981 he created *The Six O'Clock Show*, LWT's go-anywhere Friday evening magazine programme.

Two years later the first breakfast franchise on commercial television, TV-AM, was coming apart at the seams under the weight of founders like David Frost, Angela Rippon, Anna Ford and Michael Parkinson. Dyke was called in as editor-in-chief to rescue the ratings. His answer was Roland Rat. 'I spotted that the viewing figures went up at half-term,' he recalls, 'and realised the audience was made up of kids.' Before long Anne Diamond and Nick Owen were reading out horoscopes and bingo numbers. It worked, but Kerry Packer became a TV-AM shareholder and sent Bruce Gyngell over from Australia to be managing director. Dyke left to be director of programmes at TVS, the then southern England franchise-holder. Three years later, in 1987, the chairman of LWT, Sir Christopher Bland, summoned him back to do the same job there. In 1990 he became chief executive, after the urbane, Oxford-educated Bland had sent him to Harvard for three months to brush up his corporate table manners.

Dyke's 'gerrtcha' attitude might have made a better starting point than Mark McCormack's for writing the best-selling *What They Don't Teach You At Harvard*. 'It was terrifying,' he says. 'I was very nervous. But it's only later that you discover so are most of the others there. It really surprised me, because the course was a massive attack on American management. In many ways it reassured me about many of the things I believed about companies, with my background in the Labour Party and all that sort of stuff. It was about believing that many people worked in appalling jobs, and their skills and talents weren't properly used. It seemed to me that the way to make organisations work was teams. TV programme teams are wonderfully efficient. There are twenty people and everyone's involved in the meetings, everyone's involved in the discussions, everyone takes part, feels ownership of it, everyone knows what the goal is. And that seems to me a brilliant way of running an organisation. And I suppose the other thing that Harvard said to me was that leadership was more important than management. Companies have to be led, not managed. It's not that difficult to manage companies. What they've got to be is led. And that leadership quality you want to get in all levels of the organisation. That came as quite a surprise to me, but appealed to many of the things I've believed in. It always struck me, the number of times you met people who said: "I know how to make this work, but I'm not telling those bastards." There was a conspiracy between middle management and trade unions that stopped people with good ideas from carrying them out. That's what you've got to break down. What you want is multi-skilling, so people with good ideas get the opportunity to put them into practice. The third thing that Harvard taught me was that ten-year plans don't work, because the macroeconomics always drives them off course. You can't predict what's going to happen.'

Nevertheless, if you are running a business you at least have to have a guess. Dyke is placing his bets on the present ITV companies going into either pay-television, with ITV2 as a satellite channel, or cable.

'There are a lot of opportunities,' he points out. 'The question is when: that's the hard one. If you go in early you can get a very good price, but there's very few people receiving you. If you go in late, you don't get such a good price, but you reach many more people. So it's a question of when you move into these markets. But I have no doubt that that's what some ITV companies will do. I think cable is going to be a more significant factor in this country than a lot of people do. Most people seem to think that by the end of this century cable and satellite will be available in about fifty per cent of homes. Up to now it was seen that that was predominantly satellite, with dishes. There's now quite a lot of work being done that seems to think that actually the change in the rules on telephony, which allows cable franchisees to sell telephone services, means that the pickup of cable will be much bigger. And it could well be that, by the end of the century, of their fifty per cent overall share cable and satellite will be fifty-fifty. Now, if that's the case, there are real opportunities in cable over the next ten years, as a programme provider.'

A consortium called London Interconnect is joining up all the London cable stations, passing its lines quite near LWT's South Bank headquarters and studios, so the group would easily be able to tap into the pipeline with a supply of its own programmes.

Dyke compares the growth of satellite and cable to the explosion that happened in newspapers after Rupert Murdoch took his national titles to Wapping in 1986, breaking the production unions in the process and enabling national newspapers to get their hands on computerised technology for the first time – even though it had been available years before.

'Exactly the same is happening in television,' Dyke asserts, 'and therefore the value of companies like LWT are, firstly, to be part of the major commercial channel – and still will be, but with much smaller audiences. Secondly will be the ability to understand what people want to watch and how to make it and all the rest of it. What you've got to do is to make sure you can make it effectively and efficiently, which companies like LWT have done over the years, but they can get much better at it. The next question will be, where else do you use the product that you make? The days when you made a programme and it went out once are going to disappear. Sky Movies Gold is a classic example: it's getting six to eight per cent of viewing in satellite homes by showing old films, which is less than one per cent of all viewing. What they are paying for programming is peanuts, about £4,000 an hour against more than £500,000 for the average drama. However, when that can be used ten different ways, picking up that sort of money over a period of years, then it becomes significant.'

What is exciting Dyke and his executives in the main television franchise groups is that BSkyB has turned out to be a pay-television business, rather than an advertising television business. The advertising revenue is tiny compared to the pay-television revenue from subscribers.

'All the research suggests that pay-television will be a third major source of income in television by the end of the decade' he says. 'By the year 2000 that could be as high as advertising revenue. So it is a major source, but it's not a source that threatens the ITV franchise holders, other than through reduced viewing levels. But even then, if you're the major player, advertisers will want to be with you. And as those changes of structure will come gradually, ITV can cope with them. They're aware of it and it certainly can't be the ITV it was in the 1970s and 1980s, in terms of staffing and all those sorts of things, but they can cope with it. I'm not worried about that.'

If Britain follows the American pattern, companies like Granada/LWT could end up with a foot in each camp like the major American television groups, offering TV through land-based transmitters or by satellite or cable. That is already beginning to bring US network stations over to Britain looking for material to fill their yawning hours of scheduling.

'If you can come up with a great co-production deal that works in both markets, it's worth a fortune,' says Dyke. 'That's what everyone's looking at now, so long as you can avoid mid-Atlantic crap television. We've all made some of that, and the trouble is it doesn't work in either market. *Kennedy*, LWT's documentary on JFK, worked in all markets when it was shown in 1992. But oddly, at the time when the economic necessity is to find more international co-production deals, more and more people across the world are more interested in indigenous product. So there is a difficulty. There was a time when you could play American series in peak time on ITV and do quite well. Those days have gone. Not one now, apart from *Baywatch*, which is basically sex on the beach. The Americans pulled out of it, and LWT and the Germans funded it to keep it going.'

But not for long. Dyke reckons that the pressure to improve programme quality will intensify during the 1990s. He gives the present crop of television companies until about 1997 before the forces of competition break down their quasi-monopoly – which is when the value of the regional franchises will begin to shrivel dramatically. Just as the satellite channels will be building up big enough audiences to justify buying high-quality original programmes, instead of the early 1990s diet of repeats, films and sport, so the traditional channels will find their audiences deserting them. LWT took steps in 1991 to cut its overheads by bringing Carlton and GMTV, the breakfast channel, into the South Bank complex.

'For years you made money out of television because you were a monopoly supplier,' says Dyke. 'You were the only way into a home. In other words, the engineering made your profit, just by being able to deliver anything, almost, into the home. Once that's gone, and it'll be gone by the end of the decade, what will matter will be what you deliver into the home. A lot of the stuff that was talked about television was terribly arrogant: the "we'll deliver them what they ought to have" crap. But there is no doubt that the more affluent and the better educated you get, the less television you watch. So it has to be good.

'People haven't recognised the changing nature of advertising. Basically, advertising has changed from being predominantly fast-moving consumer goods to being a mixture of fast-moving consumer goods, financial services and cars. They're not after the same people the soap-powder companies want. If you're selling BMWs, there's no point putting an advert in a daytime soap. So you've got to have the sort of programmes that the more discerning viewer wants. The great danger is that what the more discerning viewer wants is intellectual programming. What they want is something that is quite stimulating, well-made drama or well-made entertainment. That's the future, and you've got to have the money to make that. That money comes from the quality of advertising you can get. So the pressure is not to go downmarket at all. You might do that at certain times of the day, but the pressure is to reduce your costs in certain areas. At the end of the day it's going to come down to competitive programming, and the belief that ITV is going to go plunging downmarket with loads of crappy old game shows is just not there. The audiences for those shows are not who the advertisers are trying to appeal to.'

This may not mean that LWT necessarily keeps *The South Bank Show* or even carries a news bulletin at all, for the simple reason that there will be specialist arts and news channels doing nothing but covering those areas. The future, according to Dyke, lies in narrower programming pushed through a wider range of hardware.

'The ITV companies must get closer together with the telecommunications companies,' he predicts. 'I have no doubt about that whatsoever, that telecommunications must become much more integrated. But the programme-makers could rule the world, because all those people with boring cultures aren't going to survive. Because someone's going to come along with a good idea, in a much freer situation, and jump them. It's a world where the value-added now is about style, marketing and ideas, not about making steel. Nobody's going to make money out of making steel. You'll make money out of thinking of what to do with it.'

Dyke's is very much a programme-maker's view of how events are likely to work out in what is clearly going to be a highly volatile market over the next decade or two. While prizes will go to the companies that can capture the best writers, actors or directors, the challenge for each television management is even greater: how to come up with a survival plan for the worst case – that their chequebooks are not big enough to snatch the share of the talent they will need to survive.

CHAPTER 5

PETER ELLWOOD

of TSB Group

'W E'RE NOT running an Oxford college here, we're running a business' was Peter Ellwood's memorable remark when he was appointed to the chief executive's chair at TSB Group, the high street banking chain. His briskness was understandable: the company had been burdened in the early 1990s by several self-inflicted wounds, notably Hill Samuel Bank, Target Group and Mortgage Express, which might have owed more to the high-flown theories of a senior common room than the practical know-how of a commercial organisation. The immediate task confronting the board when Ellwood took over in 1992 was to wipe the slate clean on the rather messy recent past and position TSB for the next century. But that proved easier said than done, thanks to the recession, the housing slump and the huge overhang of bad debts at Hill Samuel, once one of the City's premier merchant banks but bruised by a succession of senior departures after it ceded independence.

TSB suffered from a bad attack of over-indulgence when it was floated on the stock market in 1986. It nobly insisted on paying £777 million for Hill Samuel, even though the stock market crash of 1987 intervened between conception of the deal and consummation. Such an upheaval would have been more than enough excuse for slashing the price in today's more hard-headed times, and probably ranks as one of the last significant examples this century of a City gent's word truly being his bond. The inflated price was not just an accountant's nicety: the crash severely reduced the value of Hill Samuel's loans and its opportunities to generate business through takeovers and flotations. All in all, continuing losses and bad debt write-offs have added as much again to the price of the original deal. As if that were not enough, in an effort to broaden its range of financial services TSB paid £229

Peter Brian Ellwood

BORN: 15 May, 1943

EDUCATED: King's School, Macclesfield

MARRIED: Judy Windsor, 1968. One son, two daughters

CAREER:
- 1961 Barclays Bank
- 1983 Chief Executive, Barclaycard
- 1989 Chief Executive, retail banking, TSB
- 1991 Chief Executive, retail banking and insurance, TSB Bank
- 1992 Group Chief Executive, TSB Group

OTHER INTERESTS: Director of Visa International

TSB GROUP PLC

HEAD OFFICE: PO Box 260, 60 Lombard Street,
London EC3V 9DN
Tel: 071-398 3980

MAIN BRANDS: TSB, Trustcard, Hill Samuel

million for Target, an insurance and unit trust management business. But that too went sour, and TSB was glad to get it off its hands for next to nothing. Then the group got caught up in the rush by banks to break into the mortgage market. The result was Mortgage Express, a centralised lending operation developed from scratch in-house, but which had too little direct contact with the borrowers. It became an easy touch for those who could not obtain mortgages elsewhere in the depths of the housing crisis. Losses ran up fast and Ellwood had no option but to run down the operation, slowly nursing the repayments out of the borrowers until the books were squared.

So no wonder Ellwood, who left school to join Barclays Bank in Bristol at the age of eighteen, has taken an earthier than earthy approach to his job. He was soon whisked out of the relative obscurity of a Bristol backwater and found himself becoming personal assistant to Barclays' UK chief. After a spell managing a branch in the City, he got his real insight into how the customer ticks by being transferred to Barclaycard's headquarters in Northampton. Four years later he became chief executive of Barclaycard and was responsible for introducing the Profiles scheme where card users were credited with points from which they could choose catalogue gifts. So he became steeped in the drum-banging, 'come and get it' school of marketing – not fashionable in polite banking circles, but highly effective if you want to get the punters through the door and opening accounts. 'It was clear,' Ellwood recalls, 'that the TSB had only a minority of its total customers' financial relationships. I saw a great opportunity to help the organisation fulfil its potential in that regard.'

As his remark about Oxford colleges suggested, his strategy is remarkably simple: cut out the hot air which infuses many banking parlours, cut costs and bring in as much technology as possible to woo the customer.

Ellwood explains: 'If you look at it in terms of the four stake-holders in the business – customers, shareholders, community and staff – then we think that you can't start off by saying that we must look after the shareholders. We've got to look after the customers first. Therefore staff have to feel customer-orientated and be proud of the organisation, proud of service, not confuse service with servility, care about the customer, care about getting things right the first time. The thrust has to be on a greater preoccupation with the customers, understanding their needs better and then meeting those needs.'

He is ahead of several of his competitors in recognising that although TSB is one of Britain's leading banks it is really a financial services retailer – and as such is increasingly coming up against other retailers and big consumer names. In 1992 General Motors of the US brought out its own credit card, bringing it into the same arena as banks, building societies and the major stores groups. A UK version was launched the following year, carrying a low rate of interest and offering a loyalty bonus of up to £500 a year off Vauxhall vehicles. American Telephone & Telegraph has also gone down the financial services route with a plastic card and General Electric Company of the US has one of the biggest leasing companies in the world. In Britain, the tobacco giant BAT Industries is in insurance and Marks & Spencer sells its own unit trusts and pensions. Whether they are selling cars or cashmere, all these businesses are fighting for the same pound, and for them financial services are just another way of competing. The now almost obligatory offers of nought per cent finance to help purchases are just the thin end of a long and widening wedge.

Ellwood is among the growing band of younger and more progressive bankers who realise that some of their non-financial rivals are better at the consumer fight than they themselves have been.

'I don't think one can say "Oh, well, we're banks, we're inviolate, nobody comes into our patch because the barriers to entry are too high,"' he observes. 'Not so: consumer banks like TSB are retailers just like Marks & Spencer. If you look at banks, closed half the day, some of them not even open on Saturday mornings, and compare them with retailers, you can see how far we have to go. If you look at the mission statement of our retail bank and insurance business it says we aim to be the UK's leading financial retailer. It doesn't say anything about the bank. It then goes on to say we must do that through understanding and meeting customer needs, and being more innovative and professional than our competitors. We're there to meet the basic financial needs of the customer, whether it's moving money through cheques and direct debits, whether it's saving or whether it's borrowing. So let's keep it basic, let's keep it simple, let's keep it straightforward and let's do it right.'

It is a striking commentary on the self-satisfied attitude of some bank managements that preoccupation with the customer should be presented as daring or innovative. But that is still so in many corners of the City of London, thanks to centuries in which only the rich and prudent could aspire to being granted a bank account and the bank manager ranked with the vicar and the doctor as pillars of their local community. Although many retailers have been wary of trespassing on financial territory, consumer taboos about banks broke down long ago.

'The barriers to entry are coming down as a result of technology,' says Ellwood. 'I guess twenty years ago, if somebody wanted to borrow £5,000 they'd go and have a long session with their bank manager and he'd probably mark a £5,000 overdraft limit in his book and it would all be discussed in very heavy terms. Now, people who want to borrow £5,000 borrow it on a personal loan. They fill in a questionnaire and it is points-scored, credit- scored and it comes out either yes, no or do some more enquiries, and you don't have to be a genius to get into that game. It's closer to selling socks than some bankers would like to think. If you take socks as the product, you've got to make sure of the quality of the sock, that it's not going to fall to pieces, you've got to make sure that when you sell it you're making a certain amount of profit, and that it's what the customer wants. It's no use making red socks with pink stripes if no one wants to buy them. Equally, it's no use having a cheque account that doesn't pay interest if that's what people want. It's no use having a facility where you say you can have a loan but we're going to take three months over it. The same with the socks, they've got to be readily available. You've got to be able to give quick decisions and you've got to have the kind of product mix that is exactly what the customer wants. You've got know that the thing will work. If it is a loan, you will know that we will have, say, £50 a month out of your cheque account. In other words, the product and the mechanism has got to be robust, so there are a number of similarities there between socks and loans.'

TSB's research shows that its customers want certain fairly fundamental things from their bank, such as competence and consistency. If they want a standing order or direct debit changed by so much with effect from the fourth of next month, they want to be sure that precisely that will happen.

'It does not always happen,' Ellwood admits. 'And customers also want what I'd describe as care, a feeling of being valued, and this manifests itself in a number of ways. One of the things that customers say to us is that they don't want to transact non-routine business in the banking hall. They don't want one of our people coming up to them and saying "Can we talk to you about your account?" or any aspect of banking that might relate to them. They want to sit in a room to talk about that and be taken seriously. Consequently we have put in a thousand more interview rooms.'

However, it means much more than that. In 1991, when he was running the retail part of the bank, Ellwood saw that what was needed was a complete change of attitude. So he imported the Japanese idea of Total Quality Management, which means getting everything right first time, every time. That is a tall order, but companies which have adopted TQM have found that it raises standards, simply because it gives everyone something to aim at.

'Our customers naturally want to always get cash out of our cash machines,' Ellwood points out, 'and it's no use our saying the system is ninety-nine per cent up the whole time. If you look at the hundreds of millions of transactions that go through the system, if it's ninety nine percent up then that means that one in every hundred of those millions is not being properly serviced, and that's nowhere near good enough. So it can't even be 99.99 per cent right, it's got to be 99.9999 per cent or even, ideally, 100 per cent. It comes back to care. We've got a team saying "Why isn't it up the whole time? Why can't we have it 100 per cent right? What's wrong? Why can't we have these cash machines working right the whole time?" So it's getting closer and closer to an error-free organisation. It's showing respect to a customer, but it comes back again and again to having a demand-driven type of environment where we're much more conscious of the consumer than we were before. We will move increasingly towards an error-free society – we're far from that now – and to a situation where it is very unusual to have poor service, whereas now far too much ordinary service is considered good and we don't do enough about bad service to stop it becoming unacceptable. That means more training. TSB has increased its training spend considerably and will go on increasing it over the next decade.'

Ellwood is well aware of the penalties of failure: the threat from the likes of Marks & Spencer is all too real. Although they may have taken their time about going further than unit trusts, they have established their own in-store credit card and have a banking licence, so most of the elements are in place for M&S to stand in the market place as what would surely be one of the most popular banks in the world. 'They've got the customers' trust and that's why they're so much of a threat,' Ellwood concedes. 'I'd be surprised if they weren't more into it in a few years' time.'

The most important thing that consumers want, from TSB and other banks, is value for money. One of the big changes in banking over the last two or three decades has been the move towards interest-bearing cheque accounts. Bank customers understandably do not want to feel that they've been fleeced or that they've not had the best value for money. TSB has taken steps to stamp out that corrosive thought by deliberately starting to steer customers towards its most competitive accounts, even though they are the least profitable for the bank. 'We've seen billions of pounds moved from old-style accounts that we're not marketing any longer into new accounts that we are marketing very aggressively,' Ellwood reports, 'knowing that it will damage the bottom line but also knowing that if we don't do that in the consumer-orientated environment in which we live, we'll not only lose the balance but we'll lose the customer. So we're saying that it's not all about short-term profits, it's about the customer. You'll get the bank profits right if you look after the customer. If we're going to be driven by the demands of our customers then we've got to understand our customers and be on their side and we've got to meet their needs. So it's this preoccupation with the customer which is the biggest change and will continue to be the biggest change of attitude over the next decade.'

Such fine words are even more impressive when accompanied by matching action, and in 1993 TSB began experiments in Watford, on the north-west edge of the M25, and Tyneside. In each community a spectrum of branches has been set up, from a flagship offering the full range of services, to fully automated branches and cash dispensing machines in supermarkets. All the customers in those areas who bank with the TSB can use any branch. All the branches open full retail hours and customers have access to a seven days a week, twenty-four hours a day telephone service, aping Midland Bank's First Direct system – except that First Direct operates without branches.

'Our customers can talk to someone who knows what they're talking about because their account information is on a computer screen and they know about all our products,' explains Ellwood. 'If they want to ring up at three o'clock on Sunday afternoon and talk about a personal loan or insurance or about changing a direct debit then they can. I believe that offers a real way forward. In Watford we've got interactive screens where you can see the person you're dealing with for specialised inquiries, so we're using technology. Somebody phoned up on a Friday and said "I want to see somebody, but I can only see them on Saturday afternoon", and we said "No problem, we're open on Saturday afternoon." We got a fantastic response from that customer.'

Ellwood's thinking behind this sort of approach is to warm up the relationship with customers. Like his banking rivals, he wants to see TSB's customers going there for all their financial needs. That means moving out of other areas which, although related, have their own culture and carry their own pitfalls: hence the troubles with Target and Mortgage Express. Ellwood blames the latter's failure on the failure to build relationships with its customers. On the other hand, the group has done much better with the own-branded TSB mortgages it has sold through the branch network. 'Why?' he asks: 'because we know the customer. The provisions for bad debts that we have been writing on that business have been tiny.'

That success has emboldened Ellwood into making the most of TSB's strong position in so-called bancassurance, the piece of mangled franglais which is used to describe the banks' invasion of the life assurance market.

The principle is that if people want to borrow or save in the short term they will use a bank account, but for longer-term investments most of us go for an insurance or pensions policy. For generations banks have watched their customers walk out the door and round the corner to the nearest insurance broker: now they are trying to prevent that by keeping the business under the same roof, to the consternation of some traditional insurers.

'I think that insurance companies that don't have a real distribution network have got a real problem,' Ellwood declares. 'The bancassurance cross-fertilization policy has worked very well for us, but that's because we started twenty years ago and we have a higher level of penetration of insurance products into our banking customer base than any other financial institution. About a third of our customers who buy life and pensions policies buy them from the TSB. I think the secret is that they buy from the same brands, the same organisation. They are all TSB and we sell insurance only to TSB customers. We don't have an insurance business that goes and knocks on doors, so it's our customers, we know them and it's that closeness and that relationship that has facilitated our success in that area.'

Ellwood's experience with Barclaycard Profiles has convinced him that there is much more bank customers can be sold. But any such innovations have to be handled delicately, for people are naturally cautious and conservative about who meets their financial needs and whether they have their mind fully on that important job. So bank customers usually say no to any new suggestions. They didn't like cash dispensers before they were introduced. They said they wouldn't like home banking, either down a telephone or through a computer screen. Both have been successes, so innovations can work even though the advance research is unpromising.

'I think that it's likely that all that will change in the next fifteen years,' Ellwood insists. 'I think I am a lone voice on that. Most banks don't think that will happen, nor do most customers, but if you look at the customer bases, the power of telecommunications and information technology, then I think it's more likely than not to happen. Putting catalogues in mail shots has been relatively peripheral: it's not been quite what customers expect of their bank. But I think a wider product range will become more mainstream by the turn of the century. After all, banks have strong brands, good capital bases, good telecommunications links and broad distribution.'

One way in which TSB has been using its computers is to offer what it calls a Family Bonus. Most banks nowadays pay higher interest on successively bigger deposits – £20,000 earns not just more interest but a better rate than £2,000. Family Bonus gives all the members of a family the top rate for their total funds, without giving any information to the other members of the family about any individual account. TSB's cash dispensers have been made smarter, giving full statements if required. And, although Ellwood promises not to put an annual charge on Trustcard, the group's credit card, applicants must plug into the whole system by opening a TSB bank account.

Once he has got TSB up and running the way he wants it, Ellwood is setting his sights on Europe. 'All my experience and reading of banks moving into foreign fields is that they have not made a great success of it,' he observes. 'There are a lot of savings banks on the Continent that are at the stage that TSB was at in the 1980s, in that they are still owned by quasi-government authorities. A number of them around the world are now becoming PLCs and I suspect that they will go through what TSB went through. They'll need to get fitter and slimmer and more focused on service, more competitive. But there is a strong savings bank ethos in Europe, typically in the Low Countries and Germany. That could be a great opportunity for us in the long term.'

CHAPTER **6**

SIR ALISTAIR GRANT

of Argyll Group

All men who have turned out worth anything have had the
chief hand in their own education – *Sir Walter Scott*

SIR ALISTAIR GRANT, chairman of Argyll Group, the Safeway, Presto
and Lo-Cost supermarket company, is unusual among leading businessmen
in having a deep interest in literature, particularly that of his Scottish home-
land. He has read the entire works of Sir Walter Scott several times, can
recite Burns at length and is fond of such Victorian scribes as George Eliot,
Anthony Trollope, Anton Chekhov and Leo Tolstoy. Yet he has had to have
as much a hand in his own education as Scott implied was necessary in a
successful career. The eldest of six children, he spent his first nine years in
East Lothian (he has retained his soft Lowlands accent) before the family
moved to Yorkshire. There he won a scholarship to a minor local public
school. A superb set of papers in S Level English won him a place at
Edinburgh University. But National Service intervened, and like many in his
predicament he decided he could not afford the time to spend three years
studying for a degree on top of his two years in the Middle East with the
Royal Corps of Signals. A chance meeting with Unilever trainees after a
rugby match led him to the Batchelors soup and peas factory in Sheffield.
Academe took a back seat.

But years of making up for lost time have left their mark as Sir Alistair
has made the transition from executive raider to boardroom statesman.
'Opportunity comes out of the wings at Argyll,' he says in a phrase that
whispers his literary bent. 'Safeway came out of the wings. Our next major

Sir Matthew Alistair Grant

BORN: 6 March, 1937

EDUCATED: Woodhouse Grove School

MARRIED: Judith Dent, 1963. Two sons, one daughter

CAREER:

1958 Unilever
1963 J. Lyons
1965 Connell May & Steavenson
1968 Director, Fine Fare
1973 Managing Director, Oriel Foods
1977 Argyll Group
1986 Chief Executive, Argyll Group
1988 Chairman, Argyll Group

OTHER INTERESTS: Visiting professor, Strathclyde University, president of Instute of Grocery Distribution, president of Advertising Association, member of The Stock Exchange Listed Companies Advisory Committee, chairman of Agricultural and Food Research Council

ARGYLL GROUP PLC

HEAD OFFICE: 6 Millington Road, Hayes, Middlesex, UB3 4AY
Tel: 081-848 8744

ACTIVITIES: Food retailing

MAIN BRANDS: Safeway, Presto, Lo-Cost

development will come out of our readiness to do something with somebody who sees us as a competent business. It seems to me there are four or five businesses in Britain that are in the shape that would enable us to form part of a merger or acquisition. We continue to do massive amounts of research work on mergers and acquisitions but we have very, very tightly-drawn criteria. We won't buy anything that needs to be rescued. We won't buy anything that hasn't got the capacity to make certainly more than £50 million pre-tax in the short term. We wouldn't buy anything where we don't believe the existing management to be capable of becoming colleagues of our own. We wouldn't buy something where, by Day Two, we'd be running it ourselves. Mind you, it could also be that Argyll is part of someone else's strategy. We're big, but we're not so big that we'd be a daunting opportunity for someone else. That's a concern of mine because the food retailers have been somewhat undervalued. We're certainly worth more than the average, based on our knowledge of what we're going to do, but we've got to keep plugging away.'

That strategic outline says much about Sir Alistair's complex character, at once arrogant and cautious, presuming successful expansion but fearing an irresistible onslaught. On the prompting of his wife, Judi, the then 30-year-old Grant answered an advert by fellow Scots entrepreneur James Gulliver challenging 'future chief executives' to apply for a job. After eighteen years as Gulliver's apprentice and then loyal lieutenant, Sir Alistair took the top job at Argyll when Gulliver retired a beaten man from the fight with Guinness for control of Distillers Company in 1986. With former merchant banker David Webster, Gulliver and Sir Alistair had formed a formidable tri-umvirate at what was first James Gulliver Associates and became Argyll, buying their way onto the top table in the supermarket industry through a string of takeovers. For most of that time Gulliver was the shrewd if abrasive leader and Webster the cool analyst, while Grant was the one who was always eager to get things done. But now it is Sir Alistair who boasts the knighthood which Gulliver once craved and realistically envisaged gracing his own name.

'The reason Argyll flourished,' Sir Alistair explains, 'was simply that James was clever and David and I felt no embarrassment in having him as our leader. No matter what business issue he raised, there was a level of con-trolled discussion that was always fruitful.' But Sir Alistair was appalled by the revelation during the Distillers campaign that Gulliver had falsified his entry in *Who's Who* to suggest that he had been to Harvard Business School when he had not. Within a year of Guinness winning the prize – and later paying Argyll £100 million to settle litigation arising from dirty tricks during the bid – Gulliver had gone and Argyll had bought the UK end of the US-owned Safeway chain. That established Argyll as the country's third-biggest supermarketeer, behind J. Sainsbury and Tesco. Sir Alistair sees little scope to alter that pecking order. 'My view is that Sainsbury will be the industry leader at the end of the decade,' he predicts, 'but you mustn't believe that our industry is set in stone. In 1979 Asda was the top company in terms of profits, Tesco was next and Sainsbury number three. I would hope that we will be a strong number three in our industry with Tesco still being number two. But I think Asda will still feature in the market and that Kwik Save Group, William Morrison Supermarkets and Iceland Group will still be around. Morrison is clearly the company with the most potential to grow organically from its regional base in Yorkshire down to the rest of the country.'

Although he may feel that the retailing hierarchy is not set in stone, Sir Alistair seems resigned to settling for third place, both in the supermarket league and as a retailing brand. Just as he does not see Safeway overhauling Sainsbury or Tesco in the supermarket league, he does want it to be regarded as the nation's third best brand, after Marks & Spencer and Sainsbury. That, he believes, will involve a change in the order, for Safeway would have to overhaul Boots.

'Our challenge is to become an elite retail brand,' he declares. 'My perception of the brand hierarchy at the moment is that Marks & Spencer is at the top and Sainsbury has probably replaced Boots in the second position. I think Boots now are probably number three in terms of scale and in terms of consumers' perception. They've got some advantages: they've got many more stores than anybody else, they're involved in healthcare and they've been around for a long time so the consumer tends to love them. But I still think that the intensity of the relationship that the consumer has with the food operator and the quality of product and service that Sainsbury provide have put them probably number two in that hierarchy, whereas ten years ago, Boots and M&S would have been vying for number one. Our ambition in the next few years is to edge ahead of Boots. We're already a much bigger retailer than they are.'

The reason Sir Alistair is talking in those terms is that he sees the end of the great supermarket boom and realises that the leading groups can retain their position only by adding value, to use the standard management euphemism for raising profit margins, and fostering loyalty.

'The profit margin on the core range of proprietary groceries has probably stabilised,' he says in what may turn out to be something of an understate-ment. 'The growth of profit margin will come from adding own-brands in substitution for the proprietary brand, adding fresh foods, exploring the full range of product options available in the superstore.'

The arrival of the US-based Costco in the UK in 1994, following hard on the heels of Aldi and Netto from the Continent, meant that the meaning of value was being put to a severe test. In common with Sainsbury and Tesco, Sir Alistair maintained that his customers would prefer to pay a few pence more for assured standards, greater comfort and a wider range.

'I think discounters will continue to grow,' he concedes, 'but their main interface will be with Kwik Save. They will not take major market share away from the leading businesses, providing the top companies attend to their cost-base and improve efficiency. I believe that there is evidence in North America that the large-scale discounters are a phenomenon that hasn't got a very powerful long-term future, particularly if we and the non-food retailers, whose markets they're attacking, are willing to match their prices on large product sizes and case quantities when they arrive. And I'm sure we're going to do that. Discounters often take over the premises of a failed small retailer. In that way, they're not actually adding to the space devoted to food. They're very limited in their product offer. They're very committed to dry grocery and a very narrow range of fresh foods. We've found that our sales are little changed by the arrival of a discounter, but our net margin is actually improved because of its impact on other weaker retailers than ourselves.'

To make up for the sustained attack on Safeway's sales of the basic baked beans and sliced bread lines, the group is going to have change its act and stop pretending that it is the lowest-price option. Instead, it must claim the best value.

'I think that the scale of our operations per store, our unit size of the store, the quality of management that we can put into a store that's doing sales of £25 million a year, give us the opportunity,' Sir Alistair explains. 'Our chal-lenge is to be a performance-based business where shoppers say, "You're in stock, your prices are good, your fresh foods have been brought in fresh and are being sold fresh." And then we've got to add our product-based con-sumer franchise to that: our baby foods, wines, olive oils, breads, dairy prod-ucts have to be comparable with the best. My challenge is to manage the company through to the point where that is achieved.

'If you look at the great retail brands, M&S and Boots, they did have a period in their early life where they grew rapidly. M&S built 120 stores at the beginning of the 1930s and had a rush for growth. It is selling in an interesting position in the food market, because it's still got a pre-eminent product franchise for its chilled products and its general range of own-brands, but its commitment to the high street means that it's far less convenient for a housewife to shop there than it is to shop at Sainsbury's, Tesco, or ourselves, and each of us has got a much bigger food business than M&S. Once they got to a certain size, they looked at that very large scale and saw that what they needed to do was to manage their product portfolio within that scale very adroitly. They have to watch those products that are in decline, and those that are growing. They have to use expert systems in supply and merchandising to squeeze down the proportion of the store which is given to their core range, and if chilled foods or kitchenware is a growth area then they've got to be able to manage that for growth within a fixed real estate environment.'

That is why Safeway has led the way in opening dry-cleaning shops in its bigger stores, along with a pharmacy, a café/patisserie and a health and beauty shop. Although Sir Alistair has his discount chains up his sleeve – Lo-Cost and Presto – he knows that they will not be enough to enable Argyll to withstand a really vicious price war. So, as he graphically puts it, he has set about 'changing the tin whistle for the full orchestra'. Some of his competitors do not agree about every one of Safeway's innovations, especially the dry-cleaning outlets, but Sir Alistair can point to evidence of solid demand: since 1990, ideas for new stores have come from customer panels. The stakes are high. Safeway research shows that if a petrol station, a café/patisserie, a pharmacy, a dry-cleaners and a post office are added to a basic retail operation, total sales can increase by nearly fifty per cent, taking together sales of the new specialities and the extra sales in the core business from the additional traffic the specialities attract.

'The whole industry is becoming more interesting,' he points out, 'because it's putting a premium on sophisticated product management. You've got to have people who can think deeply about these product management issues. Growth won't come from a conventional range of grocery products. You've got to be very good at those, but you've got to be very expert at adding scale progressively at the other end. But if you look at things like baby foods or children's books, we've got to say that there's going to be another £10 million or £15 million of incremental business from them. If they don't achieve that then they've got to be replaced by another product which is doing a better job. In that way it's becoming like brand management rather than just retailing. By the end of the decade, we've got to be a product-based consumer franchise with the consumer saying: "We're going to Safeway because it's convenient, it's competitive on brands, it's got a wide range of goods and services and its own-brands give me value that I can't match anywhere else."'

The accuracy of such analysis depends on how the public responds to these changes. Or, looking at it the other way around, success rests on the supermarkets' ability to make the right assumptions about – or find out – what the public wants, to the extent that it knows what it wants. These are not fishing expeditions to discover the latest fad, but major social trends like more working women, more one-parent families, fewer marriages, more divorces, more foreign holidays and greater use of computer-driven technology. Then there have been the early 1990s recession and more widespread consciousness about the environment: all these developments have forced food retailers to rethink their strategies again and again.

Sir Alistair says: 'In 1988 one would have said that the irreversible trend in the market was towards green, environmentally conscious, socially conscious consumers, whereas there was a sharp counter-flow towards value for money in the next five years. But the long-run influence is towards the working woman, pressured for time and ambitious to feed her family in a more entertaining way. In the old days there were three or four formal family meal occasions: breakfast, lunch, tea and/or supper. Now everyone is taking breakfast at a different time independently. No one is taking lunch at home and the meal occasions at night can run along quite a long time-frame from the children coming home from school at half past four or five o'clock, often helping themselves to snacks, to the woman sometimes eating with them, sometimes waiting until the husband comes home, to the more formal occasions on Friday or Saturday nights or Sunday lunchtime.'

Sir Alistair admits that Safeway's management still think of themselves as aiming at the archetypal woman at home with two or three children and husband out at work. However, they are learning that their market is much more complex than that. During the week, particularly in the north, a large number of Safeway's shoppers are women accompanied by their men.

'The key things that are emerging in our market are the paradoxes between two types of shopper who can often be the same woman behaving in two ways,' Sir Alistair adds. 'You've got the working woman who's pressured for time and very interested in convenience, who will pay a premium for an assured end result or added value. Chilled meals, frozen foods, pizzas and delicatessen products are very interesting to her. That same woman, in a different frame of mind, she's educated, she's travelled, she owns her own home, she's spent a lot of money with her husband on decorating it, she's got a big sense of achievement out of what they've done together and she's increasingly into health and the environment. So she's got another mind-set when she's going around buying fresh products, looking for meal ideas and considering entertaining at the home. She's more and more confident about buying products like herbs, spices, exotic fruits and vegetables, wider ranges of meats. She's often vegetarian. She's becoming very confident indeed about buying generic wines – she's not very interested in buying branded wines.'

Another factor is the growing proportion of older and richer consumers, many of whom have retired at fifty-five. They are relatively well-off couples, shopping together, playing golf together and going on holidays together. They are interested in health and beauty products and pharmacies. They increasingly see a shopping expedition as a branch of the entertainment industry.

'In the south of Scotland,' Sir Alistair reports, 'you have people who drive down to the Metro centre in Gateshead on Sunday afternoon because of the wide range of shopping. So shopping has to be seen as the provision of goods and services, but it's also about entertainment – fresh foods, health and beauty aids, café/patisserie, delicatessen, wine products, have all got to be part of that entertainment. When supermarkets open on the edge of a town, they've either got to have that entertainment feel or they've got to have supporting retailers who provide it. So you see Marks & Spencer developing, as we have, on the edge of Edinburgh with 35 other retailers and 3,000 car-parking spaces. We're creating an entertainment area as well as a food and a non-food service.'

Safeway is having to cater for this demand for amusement by getting its act together. It is no longer enough to have a French week – it has to be a Provençale or Alsatian week. Better distribution systems and bigger stores make this an economic proposition, so long as customers are not too resentful that in the end they are paying for all this hoopla. That also gives more scope for local staff initiative.

'Now the stores are bigger,' argues Sir Alistair, 'the store managers are highly intelligent and the computer systems give you very good feedback so you can be very precise in what you offer. It's about returning power to the manager and making him the partner of the management centre of the group, where they're both debating with the same access to information. Ten years ago, the centre said, "We know it all, you know bugger all, so we'll tell you what to do." Now a manager is saying: "Did you notice that I sold seven cases of basil last week, and if you look at my scanning data, on the top three of the seven days we sold out of basil at four o'clock?" And if they can find a supply of tomatoes to go with the basil they've got a feature. Instead of the centre saying, "This sounds like wildness," they're saying: "Hey, this makes the store a lot more interesting", so it's happening a lot more.'

Sir Alistair and his top team realise that as the business gets bigger, you have to produce a career structure that lets Argyll compete for management with the likes of Unilever or Shell. In the 1990s a good store manager can earn £50,000 a year with bonuses. But, once they have got used to that standard of living, the really bright managers can still grow bored if there is not enough in the job. That comes down to Sir Alistair ensuring that there is the right balance between their capacity to influence the business and the group's capacity to influence the managers.

'They've got to feel that they've got a lot of job satisfaction,' Sir Alistair insists. 'We've also got to be willing to share the fruits of capitalism more widely. Around 300 members of Argyll are members of the stock option scheme and I hope they share with the top management the fairly educated view about short-term and long-term performance. It means that, when we have conferences and we are talking about the strategy for the businesses, people can share a common view about what we're trying to achieve. I think we will expand the 300, but it's a balance between those that you feel can influence the business and those for whom it would be seen as a form of bonus. I sort of know 300 people in the business really well. But I expect at the end of the decade there could be twice that. I think it's a good idea to make it more universal to give more people a sense of belonging.'

Naturally, a growing proportion of that top bracket will be women. Argyll takes about sixty graduates a year, of whom more than half are women. By 1994 the group had two female non-executive directors, restaurateur Prue Leith and marketing guru Ann Burdus, but no women executive directors. However, Sir Alistair was able to claim many bright thirty to thirty-five-year-old women in the business and climbing the ladder. 'We've obviously got to provide better mid-career facilities for those whose careers are disrupted through childbirth,' he says, 'but I would expect that by the end of the decade we might have two women executive directors of Safeway.'

However, the bad news for the first woman to take over as chairman of Argyll Group is that she is likely to find herself running a mature company that is gently running out of growth – unless it has diversified away from supermarkets into more general retailing.

Sir Alistair concluded: 'We've defined our corporate strengths as being that we understand retailing. We understand a business where you negotiate with your suppliers, not with your consumers. Where you manage dispersed profit centres, where the financial control and supply-chain management are important and where your core management skills in terms of consumers in product development, consumer marketing at the point of sale and merchandising. That describes what we're doing in food but that could also describe fast food, restricted areas in non-foods. If we say that by the end of the decade we'll have ten million square feet of selling space in Safeway and within that we're addressing a very wide range of product opportunities. I don't think that we will run out of growth. That might be what I have done to my successor. It's a very large retail business which is adapted to exploiting a wide range of product opportunities within the UK market.'

CHAPTER 7

TONY GREENER

of Guinness

GUINNESS is the enigma of the drinks industry. It has no pubs, no restaurants, no hotels – just the only world-renowned stout and a portfolio of spirits brands that any other company in the world, of whatever industry, would chop its legs off for. Those assets have been built carefully over more than a hundred years, but they put Guinness in the vulnerable position of having to defend what it has, rather than attacking the market position of others. As there is very little difference between its products and rival versions, even in the stout trade, it has to rely on marketing. Logically enough, in 1993 the company selected as chairman Tony Greener, who has been steeped in marketing at those corporate universities in the discipline, Unilever and Dunhill. The question is whether Greener's undoubted skills will prove wide enough for the challenges that lie ahead.

As Greener likes to point out, Guinness has a history dating back to 1759 but it was reborn in its present form only in 1986. That was the year of the ill-omened but ultimately successful takeover by Guinness of Distillers Company, owner of Johnnie Walker, Dewars, White Horse and Black & White whisky, Gordon's gin, Cossack vodka and Pimm's, but for so many years the slumbering, lumbering giant of the spirits industry. At once the deal transformed Guinness from a middle-sized proprietor of a world-famous brand of stout into a global spirits player which happened to make stout almost as an aside. The takeover temporarily achieved a wider notoriety after sparking off a complex series of criminal trials which scarred the careers of Ernest Saunders and Olivier Roux, respectively the chairman and finance director of Guinness at the time, as well as a clutch of advisers and other business figures. 'I think where the Distillers Company lost its way,'

says Greener, 'was that they made a fine product called scotch whisky and they assumed that it was something the world would always want to drink, and therefore all you had to do was put it on a boat and send it to your distributor, end of story. The reality is that scotch whisky is in competition with many other forms of alcoholic products, and on a wider basis it's in competition with a whole range of prestige products. So it's only when you look at the consumer benefits of what you're saying that you think about competition and you think about how you present your products, how you market your products to the consumer in the appropriate way, and you start adjusting the product offer.'

Like Peter Jarvis of Whitbread, Greener is a graduate of the marketing-led Unilever school of business. Leaving Marlborough College with one A Level, he went straight to Thames Board Mills, which made the packaging for Unilever's many products, from soap powder to margarine. Whereas some marketing men swear by their early days on the road, with a crate of samples in the back of a Cortina, Greener thanks his first employers for giving him eighteen months' shiftwork in the factory. 'As far as I am concerned,' he insists, 'it was the best higher education I could possibly get, particularly for someone coming out of a public school.' After a spell in accounting and sales, he was sent abroad and returned to be technical manager of a new plant in Cumbria. But eventually the lure of selling proved too much.

Greener made a Saunders-style transition from marketing to general management at Dunhill, the then family-run cigarette company. What he did, very cleverly, was to exploit the Dunhill name by stamping it on other goods that had nothing to do with smoking but everything to do with a certain smart masculine style, like aftershave lotion, watches and ties, as well as Mont Blanc pens and Chloë fashions which Dunhill took over.

Guinness and Greener joined hands when he was drafted in by Saunders as a non-executive director after the row over the removal of Thomas Risk, governor of the Bank of Scotland, as chairman of Guinness in the summer of 1986. Greener is shrewd enough to realise that the Guinness name, revered as it is in drinking circles the world over, is not strong enough to take on the stretching to which he subjected Dunhill.

'The great strength of Guinness,' he says, 'is that we are a very narrow-focused business. What we did at Dunhill was done in a coherent way so that you were just taking a property with a lot of inherent strength and developing it. We clarified the position of Dunhill to the consumer rather than changed it. I think here we're doing the same thing, we're clarifying the

Anthony Armitage Greener

BORN:	26 May, 1940
EDUCATED:	Marlborough College
MARRIED:	Min Ogilvie, 1974. One son, one daughter

CAREER:

1958	Joins family cotton waste business
1959	Thames Board Mills
1970	Marketing Director of Thames Board Mills
1972	Retail Controller, Dunhill Holdings
1974	Director, Dunhill Holdings
1975	Managing Director, Dunhill Holdings
1986	Director, Guinness
1993	Chairman, Guinness

OTHER INTERESTS: Director of Louis Vuitton Moët Hennessy, Reed Elsevier

GUINNESS PLC

HEAD OFFICE: 39 Portman Square, London W1H 9HB
Tel: 071-486 0288

ACTIVITIES: Brewing, distilling, marketing and distribution

MAIN BRANDS: Guinness, Johnnie Walker, White Horse, Dewars, Black and White, Cossack, Pimm's

image with the consumer. In industrial terms, we're saying that we've got a better chance of being successful if we focus all of our attention, all of our resources, all of our people on doing well what we know a bit about. And we're more likely to be successful doing what we know about very well rather than popping off into areas that we don't know about.'

So in recent years there has been a determined effort to brighten and co-ordinate the marketing messages of the Guinness group's portfolio of drinks, particularly the spirits. Many of its whisky brands had been competing against each other as mini-empires, which had been allowed to establish themselves across products and in different countries. The market leader, Johnnie Walker, has been exploited in a textbook marketing exercise. A progression has been laid down, from Johnnie Walker Red Label to Black Label, Blue Label, Gold Label, Premier, Honour and liqueur variants – each one more exclusive and therefore more expensive than the one before.

Greener has a touching faith that, as long as Guinness has a clear focus, with a strategy laid down for beer and spirits in every territory, and keeps doing things better, then it must prosper. 'I think there are great opportunities,' he says, 'and I think that's why one can be reasonably optimistic about the future, because by definition, if we do our job properly, we're going to be running our business a hell of lot faster and better than we are today. It's getting that integrated in a strategic planning sense, so the whole thing adds up to the top and what we're saying at the top relates to what is being done at the market place. Then it's about getting the right people in the right jobs who work sensibly together, and developing those people in their jobs so that they can get their maximum potential and have a high trade union development and coaching so that's your organisation side of it. Then you've got your brand side of it, which is the development of the brand to the consumer, and those again are part of your brand strategies and inherent market strategies, which understand what the consumer is looking for and deliver it and that's about human perception of brands.'

That summary makes Greener's job sound incredibly simple, and he has duly turned words into deeds by recruiting more than 50 senior marketing executives from the likes of Mars, Procter & Gamble and Unilever and told them to forget soap powder, margarine and chocolate bars and think drink. The trouble, as Greener readily admits, is that most people cannot tell the difference between one unlabelled scotch and another. So the manufacturers are virtually forced to deal in brands, images and other paraphernalia of the advertising circus.

And, as Greener is all too well aware, brand perception, particularly in the drinks business, changes very slowly. A typical take-home consumer might buy a bottle of scotch once a month, but a packet of cigarettes every day or so.

'I mean, why would you buy Bell's against Famous Grouse, or vice versa?' he asked. 'It's all about perception of brands. There are a whole load of different stimuli to that, making those stimuli persuade you to change from Grouse to Bell's or persuading you that you ought to change from drinking Guinness to lager and getting you to like it. That's a hell of a long-term process. It's one that's about peer pressure, because if you go to a pub and you see your mates drinking Guinness rather than lager then you might try it, and if it's a smart thing to drink then you might say real men drink Guinness, wimps drink lager, that sort of thing. But actually getting that momentum and getting to the consumer to make him behave in a particular way and start doing that is just a very, very long term process. So the brand building element of our business is not a two-year or three-year programme: it takes five to ten years to really make an impression.'

Allowing for the ups and downs of the economic cycle, Greener believes that the drinks market will become more competitive throughout the world, because if companies are going to succeed and develop then they've got to improve performance and increase market share. 'The people who continue to survive and do well will be the people who understand their consumer best and provide a package which is attractive to the consumer,' he declares.

'Not only do people want to drink high quality drinks,' Greener argues, 'it goes much deeper than that because brands of scotch whisky, like Black Label, are a badge where people can say I'm becoming more affluent, more sophisticated, I can appreciate these fine international products. The fact that scotch sells in almost every country in the world and is seen as an international high quality product, epitomises exactly what I'm talking about. I don't think the issue is about manufacturing adjustment, the issue is about a marketing adjustment and that's a critical point. The reality of life is that the world is our market place, that you only succeed in that market place by understanding consumer opportunities and understanding the needs of the market and producing that in an innovative and, above all else, in a highly cost-effective way. But the idea that you could make what you've always made and sell around the world what you've always been able to sell in the UK, is outrageous and it'll never work. I think that those UK companies that have succeeded on an international basis are those who have very clearly understood the consumer opportunities and they have got something the consumer wants to buy. As far as I'm concerned, our products are exactly what I'm thinking about, because they are products made in Britain and have a real consumer benefit around the world.'

It is clear that Greener feels that the Guinness stout is more vulnerable to competition than the group's spirits portfolio. This is as much as anything to do with the huge latent threat of the American brewers to spread their wings beyond their own shores. By comparison, the scotch market is tied up, even though most of the sacred distilleries have fallen into foreign hands. While scotch can be made only in Scotland, it is sufficiently concentrated to be transportable anywhere at an economic price. Beer, on the other hand, is too bulky to be transported very far without sending the price rocketing, but it can be made pretty well anywhere.

'There's still considerable scope for national grouping in beer,' argues Greener. 'Whether there's a lot of industrial logic to international grouping on the beer side is an open question, and international brands of beer have not been developed to anything like the extent that international spirits have. There are plenty of physical and practical reasons why that's the case so far. Marlboro cigarettes is a totally international brand, Coca Cola is a totally international brand. You could argue that if they really got behind it, Budweiser or Miller could become truly international, if the Americans really set out to conquer the world and were prepared to spend enough money on it. Given the strength of the imagery of the American lifestyle – Coca Cola, Levi's, McDonald's and all these sorts of things – then why not in beer? I think that's a very interesting, and at this stage, entirely open question.'

The Coke analogy fascinates Greener. 'How can you persuade Herr Schmidt,' he asks, 'who's been drinking this Bavarian lager for the last 500 years, that Budweiser is the beer that he ought to start drinking? Of course, the answer is that you won't. All you'll do is persuade Herr Schmidt's children that the American lifestyle is something that they would want to move to. So, it's a generational thing and it starts with people in their twenties who are coming into the market place. It'd be a bold man who'd say it can't be done. Fosters is a wonderful example of a business which is built on financial engineering and bullshit and bravado – it wasn't built on real values. That's 100 per cent different from Phillip Morris and Miller, which are very well-run businesses which understand the consumer and the industry inside out. So, you've got a solid and immensely well-run base from which to think of moving ahead.'

But could there not come a day when everyone has all the drink they can drink, and – as in large swathes of the developed world – getting tipsy becomes something that the older and untrendy tend to do, so that the status symbols that matter are cars and houses? Does alcohol then fade into the background?

One threat which could push drinks onto the slippery slope which tobacco has been slithering down for years is the relentless and never-diminishing attack from the anti-alcohol health lobby. In 1993 the pressure point was in France, where restrictions were placed on alcohol advertising. Greener is concerned to beat out the bush fires, wherever they are, before they join up and take hold.

'I think these increased restrictions are something that the industry has got to deal with,' he says, 'and the fact that that law came in in France was entirely the industry's fault, because we failed to see early enough what was happening and to do something about it. We're selling a product which is used by ninety-five per cent of people in a sensible and moderate way, but there is an element of abuse which is damaging to us and is totally not in our interests. For the ninety-five per cent of people who enjoy alcohol and use it sensibly, there is a significant health benefit from it. That is the essential difference between the alcohol and tobacco industries: I don't think that anybody can produce any evidence that smoking tobacco is anything but bad for you. There is the evidence with respect to alcohol that it is 100 per cent safe. Having said that, it is certainly not our job to persuade people to drink too much, it's not only not our job but it's something that we must not do.'

Ironically, given the level of anti-alcohol feeling in France, Greener believes that the French have got the right attitude, along with the Italians and Spanish. 'They are extremely sensible,' he argues, 'because wine particularly is an everyday part of life and children are brought up on it, and are allowed to sample it from an early age, and it becomes a natural part of life instead of this big deal that you're not allowed to touch until you're twenty-one. Clearly, what is not the answer to the problem is the World Health Organisation saying we want to drop the consumption of alcohol by twenty-five per cent. That's ridiculous, it doesn't affect the problem because the people who are alcohol-dependent are going to remain dependent. Just to say that because fewer people overall are drinking alcohol it is going to affect the hardcore – there's no logic behind that. Restrictions on our ability to trade and the anti-alcohol movement, if it's left unfettered, could have enormous consequences for us. That's where our real interest is and it's one we've all got to understand.'

Failure to comprehend and deal with that problem will leave the drinks industry open to higher taxation, just as tobacco is succumbing to in Britain.

The UK drinks industry is happily protected from direct assault by the perceived need to harmonise with the rest of the European Union, which generally has higher rates of VAT, with few qualms about taxing food, but lighter duties on cigarettes and alcohol. Indeed, Greek and Italian tobacco and grape farmers have tagged onto the agricultural lobby, while the French and German vineyards constitute an important producer interest. Greener and his counterparts in other British drinks companies naturally latch onto this different treatment.

'I don't think there is any other industry in the world in which Britain has the three or four leading companies except the spirits industry – ourselves, Grand Met and Allied-Lyons,' says Greener. 'There is no other industry in the world of which that could be said. And yet here we are, taxing spirits we make at double the rate of wine. There's just no sense in it. We go around the world to sell our products and we say to foreign governments, "Look here, you're discriminating against scotch whisky and other imported spirits in favour of your local products," and they say, "First of all, the rate that we tax spirits is a third of what you apply in the UK, and secondly, you're talking about discrimination against spirits but what we do against spirits is a fraction of what you do." So the things that we're doing domestically in the UK are mildly damaging in the UK, but they are a significant barrier to our worldwide business. The problem is that in many European countries – France, Italy, Germany – wine is taxed at a zero level or it is not taxed, and one understands the political difficulties for them in starting to tax wine. That's where we came from and that's the difficulty. I think the UK government are in an awful mess, between a rock and a hard place.'

Not surprisingly in view of these complex cross-currents, Greener confesses that he has not the faintest idea where Guinness is going to be at the turn of the century. It suits his temperament to react strongly against the wheeler-dealer atmosphere of the 1980s, when the deal was the thing and takeovers were a short cut to solid achievement. That is all to the good, but it tends to place a company like Guinness into more of a role of responding to events rather than dictating them. It may be a race against time for Greener before the memories of the 1987 stock market crash and early 1990s recession fade sufficiently for the paperchase to start up again.

CHAPTER 8

TONY HALES

of Allied Domecq

ALLIED DOMECQ is the food and drink company that aims to be everything to everyone, whether it is a cup of tea, a doughnut, a shot of whisky, gin, brandy or liqueur, a pint of bitter, a glass of sherry, a scoop of ice cream or a full-scale meal.

'What we're after is share of throat,' smiles Tony Hales, the group's keen, youthful and energetic chief executive. 'All our products go down there,' he adds with the matter-of-factness born salesmen tend to exhibit when they are off-stage, putting his index finger into his wide open mouth to emphasise the point. It is a blunt way of illustrating a basic truth about the catering trade. If you can't persuade people to put your products to their lips, consistently over a large chunk of their lifetimes, you are dead. At least, you are if you operate on the grand scale of a group like Allied.

Allied is still, like many of its publicans, trying be all things to all men. It was originally an amalgam of local breweries that came together as Allied Breweries. But then they added the J. Lyons cakes business in 1978, and more recently have gone for a huge expansion into spirits. The group now has five major spirits brands – Ballantine's whisky, the Mexican coffee liqueur Kahlua, Beefeater gin, Canadian Club whisky and Courvoisier brandy – Carlsberg, Tetley, Castlemaine XXXX and Skol beers, Tetley tea, and a retail division made up of Baskin-Robbins ice cream parlours, Dunkin' Donuts coffee-and-doughnuts bars and 5,500 UK pubs.

'They all appeal to a similar sort of consumer,' Hales points out, 'the new middle class, got some disposable income, wish to make a statement in society about who they are and what they are.' One way to do that is to have a bottle of Ballantine's seventeen-year-old on the table in the bar or the

Anthony John Hale

BORN:	25 May, 1948
EDUCATED:	Repton School and Bristol University
MARRIED:	Linda Churchlow 1975. Three sons, one daughter

CAREER:

1969	Cadbury Schweppes, Food Salesman
1977	Cadbury Typhoo, Foods Marketing Manager
1979	Joshua Tetley & Son (part of Allied-Lyons), Marketing Director
1987	Director of Allied Breweries Retail Director of Ansells
1989	Director of Allied-Lyons Chief Executive of J. Lyons & Co.
1991	Chief Executive of Allied-Lyons

OTHER INTERESTS: Member of the Institute of Marketing and the Brewers' Company

ALLIED DOMECQ PLC

HEAD OFFICE: 24 Portland Place, London W1N 4BB
Tel: 071-323 9000

ACTIVITIES: Spirits and wine, retailing, brewing and wholesaling, food manufacturing

MAIN BRANDS: Ballantine's and Canadian Club whisky, Beefeater gin, Courvoisier brandy, Cockburn's port, Harvey's of Bristol sherry, Kahlua liqueur, Tetley bitter, Tetley tea, Ansells, Ind Coope and Taylor Walker pubs, Baskin-Robins and Dunkin' Donuts eateries and Victoria Wine off-licences.

nightclub, or, at a younger level, strut their stuff at Allied's Dunkin' Donuts or Baskin-Robbins parlours.

Allied is relying on the strength of its international brands to take it into foreign markets. The brands are being used as a calling card from which Allied hopes to strike up relationships which will blossom into partnerships – an ambitious ploy, in such a fluid and fast-moving set of businesses as food, drink and catering.

The top priority of Hales, Allied's chief executive since 1991, is the international expansion of the spirits business. That's where he reckons the big bucks are to be made, in a battle fought out in global advertising space and time. 'I don't think there is a huge difference between the strategies being employed by the major drinks companies,' Hales declares. 'In the total world liquor market, seven per cent is taken up by the major international brands, so there is a hell of a lot of room for them to grow at the expense in many cases of the local rice or cane liquors, without having to directly cut each other's throats or margins. The odds are increasingly against a small operator breaking into the big league. There are likely to be more alliances.' So Hales is building Allied's existing spirits interests across the globe whilst buying into local distribution companies. That way Allied controls the marketing and distribution of its brands and takes a slice of the distributor's margin as well as the brand owner's margin. Allied, on its own, has less than a tenth of the big players' share of the market. But, if you add its relationships with Suntory of Japan and others, Allied's share is nearer to twenty per cent overall.

'It's one of the things we think we're pretty good at, partnerships,' says Hales. 'Normally our expertise would be in brands and technology, and our partner's would be local distribution and market knowledge. It requires a mutual respect where the cultures fit, and it's worked for us extremely well. We'd expect to see more of that sort of thing. It's harder for American companies to operate in that way, because they tend to say "that's our way of doing things in Chicago," or wherever, "and that's the way we want you to do it around the world". I'm not saying they're wrong, but I think there is competitive difference to be had by working well with local partners.' For the understated 'competitive difference', read 'competitive edge'. In other words, the world is still too big and diverse for one company to cover it all without opening itself to charges of commercial imperialism or colonisation – the sort of criticism that has dogged Coke and McDonald's. Partnership can achieve the same result, without so much of the mud-slinging from outraged local lobbyists.

Already more than a quarter of Allied's profits are earned in North America, a seventh from the rest of Europe, and a tenth from the rest of the world, where Japan figures large. By the turn of the century those proportions will all have grown. Most of Allied's assets – its breweries, factories and pubs – are in the relatively mature economies of Europe and the US. But the Pacific and South America are where Hales sees the major opportunities. 'They are high risk,' he concedes, 'but that is a factor one can accept with high growth possibilities. We extend our reach with local partners in a slow, careful, step-by-step approach. We have built on a drinks relationship with Suntory to sell foods with them in Australia, Korea, Thailand and Taiwan. But China is the most exciting. We have three offices in China – in Beijing, Shanghai and Guangzhou, across the border from Hong Kong.'

In South America Allied is mainly in Argentina and Brazil, but Venezuela, Chile, even Colombia, are on the list for expansion. The group has a springboard in Mexico with Domecq. 'We've worked extremely well with them in Spain,' says Hales, 'and we are building the business through them in Mexico. That, to us, would be the most exciting growth market in central or South America. It has a huge population, 85 million people, sixty-three per cent of them twenty-two years old or under.' With the completion of the North American Free Trade Area, involving Canada, the US and Mexico, Allied sees great possibilities there, and has signed a long-term distribution deal on its whisky brands for Mexico.

Hales regards Eastern Europe as probably a higher risk area than South America because most of the countries there are less stable politically. Allied has a fruit operation in Poland, and a tea factory in the Czech Republic from where it sells to Hungary and Poland. It has a fruit juice factory in Ukraine, a bakery in St Petersburg, and an ice-cream plant in Moscow. 'We're putting our fingerprints down,' says Hales. 'It's pretty small beer, but we're there and if those economies start to really show some stability and then sustained growth, we've got a springboard from which to grow.'

The second priority on Hales's list, after expanding spirits internationally, is expanding Allied's retail concepts: Dunkin' Donuts, Baskin-Robbins ice cream and its UK pubs. It has branches of Baskin-Robbins in Korea and Russia, and Dunkin' Donuts in the US, Australia and Thailand.

Hales believes that the world's taste buds are slowly harmonising, although it will be many years before they all sing the same song. McDonald's has gone well all round the world, from Los Angeles to Beijing, taking in Moscow on the way. 'Baskin-Robbins is doing well in Moscow, too – and in Japan,' Hales reports. 'But the Chinese are not going to stop eating rice, and the Brits are not going to stop eating bread and we're all going to have some sort of mixture. I think there will just be a rather gradual convergence of a minority towards international brands, particularly in growth-type areas like snacks, fast food, liquor. America is influential because it's the biggest opinion-former in the world. It's the richest economy, people aspire to a lot of American values. But if one is philosophising, I wonder if in ten years' time that's really going to be the case. One actually wonders whether America is going to have a highly competitive industry which is going to be capable of meeting the competition from the Pacific ten years hence.'

So, Hales suggests, the world's eyes might start shifting to Chinese or Japanese products and culture. 'By the year 2000 I hope and think that many of the styles of business that are in Japan will permeate to Europe,' he says. 'We need them. I hope that the days of the 1980s, of rather excessive financial engineering, high debt, inflation covering up lots of people's sins, are over. In the 1990s, as we go to 2000, we'll be in a lower inflationary climate. It won't be so easy to cover up people's mistakes through overexpansion and I hope we'll go back to building businesses with investment in productive, highly efficient capacity, more investment in innovation, more investment in building brands. This is what we are trying to do, providing that difficult bridge of delivering reasonable growth for one's shareholders but at the same time investing heavily in the business. If we don't, in the UK sense, we've got very poor prospects in the year 2000.'

A big seller for Allied in the 1990s is tea, where it has launched Tetley's round tea bags across the US against Unilever's long-established Lipton's tea. 'If you go back to 1989,' says Hales, 'Tetley was a poor second in the UK market, with a declining market share and looked as though it was going nowhere. Then we had this innovation of round tea bags and marketed it extremely well, I think, and now we're the leading tea company in the UK. We've put it into Ireland and now have over sixty per cent of the Irish tea market. We're over thirty per cent in Canada, and the big challenge is the US, where Lipton's were four times our size.'

Allied has flirted with restaurant chains and retreated. In the mid-1980s, when lifestyle catering and street theatre were all the rage, Allied sprouted several chains, Muswells, Callendars, Cavaliers and Golden Oak Inns. Its Soho Brasserie won *The Times* Brasserie of the Year award. Now they have all either been closed or are being wound down. Hales's 1992 annual report had only one sentence on such eateries: 'In the UK, our Big Steak pub brand added a further twenty-six units, its value-for-money formula proving highly relevant to consumer needs.' Big Steak does in fact go a little way beyond thumping great slabs of meat hanging over the sides of the plate, but it's straightforward pub nosh, order at the bar and the food is brought to the table. Carry your own drinks. Hardly the stuff dreams are made of.

Hales explains: 'We'd like to have had some more of the Callendars and Muswells, but the difficulty of obtaining really cracking sites held us back. Now I think we know how we make our money, which is much closer to the pub side of things. Europe-wide restaurant chains do have potential to make money, but not run by us. Selling liquor is not as complicated as running a restaurant. It arrives in a package and you have to dispense it: you don't have to create it from a whole host of raw ingredients. Doughnut and coffee – two products. Ice cream – essentially one product. Easily controlled businesses. Much more capable of being run when you're running thousands of them than restaurants, which are a lot of detail. I personally think that, in the restaurant trade, the entrepreneur has many competitive advantages over the chain. It's difficult to keep an individual flavour across a chain, and perhaps in our case it fell apart a little bit.'

So, aside from the specialised Dunkin' Donuts and Baskin-Robbins, Allied in Britain has retreated to what it knows best: its pubs, reduced to 5,500 under the 1989 Beer Orders, half of them managed, half tenanted. The approach is to let the individuality of the property and the licensee maintain the personality of the pub at the front of the house, but behind the scenes lead everything from supply lines, to information systems, back to head office. 'I think we have excellent systems in terms of our marketing, our site targeting and the way that we classify, measure and monitor our pubs in a marketing sense,' claims Hales. 'We have excellent systems in terms of the computerised Electronic Point of Sale till in the pub, which has empowered the publican. It's a tool which gives the manager a chance to run his pub, rather than a spy for senior management to run the pub. We can see that continuing, as long as the technology doesn't get in the way of the customer, and all the time it is freeing up time for the licensee to be with his customers. It will lead to automatic ordering of product. We're not quite there yet, but we're rapidly moving towards that, which will again make life easier in an admin sense for the licensee.'

Allied is also using the consequent torrent of information to measure different pricing models, different product mix, and the pubs themselves have been divided into clusters, each of a different type. A young person's venue pub is defined differently, in terms of its product mix, pricing, promotions, even staffing, from a traditional local blue-collar worker's pub. A quality suburban food house is different from a city-centre business-driven drinking pub. Allied has about ten different kinds of pub, each based on a model. Area managers are continually comparing their houses with the models. By cross-referencing with demographic and social trends, the reference houses are also used to identify new sites and decide where to invest, whether it is another disco pub in Basildon or a new business bar in central Manchester. The models are constantly changed to keep up with drinkers' new habits.

In 1993 Allied got together with the Danish Carlsberg group to bring its UK breweries under a £500 million joint-venture company called Carlsberg-Tetley, ranking third biggest behind Bass and the Australian-owned Courage. The aim of the deal was unashamedly to cut costs, so one of the first moves was to close seven depots owned by the two partners. However Michael Heseltine, as President of the Board of Trade, exacted tough conditions in return for approving the merger, including an insistence that Allied releases another 400 pubs from its tie by 1997. That in itself is no great hardship, for Hales admits that he would not want that many more than Allied is allowed.

'They'd just be higher quality,' he grumbles. 'The progression anyway was numbers coming down. The progression in the industry was towards more free trade, and more take-home trade, which is also free. What the Beer Orders did was accelerate that process and compress what would have happened anyway into a bloody awful timescale, at a time when the property market was collapsing. It couldn't have been a worse time. It was the poor old tenant who had to accommodate change at a huge rate or get out, or have his pub sold under him and all that sort of thing. We would rather have a set of rules that we know. The worst thing is when the rules change every day. A lot of these regulations are like a big jelly: push them in one side and there's a reaction that comes out the other side. So then they put another bit of law in to squash it in there, and then it pops out somewhere else. The regulators are all the time trying to hold this jelly in place. But that's not how a market operates.'

The more immediate problem has been the official opening of the European Single Market, which abolished the limits on how much duty-free alcohol, tobacco, perfume and other goods Brits could bring back from the other eleven European Union countries. As lorry after lorry trundles off the ferries, groaning under the weight of liquid, Hales reckons that as much as a tenth of the UK take-home beer trade is now coming in from the Continent, allegedly for personal consumption. Hales guesses that more than half is being sold commercially. 'Customs & Excise will do a valiant job,' he says, 'and probably catch people on a regular basis, but if they catch one in ten, people are still going to keep bringing it in, because the rewards are very high. So there has to be progressive harmonisation of duties, which hopefully will not mean people moving up in real terms to the UK level. I suspect duties on the Continent will come up: I hope we'll come down. The Scandinavians are starting to come down.'

But at least Allied is managing one export success against all the odds. It is selling pre-packaged John Bull pubs in containers to eastern Europe. 'I wouldn't say it's the height of sophistication,' Hales admits, 'but it is pretty sophisticated in these economies, which have had so little over the last few years.' But it is unlikely that Allied will repeat the trick in western Europe. They have enough of their own bars.

CHAPTER 9

MICHAEL HOFFMAN

of Thames Water

RUNNING WATER is big business. By the end of 1993, the industry was valued by the stock market at nearly £15,000 million – three times the size of ICI. Yet, until privatisation in 1989, most people never gave water a second thought. It simply came out of a tap or cistern and ran away down a drain. Indeed, until local authorities started showing water charges separately in the 1970s, some naive folk dreamily imagined that it came free. Few think that now, as the debate has raged over the water companies' campaign to push prices higher and higher in order to finance long-overdue investment in pipes, drains and sewers.

Although the National Rivers Authority and Her Majesty's Inspector of Pollution have their say, the industry is ruled by Ofwat, the Office of Water Services, whose director-general in its early years has been Ian Byatt, one-time husband of the award-winning novelist A.S. Byatt. He has declared: 'I'm here because I'm needed by customers to ensure there is no exploitation.' But no one doubted that water prices had to rise, to finance the much-needed spending on the system. So Byatt has negotiated regularly with each of the water companies to agree a so-called K factor – the percentage over inflation by which they can raise prices each year. Although they were allowed to start off with rises of between four per cent and seven per cent over inflation, Byatt has indicated that he would be unhappy with real price rises of more than two per cent in the second half of the decade. That meant the companies had to get some experienced commercial management, quick.

Now that it has broken out of its public-authority cocoon, the industry has begun to attract career managers like Michael Hoffman, a veteran of Rolls-

Royce, Massey Ferguson, Babcock International and Airship Industries. At the beginning of 1989 he became chief executive of Britain's biggest water company, Thames Water. He prefers to think of it as just another engineering concern – almost. 'I've spent my life in areas of engineering that need a lot of change,' he explains. 'I spent a year trying to rescue Airship, and another year trying to decide what to do after we sold it. Then this came along. It's a bit different from the others: I don't see any difference in terms of the engineering aspects of it, the management of costs and all those sorts of things. But there is a difference, in that you clearly can't make a decision to go and sell more water.'

In fact, quite the reverse. Any sign of profligacy with the raw material and down comes the conservation lobby hunting for blood. Yet Britain is not particularly short of water, as many a rain-sodden foreign tourist will testify.

'You really shouldn't stimulate consumption,' warns Hoffman, who includes sailing among his pastimes. 'Water's a much more valuable asset in this country than ever people realise. If you look at demand increasing all the time, the per capita use is going up and I think only the Belgians use less than us in Europe. And we're way, way below North American standards in water consumption. So the pressure has to be on to conserve.'

The trouble is that most of the country's inhabitants inconveniently choose to live in areas of low rainfall, shunning such well-soaked parts as the Lake District, Wales and the West Country. So, while the population increases and we drink and bathe in water more frequently, there is a growing problem of storing water and trying to move it from where it lands to where it is consumed. During the droughts of the early 1990s, envious eyes were cast towards Kielder Water in north-east England, the largest man-made lake in Europe. But, although it was completed in 1982, none of its 200,000 megalitres was needed by the local catchment area for several years. Meanwhile, water users in the south were enduring year after year of hosepipe bans – although not, Hoffman is keen to stress, in the Thames region. 'I have taken the view now that we will never have a hosepipe ban again,' he declares confidently. 'It's an arrogant way to approach it, but I think now that we can sustain almost any dry spell.'

Thames is fortunate, in that it is the only one of the privatised water companies to cover an entire natural river basin, from the Cotswolds to Tilbury. While it is closely identified with London, it also serves Guildford in the south, Swindon to the west and as far north as Banbury and Luton. Their nearby rivers all eventually feed into the River Thames.

Surprisingly, Thames Water captures over half the usable rainfall that

Michael Richard Hoffman

BORN:	31 October, 1939
EDUCATED:	Hitchin Grammar School, Bristol University
MARRIED:	Margaret Tregaskes, 1963. One daughter Helen Peters, 1982

CAREER:

1961	Rolls-Royce
1970	Cannons & Stokes
1971	Managing Director, Perkins Engines
1977	Chairman, Perkins Engines
1980	President, farm machinery division, Massey Ferguson
1983	Chief Executive, Babcock International
1987	Chief Executive, Airship Industries
1988	Group Chief Executive, Thames Water

OTHER INTERESTS: Chairman of Brunel University, member of Monopolies and Mergers Commission, Director of Cray Electronics, WEW Group.

THAMES WATER PLC

HEAD OFFICE:	14 Cavendish Place, London W1M 9DJ Tel: 071-636 8686
ACTIVITIES:	Water supply and sewerage services, construction and supply of water treatment products and services
MAIN BRANDS:	Thames Water, Thames Waste Management, Morgan Collis, Metro Rod, Subscan, PWT Projects, Simon Waste Solutions, Binnie Thames Water, Permutit, Hydro Aerobics

drops on the area – the amount that falls, less evaporation. The next best is Anglia, which grabs about a fifth.

'One's got to recognise that London's water supply is only really 120 days of usable water in the summer time,' says Hoffman. 'One can understand how we have run into these supply problems in the past. Because there is a problem with supply of water, one can't say "use more water, bath twice a day" or anything like that, because you are running against the long-run national resource. The raw material is limited. The only thing you can do is to interfere with the natural cycle, and the only way you can do that in our type of terrain is by a raised embankment reservoir.'

And that is currently a very sore point indeed with people living around Abingdon, south-west Oxfordshire, where Thames has sought planning permission to build a 150,000-megalitre reservoir early in the next century. It will cost half a billion pounds at today's prices and will be second in size in the UK only to Kielder Water and about four times the size of the group's present biggest, the Queen Mother reservoir on the other side of the M25 from Heathrow Airport. 'Queen Mother is just a round cauldron, basically,' says Hoffman dismissively with the merest hint of *lèse majesté*. 'The new one will need to be much more environmentally friendly than that. It will be more artistically raised.'

Nonetheless, no one wants a puddle that size on their doorstep, so the protests will continue long and loud. Thames wants to scoop out a five-and-a-half-square-mile site to a depth of thirty feet: twenty-two farms would lose land and sixteen homes would be submerged. The excavated earth would be used to build a contoured wall the height of an eight-storey building around the hollow. Thames says that the walls of the reservoir would be landscaped but villagers are frightened at the thought of living beneath such a huge mass of water.

However, Hoffman has good news for the rest of us, or at least our grandchildren. 'The water problem may be solved by the middle of the next century,' he predicts. 'Certainly, demand will go on and on. The population in the south-east will continue to rise, although there is some doubt about that. The next level of supply is a semi-overland route. The idea is to increase the capacity of one of the Welsh reservoirs, and then bring the water down into and out of the Severn, pipe it overland and then it would fit perfectly into our big reservoir down there, which would be a holding and mixing reservoir as well as a river supply reservoir. So the problems can be taken care of, but they're expensive. We'll all be long dead and buried by the time that decision's made, because it doesn't need to be made until 2030 or 2040. The first thing is to get our new reservoir in position, in the first decade of the next century.' It will take up to seven years to build. It might have been needed sooner, but for the success of Thames's leakage campaign.

When the country's water system was being starved of capital by successive governments – let's face it, there are few votes in new drains – as much as a quarter of the water made ready for consumption was lost in leakages. Thames has been bringing that rate of loss down to fifteen per cent, and the latest technology could bring it down to ten per cent.

'Leakages are all about reducing flow pressures and finding out what big leaks there are and curing them,' says Hoffman. 'Of course, that's an ongoing process and you can only do that by studies in the small hours of the morning. But now we can read these very low flows at the time we're in the street, whereas before we had to have lots of meter readings and then come back and run them through the computer. The computer would say "it's likely to be there" and then we'd go back, put all the kit up again and start to look closely in that area. Now we can pinpoint quickly where the leak is, and that's made a huge difference.'

A ten per cent leakage rate still sounds a lot, but the best rate in the world is Singapore's three per cent, and to do that they have replaced almost all of their major pipelines with stainless steel. 'Singapore can do that and sustain the disruption,' Hoffman points out, 'but can you imagine relaying all of London's mains? I think if we got down to ten per cent, that would be a stunning step forward.'

British weather fosters leaks. In February 1991 a prolonged freeze sent bursts in the Thames area from about ten a week to a thousand in one week, many in unoccupied premises where water was therefore left running for days.

'That can put your leakage programme back a year,' claims Hoffman, 'but it's the reverse in the summer where you get very, very dry periods and two things happen. One is you get ground shift, and secondly under London roads you can get much bigger shock transmission. If you imagine the earth as a spring when it's wet, when it's less wet, it's more of a harsh spring and therefore the banging transmitted from big trucks down to the mains can be more dangerous. If you have that in summertime, when you're flowing water at as much pressure as you can possibly raise, just to get the velocity and volume of flow up, then it can become very difficult. You've got high internal pressures and pounding pressures outside, so sometimes the pipes burst.'

Early 1991 was memorable for another reason: the short-lived but alarming Gulf War. Strange to think that shots fired in Kuwait should concern a

British water company, but they did. The reason: the war hit the London tourist industry because of reprisal fears, and a sudden slump in demand for water in hotels and other business premises immediately hits the company's income from water sold through meters.

'We lost about £15 million of metered income compared with the prior year,' says Hoffman. 'As there's no marginal cost on water, that was £15 million straight out of our expected profit. We had to work our butts off to try and replace most of it, as we did, by cost savings. So it's not all the soft business people might think it is. That's why prices were as high as they were subsequently.'

Thames has been making profits of between £200 million and £250 million a year since privatisation. The first £200 million is virtually guaranteed by Ofwat's K factor price formula. Good management, reckons Hoffman, can bump that up by another £50 million. But in its first four years as a commercial company, Thames was spending £400 million a year in capital expenditure, so losses of £15 million cannot be taken lightly: the pressure is on to perform.

'The criticism over prices is always going to be there,' explains Hoffman, 'because if you live in London – I live in Kensington – you have not seen a whit of change for all the expenditure that's been going on. Water still comes out of the tap, I drink it, as I did before I joined Thames Water – so what the hell's the difference? Where we have seen a difference is in a number of the more rural communities, where there were big odour problems, Reading for instance. We've got those fixed. A little place like Wargrave-on-the-Thames had an appalling sewage treatment outfall into the river – that's been fixed. Small communities see that, and indeed we've targeted our public relations activity on such issues.'

However, shed no tears for London. While rural communities may have had their mite of attention, the capital is getting a monster lavished on it by comparison. The £250 million London Water Ring Main is coming on stream during the mid-1990s, a fifty-mile circular tunnel forty metres under ground. It is the longest tunnel ever built in the UK, nearly twenty miles longer than the Channel Tunnel and big enough in places to drive a car through. The Ring Main will ease the operating pressures on the existing mains system, and at full bore it will supply half London's water, using fibre-optic technology to control the movement of 285 million gallons each day. It gets its name from the similarity to an electric ring main, in that you can tap it at any point in the system. That means that a district in trouble can easily get fresh supplies, whereas before they were isolated.

Says Hoffman: 'Our inputs are weather and likely customer demand, and the system is basically built on reservoirs that fill during the night and run down during the day. That's a gross oversimplification of it, but that's the principle. What you've got to do is fill those reservoirs to an optimum level, but not overflowing, because otherwise you're using too much energy at the wrong times. So, if we can predict demand then we can be much more effective in how much water we're going to treat today, where we get it from and which of the London reservoirs we bring it from. We're putting a lot of effort into that. We'll soon be able to get a signal coming in in the morning, perhaps to say that the Lea Valley reservoirs have got algae in them, we're much better off running the West London works absolutely flat out using the Ring Main to transmit it, and the supply that you need for tomorrow is 2,300 megalitres and not 2,400 as you might normally expect at this time of year. That is another cost saving. By the late 1990s, when London's water is free of pesticides, where I live in Kensington it'll look just the same and taste a bit better, because one of the side effects of the process that gets the pesticides out is that you actually get shot of some of the chlorine taste.'

A different taste may be left in the mouth by whatever system Thames and the other water companies come up with for charging for their services. Traditionally, domestic water charges were tied to the old rating system, on the basis that better-off folk use more water than the great unwashed. But the hated poll tax put an end to that, for where you lived within a local authority would no longer be relevant. Meanwhile, the water industry was given until 31 March, 2000, to dream up a new scheme. Then poll tax was replaced by council tax, which is basically a broad-brush version of the rates and could therefore easily be the springboard for water charges. However, in the interregnum, the case for metering was advanced. Its advantages are that you pay for what you use and it encourages us not to waste the stuff. But it is not as simple as that. Apart from the fact that meters cost over £200 apiece to install, our antiquated warrens of pipes often make it difficult to decide who is using what. Old houses converted into flats are particularly notorious for being meter-resistant.

'I don't ever see us being in a position where we will be universally metered,' insists Hoffman, an avowed sceptic of the notion that meters cut consumption. 'I think, because of the peculiar nature of water and sewerage services, you can't ever see a situation where you'd be back almost to a poll tax configuration where you'd be penalising a single-parent, three-child family in east London. I can see endless arguments there, and it seems to me for those types of areas there's a need for homogeneity. Our policy's very straightforward: at the bottom end of consumption, like a grandparent living near the family home, it almost certainly pays to have a meter. All non-domestic premises, virtually, would be metered. All new properties of any type from 1 October, 1989, have been and we shall possibly go on to meter detached houses because they've got a higher potential use for water. If we did all that, we'd still have seventy-five per cent of our connections unmetered. We think there's probably some form of banding that we can develop. If you asked me if, at the end of the century, people would be metered up to the level I've suggested, I would then think that there would be a two, three or four-tier banding structure. Maybe in the very long term there will be universal metering of some sort, but that will be in the twenty-five to fifty year time frame rather than the short term. At the moment, if a new family moves in to a house with a meter, then they can have the meter taken out. Once we move into the new environment, where we've got a full structure, from the granny flat to the detached house, then at some stage we'll have to make it irreversible but at the moment, because it's so small, it doesn't matter if it's reversible or not.'

Nevertheless, Hoffman sees the water industry coming under closer regulation, led by continual demands from the European Commission for higher and higher standards of water purity. This will add to the incentive for Thames and its rivals to diversify into related but non-regulated activities, from waste management to wind-surfing. When the industry was privatised, the general assumption was that the companies would use their vast tracts of idle land to make a frontal attack on the leisure industry. But the recession dampened enthusiasm for that tactic, as one hotel company after another went bust and would-be theme park operators from Disney downwards found it hard to part the public from their money.

'We do have a leisure officer,' Hoffman admits, 'but the practicality of what you can do is quite small. The leisure industry in water sports, which is basically where we could exploit it, is always on the edge of bankruptcy. People aren't prepared to pay the cost of their sport in this country, so you're never going to make very much out of it. Reservoirs can be used for fishing and sailing, but we're quite strict about what you can do because we don't want contaminated water. We've got lots of people exploiting scientific sites, like the reserve at Farnborough where you can go and watch birds and that type of thing, but it's pretty small beer in comparison to what people might think. Ventures like Thorpe Park in Surrey are not for us. We don't have that sort of expertise and where we would do it you can get a much better property development than a theme park. So, from our point of view, we'd rather be working with others to develop land, using our skills in preparing planning applications and getting planning through and let others control the sites, whether for housing or commercial purposes.'

Hoffman wants to concentrate on diversifying into four specific areas:

• Contracting of water and sewerage services.

• International operating and managing water facilities.

• Products and services related to the water industry, such as filtration and membranes.

• Environmental services, tied to either underground activities or the management of holes.

'There's a massive demand for water around the world,' Hoffman points out. 'The question is whether you can pay for it, but if you took a long-run view of that, then that's an industry to be in with a high level of expertise and a track record, so that people can rely on you. Secondly, as society becomes more civilised and has supplies of appropriate water, then it does want to clear up its sewage treatment discharges to get a better quality of life and environment, so again if you were taking a long-term view on the sewerage industry, then you'd say worldwide there's going to be a demand for sewerage and sewage treatment activities. While there may not be stunning growth or anything like that, there's a long-run market that will exist beyond the end of the century as people upgrade their facilities.'

But diversification is a capricious mongrel. Aside from the risks of a company going outside its basic business, which Thames Water has already discovered can be expensive, there is a double bind when that company is in a regulated industry. If the core operations make more profit than the non-core, the regulator may demand a squeeze on the prices charged by the core business. And if the non-core turns into a raging success, either critics may accuse the company of syphoning hidden subsidies from the core or the regulator will deny core price rises on the grounds that the company has a convenient kitty to draw on. I suspect, however, that Hoffman will be happy to cope with such problems, for diversification gives him one priceless asset – a part of the working week when he does not have to ask permission from Ofwat to blow his nose.

CHAPTER 10

PETER JARVIS

of Whitbread

T HE QUEUE of people waiting to get into London's Playhouse Theatre were not anxious fans hoping for a glimpse of their heroes. They were there on business. Like many young would-be actors, they were lining up for an audition. But, although the show was destined for a West End run, the public performances were not scheduled to take place in a theatre. Once the curtain had gone down on the audition, the lucky ones chosen for the cast would find their stage was a little more cramped than usual. For these performers were competing for a part in the ongoing tale of TGI Friday's, the restaurant chain that started as a New York singles bar in 1965. Just over twenty years later Whitbread, the brewery group, brought the concept to Britain as a franchise from the Carlson Hospitality Group, and opened their first outlet in Bedford Street in London's Covent Garden. It's still their most successful site.

The original American interior design is meticulously reproduced in each restaurant, right down to Tiffany-style lamps, polished wood floors, half an eight-man rowing scull and other carefully careless clutter to give the place that go-as-you-please feel. The focal point is a sunken, square cocktail bar in the middle, with raised tables that surround the bar area at just the right height for previously unacquainted singles to get to know one another, as in the original singles bar. Before the evening session all the Dub Dubs, as the full-time waiters and waitresses are known, assemble in the back yard for a pep talk from one of the managers. A bubbly personality and the ability to perform in the way that will bring the best out of any given table of diners can make a difference of £200 in the bills generated per waiter per shift. That's a lot of smiles.

102

Running the TGI chain is a far cry from playing mine host to the varied range of drinkers, young and old, noisy and quiet, who inhabit British pubs. That population has been shrinking in the past twenty years, creating a strategic vacuum. The problem was compounded by the Beer Orders, breaking the tie between Whitbread's brewing operation and many of its pubs. The group has been trying to respond to these difficulties by diversifying into other forms of catering. But that has thrown it into a highly competitive trade, relatively easy to enter, dominated by major international players like McDonald's, Burger King and the pizza chains. Whitbread, realising that it faced an uphill fight to establish eatery brands from scratch, bought the UK franchise for TGI. However, critics argue that TGI is too upmarket and specialised to offer more than a limited chain, denying Whitbread the benefits of high volume. It may be significant that Allied Domecq has all but pulled out of this sector of the market (Chapter 8).

Whitbread's problem is that most people still think of it as a brewery with pubs rather than the way its management would like it to be seen – as an international marketing business. That mismatch will persist as long as the old Whitbread family influence lasts – possibly even while the name persists. This is the challenge facing chief executive Peter Jarvis, and observers are a long way from being convinced that he can work the trick. A leading City drinks industry analyst, John Spicer of S.G. Warburg Securities, says: 'In the longer term, Whitbread's position in the industry is frequently questioned, due to the size of its brewing business compared with Bass, Courage and Carlsberg-Tetley and the strengths of its retail operations.'

Jarvis' arm was strengthened after Samuel Whitbread's retirement as chairman in 1992. He was succeeded by Sir Michael Angus, former chairman of Unilever, a global foods and toiletries giant which lives, eats and sleeps marketing. 'I think that as far as retailing related to pubs in this country is concerned, we're as good as anyone,' says Jarvis, who has been chief executive since 1990. 'The big question is, can we extend that into foreign parts? We are trying to find out if the skills we've got in this country, skills about systems, information, purchasing, training, hygiene, can be used in foreign markets like the US.' If the answer to that question is yes, Whitbread will be able to take its place on the international stage and possibly even develop a global operation. But if the answer is no, the group will be doomed to confinement in the UK and could easily become prey for a more ambitious predator in search of a well-managed but limited catering business.

But Jarvis, whose father was a Bolton mill worker, has fought his way to

Peter Jack Jarvis

BORN:	1 July, 1941
EDUCATED:	Graham School, Bolton, and Christ's College, Cambridge
MARRIED:	Yes, with one son, one daughter

CAREER:

1964	Unilever, sales and marketing
1976	Whitbread: Sales and Marketing Director Long John International
1978	Group Marketing Director
1979	Joined main board
1981	International Managing Director
1983	Managing Director of Trading Division
1985	Group Managing Director
1990	Group Chief Executive

OTHER INTERESTS:	Member of the Brewers' Society and Fellow of the Institute of Grocery Distribution

WHITBREAD

HEAD OFFICE:	The Brewery, Chiswell Street, London EC1Y 4SD Tel: 071-606 4455
ACTIVITIES:	Beer, inns, hotels, pub partnerships, restaurants and leisure
MAIN BRANDS:	Boddingtons, Hoegaarden White and Whitbread beer, Stella Artois, Heineken and Tooheys lager, Murphy's Irish Stout, Brewers Fayre pubs, Beefeater, Churrasco, Pizza Hut, TGI Friday's and The Keg restaurants, Thresher off-licences, Country Club, Lansbury and Travel Inn hotels

the top with generous helpings of Lancashire grit and perseverance. 'I'm pretty determined,' he declares. 'My mother is pretty determined. I was made like that.' He went to a local direct grant school endowed by William Lever, the soaps magnate of Unilever fame. Built like a pillar with hands like tureens, he was a promising football goalkeeper, playing for under-eighteen England schoolboys. Naturally, his team was Bolton Wanderers. Led by the legendary Nat Lofthouse, they beat Manchester United to win the F.A. Cup in 1958 when Jarvis was seventeen. 'I was good enough to play professionally,' he says wistfully. But duty came before pleasure. Instead he read geography at Christ's College, Cambridge, channelling his soccer ambitions into winning Blues for trouncing Oxford three times on the trot. He still makes himself swim every Saturday morning, and is a keen sports fan.

After graduating, Jarvis made the most of his school's connections with Unilever by working for the giant group, helping to sell such products as Bird's Eye frozen food. 'Unilever ran the best school of marketing this side of the Atlantic,' he insists. There, too, he also had his first taste of life in the United States. Coincidentally, Jarvis was a contemporary of Sir Michael Angus, who went on to become chairman of Unilever before succeeding Sam Whitbread as head of the one-time family firm. But they never met at Unilever: Sir Michael was too busy selling shampoo.

Jarvis was also a protégé of Whitbread's man at the top. In 1976 he joined the group as sales and marketing director for its whisky business, Long John International. Within three years, at the tender age of thirty-eight, he was on the main board. He had been spotted by the then chief executive, Sir Charles Tidbury, who promoted Jarvis and made sure he got a thorough grounding in most aspects of the Whitbread group. 'He's a bit of a workaholic,' says Sir Charles, 'but he has got an ability to let people get on with things. He's got a nose for business. When he knows he has got to do something unpleasant, even to get rid of people, he gets on with it. There has to be a certain ruthlessness about any chief executive, and he's got that.' Jarvis had a couple of years as international managing director in charge of all the overseas operations, when he did well to survive the failure to make Long John a true world brand. He commuted between London and New York for six months in an effort to get the all-important US distributors to stock the Whitbread tipple, but could not woo them away from established brands like Dewar's, Johnnie Walker and White Horse – now all owned by Guinness. Jarvis was able to persuade his mentors that Whitbread simply did not have the muscle to stand up against the likes of Allied-Lyons and Distillers. They tried to buy the US-based Heublein, but failed.

So Jarvis was allowed to put away his passport and run the trading division in the UK for two years. Then in 1985 he was made group managing director, a title which was upgraded to chief executive when Sam Whitbread became non-executive chairman.

Jarvis is very much an ideas man, and is credited with putting Boddington's draught bitter in cans – although this trick was first pulled off by Guinness. Nevertheless, Jarvis saw the potential of the idea in a market where the pub trade was losing out to the desire to rent a video tape and stay at home.

Now he is driven by the Big Idea of making Whitbread an international slaker of thirsts and sater of appetites. But, as he is the first to acknowledge, most retailing ideas do not export very well beyond their native land. Size is vital, to spread advertising costs and reap the benefit of bulk buying. Whitbread manages Pizza Hut UK under a joint venture agreement with the brand's owner, the US-based PepsiCo, of Pepsi Cola fame. However, in 1992 Whitbread had to pull out of the Pizza Hut businesses in France, Belgium and the Netherlands because of 'insufficient safeguards for the hundreds of millions of pounds which would have been involved in the widescale development of the brand'. In plain English, this means that, when the chips went down, they did not have enough chips to stay at the roulette wheel. As Graeme Eadie, brewing analyst at County Natwest Securities, points out: 'Throughout the mid to late 1980s, Whitbread developed a number of retail concepts, giving the company a plethora of ideas from which it could pick one or two that could be expanded significantly, leaving the others to be dropped. However, Whitbread postponed making these strategic decisions, thereby getting caught out by the onset of recession. The only reaction was to axe Pizza Hut in France, Belgium and Holland – which unnerved investors even further, as it had seemed the concept with the most potential. This leaves a major question mark over the group's future retail strategy.'

Whitbread had a few Beefeater restaurants in the London area when Jarvis joined the company, but through the 1980s the focus of expansion was out of managed houses into shops and free-standing restaurants. Now they have TGI Friday's and a half-share in the British end of Pizza Hut, as well as three hotel concepts: Country Club, Lansbury and Travel Inns. More are on the way. Jarvis carefully categorises the inevitable failures as experiments – which at least deserves a prize for positive thinking.

'Around eighty per cent of our retail businesses are well established,' he explains, 'and there's another twenty per cent in newer businesses which are not yet proven. So if you look at the number of concepts that we have, then as far as retail is concerned, there are a lot of small things but they are being tested out for future growth, God being willing. People who talk about our retail business tend to say "half the things they're doing are good, half are bad": they forget about this testing of new ideas and new concepts.' That philosophy is central to Jarvis' ambition to make people think of Whitbread as very much a marketing-orientated company. If he could achieve that, he would be able to distance the central management from the operations in the field. Whitbread would become the investor, its retail brands would form a portfolio, to be treated as dispassionately as any shareholder's – providing the bottom line delivered overall success.

'We're very, very close to customers, we do a lot of consumer research, we come up with a lot of new ideas,' Jarvis insists. 'We've been quite successful in introducing new retail concepts into this country. Some have failed. Often when we have failures, we have reluctantly walked away from the market. We've tried consistently to get into the fish restaurant area because we feel there's a big opportunity. We had a concept in the mid-1980s called Hungry Fisherman which we trialled and we couldn't make succeed, so we closed it down at a cost. We sold off our carvery operation, Roast Inn, because after many years we couldn't get a return as good as we could get from Beefeater. We had a café bar concept that was good, called Henry's, but it was not as good as Friday's so we sold it. So we will continue to look for new ideas that will bring non-users into our market and we've been very successful at doing that.'

The trouble with that strategy is that Whitbread is a middle-sized operator in what is becoming a big international league. The giants are tending to leave the solo operations alone – indeed, a branch of McDonald's can spawn a rash of burger lookalikes in a district. But a business of Whitbread's size is there to be crushed or taken over, unless it can graduate to the premier division. In recent years, profits from Whitbread's retail activities have grown faster than the rest of the group, but so has capital expenditure on these projects. According to Graeme Eadie: 'Whitbread suffers disproportionately high central overheads due to the running costs of developing and managing all its diverse retail concepts. Each has different management, separate systems and disparate marketing objectives.' The group's highest-profile success, Friday's, still has only around a dozen branches in Britain. Each costs something like £5 million to open, since they have to be prime sites capable of feeding up to 250 diners at once. But a dozen branches is not enough to earn the best discounts on buying cutlery, crockery or food, while the countrywide spread stretches the management.

'If you take our pubs, restaurants and shops together,' says Jarvis, 'I don't think anyone would suggest that we're in the second division. I mean who's better? We're bigger. We dominate the family restaurant market with 300 Beefeaters, the next biggest player has less than 100 outlets. Pizza Hut dominates the pizza market with a thirty-three per cent share. Thresher dominates the specialist off-licence market and is the biggest purveyor of alcohol in this country. They are very big businesses. Thresher turns over £700 million a year or thereabouts. So in those areas there's no question about us being second or third best – we're clearly not. If we can manage to get twenty-five good sites for Friday's in this country then we have a very good business. We'd never have got where we got to if we didn't put the overhead in first, because we'd never have got the standards, we'd never have recruited the staff, we'd never have trained the staff, we would never have got the environment that we've got in the restaurant. But we don't need any more staff at HQ to produce that in the new restaurants, so a much bigger proportion of the sales fall through the bottom line. We believe that's the way to build successful businesses in this area, and that's essentially what we're trying to do.'

Jarvis proudly cites the transformation of Thresher from being one of the most anonymous chains on the British high street to dominating its sector and making very good profits, too. And a lot of Threshers in the north of England are being turned into convenience stores, rather than just off-licences.

'All the customer trends, all the margin trends, are very good and it's a good business,' purrs Jarvis. 'We've moved it on from 300 shops in the south east of England to 1,700 shops that cover the nation and are plainly brand leader in that sector. Most of that work has been done by talking to consumers and planning ahead with the way the markets have been going. The process isn't finished yet, but the players are in place, the techniques are being used and quite a lot of benefit is already visible.'

Internationally, Whitbread has done little more than dip its toe in the water. Its steakhouse business in Germany, Churrasco, has only forty outlets. The Keg, a ranch-style restaurant selling steak and seafood, has sixty branches in Canada, a couple of dozen in the north-west US and a dozen in Australia. 'The Keg style, high service standards and food quality have a powerful appeal,' says Jarvis, 'and the chain is set to trade vigorously when the recession ends. We have enough Churrascos to learn a lot about the

German market, but we're not ready to go for 400. We'll only go to 400 if we prove that we can run those forty as well as anyone else. New initiatives, including fresh menus, better service standards, consistent signage and marketing activities are increasing customer satisfaction and building brand awareness.'

Pubs are still the core of what Whitbread is about. If they are doing well, Jarvis has a credible base from which to expand and diversify into other types of outlet, fast-food, café, brasserie, restaurant or hotel. So he concentrated first on widening the pubs' appeal. Until the 1970s Whitbread's pubs were really outlets for the group's beer production, rather than the other way round, relying on the relentless drinking capacity of manual workers and young men. But those groups were in decline. As the nation's heavy manufacturing activity has shrunk, so has the pool of thirsty labourers keen to stay away from drab homes. The DIY revolution saw to that. Young people began to desert pubs in favour of clubs, discos or simply staying at home to watch television or indulge in recreational sex. But everyone has to eat, so Whitbread decided to offer better food through a chain it developed called Brewers' Fayre. That theme now runs to 200 of the bigger pubs. Another group that were staying away from pubs were middle-aged and retired people, many of whom were complaining to anyone who would listen that their local had become noisy, smelly and plagued with a rash of Formica. Jarvis listened and introduced a concept called Wayside Inns, a cosier style of hostelry with thatched roof, homemade food (or something like it) and no jukebox.

Jarvis points to these successes as evidence of Whitbread's ability to expand on a broader front. 'We have been able in our managed pubs to pick up market share on a fairly consistent basis,' he says, 'because we've been appealing to a wider range of people and it's that sort of restlessness and inventiveness and interest in consumers that leads to these new retail concepts, leads to the risk of failure but if you're clever and lucky it actually leads to success. Our customers now are a much wider range, but we have much less heavy users of beer and many more infrequent users of food and the facilities that we provide. I think that as far as our kind of retailing is concerned, retailing related to pubs in this country, we're as good as anyone.'

Like the other big brewers, Whitbread has had to cope with the UK government's 1989 Beer Orders, which were intended to cut prices and widen consumer choice, but have done the reverse. 'I think that we will come out of the Beer Orders a better competitor,' says Jarvis. 'We might have been just as good a competitor left to our own devices, but we will certainly come out better equipped to deal with anything that the world throws at us, because the Beer Orders are very, very complex. They were a very difficult thing for us to deal with and we have been pretty inventive in the way that we have managed the process. We have developed with our licensees a much more contemporary business relationship, these are our tenant licensees, so there have been benefits, but there have also been huge costs.'

Jarvis believes that measures like the Beer Orders are in danger of weakening the very notion of a pub, which could in turn leave it vulnerable to interference from the European Union authorities.

'The real issues are as much to do with Brussels as they are to do with Whitehall,' he claims, 'and we want to preserve the British pub. It is plainly the most successful of its kind in the world, and above all else we don't want bureaucrats in Brussels telling us what to do with our pubs. So I think the government and the brewers together have quite a thing to defend on behalf of British consumers, because I can promise you that as far as French consumers are concerned, they're not going to care about pubs because they're not important to them. But they're very important to us. When visitors leave this country, the two things they like to take home with them are pubs and policemen, and long may it be so.'

The Jarvis marketing-led strategy still has some time to run. But he has a fellow marketeer sitting at his shoulder, in the bulky and respected shape of Sir Michael Angus. They may be allies in spreading the marketing gospel throughout Whitbread, but Sir Michael can also judge better than anyone else in the company the success of what Jarvis is doing.

Should the push for growth be given the thumbs down, then either Jarvis goes or plans for the long-mooted merger with Scottish & Newcastle, the brewer, distiller and hotelier based in the north, are liable to be dusted down and given another glance.

CHAPTER 11

ROBIN MILLER

of EMAP

ROBIN MILLER is an unlikely Sign of Things to Come. But the way he runs Emap, the Peterborough-based newspaper, magazine, local radio and exhibitions group, is attracting increasing attention from management sages. The point is that he is so incredibly *normal*. If he wants to get about he walks. Faster than that, and he climbs onto his beloved BMW 1000 motorbike. His office is whatever room he happens to walk into, but above all he has the elusive knack of letting everyone else get on with it.

'There's no magic here,' he says. 'We're all just enthusiasts, and we do like publishing. I'm a hack by trade, and I'm enthusiastic about newspapers and magazines. I think everyone who works for Emap is.' It is a simple philosophy, and one which has increased the group more than tenfold since he became chief executive in 1985.

'I just dropped into one of our offices this afternoon,' Miller recounts. 'We don't have an Emap Towers with a thousand people in it and Lord Emap sitting at the top – we have a whole series of offices, including about a dozen in London. I just wanted to know what was going on, apart from the fact I was blagging a couple of free computer games for my son. This is what I mean by enthusiasm and creativity. Coming up with the ideas, doing the layouts and putting the packages together can only be done by people who are really into the games but also enthusiastic about what they're doing. They're fired up and they're keen to know what the next issue's selling. They're really involved. We keep telling them the good news and the bad, but they know everything. They're part of it.'

He is referring to computer games like Nintendo, for which Emap publishes user magazines which sell by the tens of thousands to fanatical teenagers.

Miller explains: 'If people have ideas, we like to try to enable them to actually do them – or explore them so that they recognise that it isn't going to work. Most of our ideas haven't come from business graduates sitting in a darkened room, they're editorial or ad guys who are saying "why don't we do that?" Most of our ideas have come up that way, and we like to encourage it. My colleagues and I don't have a monopoly of good ideas. In fact, we still have a huge number of pretty bad ones. Sometimes, one or two launches we've done I thought we shouldn't have done. I was wrong. Now, I'm delighted to say I've been right on one or two occasions as well. It's very satisfying to be right, but at the same time there are a number of things that, left to me, I wouldn't have done but the group of people contributing to it thought we should, so we did.'

Such a laid-back attitude will tell any formally trained business manager that Miller is, to put it politely, self-taught. In fact he is a journalist made good, who started on *Motor Cycle News* – still a flagship title – and graduated to the management ranks courtesy of the group's former boss, Sir Frank Rogers. Like all the best success stories, Miller paints it as a career that happened by accident. He comes from the Lake District and started as a journalist in typically humble style, on the *Penrith Observer*. Then he saw an ad for a job on *Motor Cycle News*. 'It was in Kettering, Northants, a town I'd never heard of before,' Miller remembers. 'I got the job because I said that I liked the odd drink and the other candidate was a Welsh Methodist who never touched a drop. *Motor Cycle News* is still the most profitable title in the group. It has knocked out all the competition, and it's the Bible of the business. There is a huge classified section: if you want to sell a motorbike in the UK you have to advertise in this magazine. So it carries twenty-eight to thirty-two pages of classified and sells 130,000 copies a week. Since then I've just taken any job that was offered. I went from *Motor Cycle News* to *Angling Times*, though I knew nothing about fishing. But you pick things up quite quickly. Then I went back as editor of *Motor Cycle News*. It was the greatest job I'd ever been offered, and the fact that the editor I had fallen out with had gone made it that bit sweeter – although we are very good friends now. Then I was made editorial manager of all the magazines.'

That was in 1974. Eleven years on, he was running the whole group. Rogers was careful to put David Arculus from the BBC's planning department alongside Miller, and when they got to the top they hired David Grigson from Saatchi & Saatchi as finance director. These three make the big decisions.

Robert William Miller

BORN:	19 December, 1940
EDUCATED:	Queen Elizabeth Grammar School, Penrith
MARRIED:	1973. Two sons

CAREER:

1958	*Penrith Observer*
1965	Reporter, *Motor Cycle News*
1974	General Manager, magazine division of Emap
1976	Director of Emap
1985	Group Chief Executive of Emap

OTHER INTERESTS: Director of Trans World Communications

EMAP PLC

HEAD OFFICE: 1 Lincoln Court, Lincoln Road, Peterborough
PE1 2RF
Tel: 0733-68900

ACTIVITIES: Publishing, managing and organising exhibitions, printing, broadcasting

MAIN BRANDS: *Angling Times, Motor Cycle News, Kerrang!!, Smash Hits, New Woman, Elle, Just Seventeen, Slimming, Q, Mean Machines, Fleet Car, Public Treasurer, Broadcast, Media World, TV World, Screen International*

By 1994 those decisions had taken the group to control of around 150 magazines, more than seventy newspapers, over thirty exhibitions and two local radio stations, Kiss FM and Radio City. In 1991 Emap bid for the Anglia TV franchise in tandem with CLT, the Luxembourg television group, who wanted a UK partner.

'In the event we didn't get it, and I'm glad,' Miller insists. 'ITV is dominated by the big players and I guess the outlook isn't so bright and breezy as it was a few years ago. Transparently, the competition from satellite and cable is going to be stronger than was thought then, and maybe ad revenues aren't going to be so frothy. Nevertheless, television is the most powerful medium. The growth of television in the world has been quite remarkable, and it's still growing. We're just seeing the tip of it, quite frankly. There are cable systems in the US which give literally hundreds of channels. That will happen here, and it's going to gobble up software. What we're seeing now will be dead as a dodo in ten years' time. It will be dramatically different. Any publishing company must be interested in that, as providers of the programming, the software, whether we make the programmes ourselves or just use our knowledge of the markets to publish them, whether it is gardening or whatever, to provide the information and pictures to be published through another medium. So I see that as a role for Emap in the future as this whole proliferation of information systems explodes, as it undoubtedly will do. In the States a number of media owners like Hearst have gone into cable in a big way, and American companies own most of the cable franchises over here. What is now driving that market is that you can hook up telephones through it, and when you can do that the churn factor, the fall-off in subscription, is much lower. And with fibre optics you can put through so many channels through one piece of wire that it's unbelievable.

'I just have a very open mind about Emap's role. But I am clear that we should own the software. What will change is the way it is distributed. We don't own the newsagents, we don't own the wholesalers, but we do own the product, so we are not in charge of distribution in that respect. We have to negotiate with those people to get our magazines on the shelves. But if you have the knowledge and authority, you can produce programmes that these people want to use. Our radio stations are a toe-dipping exercise in that respect. In ten years' time the magazine market will be very different from today, in that there will be more of it. But there will also be many more specialist programmes on television through cable. The same applies to business information. Much that is now held on file and on paper will be held in on-line systems, by CD-ROM and all that sort of stuff.'

Miller is characteristically down-to-earth about Emap's role in the great scheme of things, describing it as a gatherer of information, which it dresses up in attractive packages and distributes to a receptive public.

'I don't think the first part of that is going to change,' he argues. 'What is going to change is distribution methods. While the rumours of the death of print have been greatly exaggerated and I personally don't see magazines or indeed books being usurped by screen-based information, undoubtedly that screen-based information is going to become more and more significant. I can see a time when kids in school are learning much more from screens, using this CD-ROM stuff, and where businessmen are going to be prepared to pay for high quality business information which will be screen based. It's arguable that newspapers at some time in the future may not be distributed through the present methods, and your television set could become some form of printing press because you'll be able to print what you want from a menu on the screen. If you want to know what property is available in a particular area, or what cars to buy, or what the latest market information is, you will press a button and have it printed out for you. That is why the *Daily Mail* group has gone into Teletext. So the packaging and distribution will change. But the important thing will be the ownership, authority and expertise in generating and producing the information.'

However, until we are all peering at screens instead of turning over printed pages, Miller is adamant that Emap will remain basically a publisher of consumer magazines. Back in the 1970s, when Rogers was beginning to weave his spell, Emap was seen as very much a regional newspaper publisher with a few specialist magazines tacked on. Miller's achievement has been to give the group national coverage by filling in the gaps, mainly for special interest and business titles from *Horse and Pony* to *Middle East Economic Digest*. Some have been dreamed up in the haphazard way Miller describes, but others have been bought in blocks from Maxwell or Thomson as those companies dropped out of the race. In the process Emap has become one of the most all-round magazine publishers, keeping its different activities carefully balanced whilst making small forays into new areas.

'Consumer magazines really has been the main thrust of the company, and I think it will continue to be so,' Miller declares. 'We've proved to be reasonably good at it, and we want to continue doing it, both at home and abroad. What is interesting over recent years is that people have said consumer publishing is very, very cyclical because of advertising. But, because the bulk of our revenue comes from cover prices, that has remained relatively immune from the economic cycle. What have been hit hardest have-been those publications which rely very largely on advertising for their revenue. So consumer information is much less subject to cycles. W.H. Smith moved away from magazines a few years ago, but have moved back and are giving magazines much greater display space. They held up extraordinarily well over the recession. That is because people are not easily persuaded to do without what they like, and magazines are not a commodity. They're very personal, very special and they provide what people require. Looking at the longer term, I think the trend is that markets will become more segmented and specialised. Magazines, in terms of all forms of media, have grown quite considerably and I think will continue to grow. There will be more magazines, more specialist, more tightly targeted, lower circulations, better quality and better directed.'

While it is all very well to become more and more specialist as the economics of magazine production allows titles to break even at successively lower circulations, worries have surfaced about Emap's exposure to the country's children. While ever-improving GCSE and A Level results are encouraging, children's publishers must increasingly try to appeal to the underclass who may not even sit these exams, let alone pass them.

'I don't fully subscribe to the view that kids don't read any more,' replies Miller. 'We are selling more magazines and books than ever before. But it doesn't really matter, because we must simply package information the way that people want to receive it. If they want to get it off a screen or some other method, our method is to distribute it in that way. We are not printers, we're publishers, and however we publish the software must simply fit the market. People will want this information. Kids who are interested in computer games want to read about them, and the only way they can do that at the moment is by buying computer magazines. They sell like hot cakes.'

And long may they do so. But Miller is canny enough to realise that all these impending changes in the delivery of ideas and information will mean corresponding changes in the way publishing companies are organised. It is not entirely coincidental that his forecasts of how Emap will have to adapt fit fairly closely with the sort of informal setup that he himself feels most comfortable with: flat, flexible, unhierarchical, unbureaucratic, with decisions pushed as far down the organisation as possible.

'People in individual markets will be much more powerful, much more able to do their own thing, which will need to happen because markets will be much more competitive,' Miller points out 'It won't be possible for little groups of people sitting in offices to run these operations in tremendous detail. You will have to be extremely flexible in order to compete. I would describe us as informed bankers. We have 200 profit centres with the central organisation providing the finance for the subsidiary activities, and it will probably become more and more like that. Launching a new title always gives people a big thrill, but it will become less of an event for the corporation, and it should be. Unless you push decision-making much further down, you're going to become hopelessly bureaucratic and nobody will want to work for you. You're going to get a much higher quality of person making those decisions, because they'll be much closer to the market and a much higher calibre.'

Not only does this match Miller's temperamental preference for the informal, it is an implicit snub to many of the traditional attitudes still prevailing in British business.

'Arguably one of the greatest problems of British business is that you have had to be a generalist and come up through a particular structure to come up through a company and to be perceived to have succeeded,' he argues. 'That undoubtedly is a great weakness, because it does mean that some people who are very good specialists have to become a generalist to get on. I believe people should get lots of recognition and be highly rewarded for being very good at a particular thing, whether it be editorial or whatever. They should be hero-worshipped for what they are: we don't do enough of that. So you tend to get bloody good editors becoming poor publishers. Because that's the way companies operate. We have a guy called Dave Hepworth, who came into our business to work for *Smash Hits,* then became editor of it and now sits on our consumer division board, not as a generalist but as an editorial genius. He is recognised in the company, and his status is almost the same as the MD. People say, "Ooh, Dave Hepworth – wonderful, wonderful", and I think promoting that sort of thing is very important, or you lose people or they take the wrong job. Hepworth happens to be bloody good at what he's doing. He recognised that he didn't want to become a generalist. I think companies should be able to do more and more of that and if you don't you just miss tricks. I think letting people do what they're good at – and giving them recognition, which we all crave – is very important. Many of our systems, Emap's as well, don't cater for that. There must be room for excellent people. It's a fantastically important role, as editorial excellence is our be-all and end-all. Hierarchy is tradition, history and the way we've all grown up. That's one of the reasons why the level of management in British industry isn't good enough. It's too generalist, it's too often, in a strange way, class-based, and we very often aren't getting the right people to do the right jobs. It's a big subject, and no one's quite cracked it yet. Why does the chief executive's office have to be on the top storey, for Christ's sake? Why not the bottom storey? Why do people have their desk facing the door? I often wonder if it's to protect the executive from people coming in. It's an interesting psychological play, a bit like a bar in a pub. It bars contact. It's much better to have a desk set against the wall, and if someone comes in, they can sit alongside, then there's none of this business of getting up from behind the desk, or staying there with this great barrier between you.'

Hepworth loyally boasts: 'We produce magazines for people, not for other people in the media. It's that chip on the shoulder that gives us our edge.' But every so often employees in this highly profitable but unbusinesslike business display another side to that chip – complaints about long hours and low pay. Miller shrugs off such grumbles philosophically.

'You can't keep all the people happy all the time,' he observes. 'You can just try and keep most of the people happy. If we aren't capable of providing enough growth for people, they will leave. My job, and others', should be trying desperately hard to keep the top ten per cent of our people happy, and keep them with us. And you won't do that by bashing them over the head with pound notes all the time: it's something else. Pound notes are very nice, thank you very much, but they need something else – they need satisfying. We're all tempted by pound notes at the end of the day, but I think people who have certain kind of creative desires also want to see those desires satisfied in some way and sometimes pound notes just don't do that. It might be that a journalist just wants to write for a particular paper, or he might want to edit. Now, we've got to provide the environment to do that, or he may go somewhere else. We've lost one or two to the national newspapers, but it's a game and we win most of the time.'

CHAPTER **12**

SIR GEOFFREY MULCAHY

of Kingfisher

THE BIGGEST surprise about Sir Geoffrey Mulcahy is that he is in retailing at all. Nothing in his previous career – a physics and chemistry degree at Manchester University, a Harvard MBA, then management jobs at Esso, Norton Abrasives and British Sugar – prepared him for becoming successively finance director, chief executive and chairman of Kingfisher, a holding company for a mini high street of retail names, including Woolworths, B&Q, Comet and Superdrug.

'I am a cold and logical businessman,' he once claimed, possibly with a hint of self-caricature. That superficially grim assessment belies a Sunderland-born shrewdness and a refusal to be bewitched by the baubles of the business world. He looks at the ground and changes the subject when the subject of his knighthood comes up.

Mulcahy was most visibly irritated back in 1986 when, as part of the ritual pie-slinging surrounding Dixons Group's attempt to takeover his company, Dixons circulated the slur that he was not really a retailer. 'As if you had to be born with an apron on, standing behind a counter to qualify,' he scorned his detractors. But he saw off Dixons and four years later was prevented only by the Monopolies and Mergers Commission from turning the tables and having Kingfisher buy Dixons.

True to the serious side of his nature, that warning shot from officialdom set Mulcahy dutifully looking overseas for expansion opportunities. It was a long search. Dixons was one among many British retailers which had found offshore expansion to involve a long and chilly swim. More like a cold bath, really. But in February 1993, after seven years of getting acquainted, Mulcahy eventually landed what has been generally hailed as a prize catch:

Sir Geoffrey John Mulcahy

BORN: 7 February, 1942

EDUCATED: King's School, Worcester, Manchester University, Harvard Business School

MARRIED: Valerie Elizabeth, 1965. One son, one daughter

CAREER:

1964	Esso
1974	Finance Director, Norton Abrasives
1977	Finance Director, British Sugar
1983	Finance Director, Woolworth Holdings
1984	Chief Executive, Woolworth Holdings
1990	Chairman of Kingfisher

OTHER INTERESTS: Director of Bass, British Telecommunications

KINGFISHER PLC

HEAD OFFICE: North West House, 119 Marylebone Road, London NW1 5PX
Tel: 071-724 7749

ACTIVITIES: Retailing, property management

MAIN BRANDS: Woolworths, B&Q, Comet, Superdrug

Darty, the biggest electrical retailer in France. That is likely to be only the beginning of a long, slow move into the main markets of the rest of Europe, absorbing the cultures, overcoming the regulatory hurdles that hamper the Single Market from becoming a reality.

Says Mulcahy: 'I've long maintained that expansion overseas – even within Europe – is difficult for retailers. My reason is simple: to be a really good retailer in your chosen market you have to be extraordinarily close to your customers, and this is not easy in a greenfield situation in a foreign country. But that's one thing that to my mind's going to happen, because you've got forces driving you that way. Consumers are becoming more international. Suppliers are operating on a global framework. And retail formats are developing in similar sorts of ways. The opportunities are growing. But we'll make sure we understand our markets and we'll choose our moments carefully.'

A proud manifesto, and no more than meet for a retail organisation valued on the Stock Exchange at more than £4 billion by 1994. But when John Beckett of British Sugar persuaded Mulcahy and their colleague, Nigel Whittaker, to take part in what was effectively a management buy-in of Woolworths in 1982, they were freely warned that their careers could be finished in the extremely likely event that they could not revive the ailing high-street sluggard. The group was then valued at £310 million, and that mainly because it was sitting on a vast pile of freehold sites.

The Woolworth concept had been brought over from the United States in 1909 - everything for 3d or 6d, big stores with wide aisles, where customers were encouraged just to come and browse, no need to buy. That was a sharp contrast from the dour attitude to their patrons that most turn-of-the-century British shops exhibited. But after the Second World War the chain failed to keep up with the times. It went further and further down-market, at least in the public mind, and a 1970s attempt to import the Woolco out-of-town hypermarket idea from America was poorly received.

A London property developer, Godfrey Bradman, had the idea that if a group of City institutions bought the American Woolworth's fifty-two per cent stake in the British end of the business, they could inject fresh management and make a huge profit, with the freehold sites as security. The key was to find that fresh management. The snag was that no established retailers would touch it. Luckily for the institutional consortium, British Sugar was taken over and Beckett, Mulcahy and Whittaker were suddenly jobless. They had nothing but their reputations to lose by joining the Woolworths party.

That story is worth retelling because it shows why Mulcahy is so dispassionate about Woolworths – and why he was sneered at as a non-retailer. But that apparent drawback has also meant that he has been able to see retailing with clear eyes.

'The underlying trend, as I see it,' he explains, 'is people wanting more value for money. But I think the UK, to be honest, is a slightly odd market. In several of the other large markets, like Germany or the US, people are already far more value-conscious. I was over in Seattle, in the north-west US, being driven round by a chap who took me into a Costco. We went round the store and he knew the prices. He knew where to get the best value, and was talking about buying in bulk to split up with his family and neighbours. Similarly, in Germany you see new Mercedes parked outside Aldi, their big discount chain. Here, the perception is that you only shop at Aldi if you can't afford to shop at Sainsbury or Tesco. But I think the British consumer will change. We will see the value thing coming through. I think the other trend will be convenience, by which I mean being able to get to the place you want to get to and buy what you want there, rather than having to stagger round with large parcels looking at incomplete ranges. That means a continuing move to edge-of-town, backed by service.

'Again, if you look at what's happening in the US, you can see this polarisation between the sectors. DIY and electricals are two winners in the States, with chains like Home Depot and Circuit City. They have dominant product ranges, better than their competition, backed up by a high degree of service. In Circuit City you find salesmen who actually know about the product, and can actually help you select what you want. Similarly in a Home Depot you not only have people who know about a product, but they are also getting into installation. You can have your garage doors or kitchens fitted for you. And the third thing is that the whole thing is backed up by the best prices on the street. They're talking about selling on gross margins of ten per cent, which is less than half the gross margin that the UK food retailers operate on. So I think the shifts in the economics are quite substantial. These forces haven't applied in the UK so much, partly because of what the consumer has been given. I don't think the retailers in the UK have been as aggressive at pushing value. In food, I would argue that there's a lot more competition in Germany and the US. This is partly to do with planning permission, which is one of the difficulties in the UK. Permission to sell food is quite difficult to get, which means that the food retailers tend to spend a lot of money on prime sites and then have to charge prices which give them a reasonable return on capital employed.'

Mulcahy realises that retailers will be up against increasingly

124

discriminating consumers as the 1990s proceeds, mainly because they will on the whole be older and therefore better off. The 35–60s will outnumber the 16–25s. But, he argues, the 35–60s are precisely the group that has been hardest hit by the recession, because they are suffering most from big mortgages and falling property values.

'The memory of that pain is likely to remain with them for a very long time,' Mulcahy points out. 'On the other hand, this same group is wealthier, with higher disposable incomes, more leisure time and a greater ability to exercise choice in everything they do. The result is bound to be an ever more cautious approach to spending, with a far greater emphasis on price-led propositions and value for money. I believe we're in for a long period during which people live within their means, save more and buy less on credit, less on impulse.' And it goes further than that. 'The growth in wealthier mid-life consumers will lead to a shopping population with far higher expectations of improved service, better advice and more perceived value.'

Kingfisher has found itself increasingly playing cat-and-mouse with its customers. They delay Christmas purchases until after Christmas, when they think there is going to be a sale. 'I think sales are a bit of a con generally,' muses Mulcahy. 'Some stores make more money during the sales than at other times, because basically what they're doing is buying merchandise in specially for the sales and charging quite good margins. But people are seeing through that. What you want is for people to be convinced that they're getting value, not that they're being suckered by a sale.' At B&Q, there was so much discounting going on that people were coming in the stores and asking when the next sale was. So the management responded to that by moving on to continuous low prices, to remove the deterrent.'

Kingfisher has also cut customer complaints at Comet by putting service centres in the stores. That means there is a qualified person in the store to sort out a problem instead of an item having to go back into the system for repair. 'A very high percentage of faults can be fixed quite quickly,' Mulcahy reports, 'because people simply haven't pressed the right switch. But I'd say people expect more service than they did. Post-war, you were glad to be able to buy something at all. Now there is plenty to buy, so you are much more demanding – and less likely to forgive those that let you down.'

Demand for better service has also meant that Kingfisher has had to devote more time and money to training the staff, so they will be more on top of their jobs. That in turn should enable decisions to be pushed further down the organisation. 'You want people who will help to sell the gear and respond to the customer in a positive way, meet customer needs and feed back to the centre the additional sales opportunities,' says Mulcahy, 'so there is a cultural shift in retailing which is in one respect quite difficult to do because retailing has traditionally depended on a low-paid, low-skilled workforce. That results in high staff turnover. What you now need is a better trained and more stable workforce.'

Mulcahy has been clever enough to recognise that, although he can manage a business as well as any dyed-in-the-wool retailer, he did need to import some of the creative flair which makes the difference between a dull shop and one that the public feel excited about visiting. So he has had no qualms about buying the best advice. One of his top sources has been Crispin Tweddle, a former designer who runs a consultancy called Piper Trust from trendy pitch-pine offices in London's Notting Hill Gate and has come up with some of the ideas which enabled Mulcahy's team to update Woolworths and the other Kingfisher chains.

One of Tweddle's favourite sayings is that 'successful retailing is about having a dream,' but he accepts that the early 1990s recession has brought that dream down to earth. 'Customers and shop employees want stable relationships,' he says. 'Customers in particular want recognition for bringing their business to your shop. But it's now technically possible to dovetail relationship management with database management and database marketing to give the customer individual treatment. Personal service is information-related: people make purchases to fit in with hobbies like golf or gardening. So we will start to see different ways of managing the relationship, and that in turn means a huge agenda in terms of human management resources, recruitment and training. It's going to require some real courage, real leadership.'

Mulcahy has imbibed these thoughts and is convinced that technology holds the key to the future of retailing.

'If you look at what you can do with modern computer systems, faxes, videophones and cable television,' he points out, 'you can see how much cost you could take out of the system if you could get people into a direct marketing operation. Our whole way of interacting with the world around us is changing. Interactive information services are already commonplace, home shopping is becoming ever more popular. Banking and investment can be done from your armchair. From raw material to getting the product to the customer, we're already into the game of tying much more closely in with manufacturers, so that they can plan their production better and we cut out waste by having far faster feedback from what is selling. Before, retailers would order a full season's merchandise six months before the season commences, when you never know what's going to sell. If you order too much you have to mark down, too little and you can't reorder. Now we're in the game of having much faster information transfer and improving the production processes. We can now get feedback as to what's selling at the beginning of the season in order to influence the production runs. That's simple, but if someone could order a washing machine from their house and have it delivered, you can start taking huge amounts of cost out. People want to save time, and technology is going to make that a lot more possible.'

If that sounds like dear old mail order with an electronic twist, you are not far wrong. Mulcahy sees his customers becoming rushed off their feet, with a growing feeling of so-called time poverty: surveys shows that working women have an average of thirty-seven hours' free time a week, compared with forty-seven hours for working men, mainly because more than four-fifths of housewives are responsible for doing the household shopping. So it is tempting to see them reaching for the phone or the TV remote control to solve their shopping problems. But the savings made by the shops, in terms of better stock control and more deliveries direct from the factory to the home, will increasingly have to be passed on: no squirrelling away by shop-keepers eager to turn every penny, because competitors will take the opportunity to undercut.

'I believe firmly that the days of increasing gross profit margins have long gone,' insists Mulcahy, 'but get the volume right and there's no reason why net profit, and therefore earnings, should suffer. In fact they should actually improve. The key from now on will be generating more volume to improve better use of space. If increases in volume sales come from lower prices, then lower costs and higher productivity are more important today than they have ever been before. The race for space is now behind us: the 1990s are about driving higher sales across the same or a smaller store base. And to stimulate sustainable customer loyalty, we must be synonymous with the products we sell. We must dominate our chosen product categories, and it is no coincidence that the great majority of the products sold in Kingfisher group stores fall into the "growing market" categories: DIY, out-of-town electricals, confectionery, recorded music and videos, and drugstores. But those categories are not going to stand still. There are going to be continuing rapid changes within individual markets and product sectors. So we must deliver what consumers want rather what we think they ought to want.'

Although businessmen tend to play down the good times and exaggerate the bad, Mulcahy's time does seem to have arrived. Dodging consumer bullets is a tactical role that fits his lugubrious character, although he makes capital out of this public persona in private with a dry sense of humour. Certainly by assuming the worst he is unlikely to fall into any corporate elephant traps. And, behind the gloom, he is quietly confident about Kingfisher's chances.

'We are more convinced now than we were that we can achieve growth in our mainstream businesses,' he declares, moving quietly into the first-person plural for the upbeat message. 'I think we're in quite a good position to do that, because we're in reasonable growth markets. I suspect we will become more customer-focused, even more decentralised. We will be seeing a far higher rate of change in businesses. The question will be how fast you can evolve the organisation to provide the customer with better value for money, how much more efficient can we become. It's difficult to see where we will be in ten years, but if we are to be successful you will see us operating to a number of underlying principles: bigger, more decentralised, international, possibly more retail brands. I think it's very important to be highly focused on your particular customer segments. If you take Sainsbury's, they developed Homebase and Savacentre and Shaws when they didn't think the growth was there in the food business. But they've been hugely successful by focusing on what the customer wants. That's extremely important.'

Above all, Mulcahy rates the value of having a clear vision of the organisation which can then be communicated to the rest of the staff so that everybody knows what people at the centre are trying to do. 'People are a lot more intelligent than they are generally given credit for. If you have a clearly enunciated set of ambitions and values for the business, and you put a lot of effort into communicating that, making sure people understand the standards you are trying to set, then it helps people to perform better. You can't manage these days by diktat. You actually have to have people understanding and agreeing with what one is trying to do.'

CHAPTER 13

MICK NEWMARCH

of Prudential Corporation

MICK NEWMARCH, like the Prudential Corporation he heads, is larger than life. The Pru bestrides the life and pensions market and, because of the inflow of premiums that brings in, the group is also the biggest single investor on the London Stock Exchange. The rotund figure of Newmarch has ruled over the Pru's affairs since he was promoted to the chief executive's handsome panelled office in 1989. But he was well known in the City for years before that, as the man directly in charge of those investment billions.

Like David Prosser, his counterpart at Legal & General (Chapter 16), Newmarch will spend much of his remaining time at the Pru dealing with the problems raised by bancassurance, the French phrase for banks' incursion into the life assurance business. But, despite his background, he has not followed Prosser down the route of trying to fight back through the sheer weight of investment performance. Instead, Newmarch has concentrated on taking his own organisation away from the 'Man from the Pru' image without ditching the sense of integrity which went with that.

He says: 'I hope shareholders towards the end of the decade will see a corporation that has been well managed, has taken a clear look at its opportunities, resources and controls, got those resources honed into a highly competitive mode and is using them in an efficient way to the benefit of shareholders and markets. It will be about quality of service, quality of returns, packaged in a way which causes the consumer pleasure rather than pain.'

He inherited Scenario 3, an internal programme which was started in 1988 by Keith Bedell-Pearce, chief executive of Prudential Financial Services. It was designed to turn the Man from the Pru from a cash collector into a

clued-up insurance consultant. The idea was to maintain the existing door-to-door cash business, known in the Pru as the Industrial Branch, and simultaneously encourage customers to pay by direct debit, cheque or credit card. Since 1988 the volume of cash collection has dropped sharply, so the Prudential's Home Service Division needs many fewer admin people and many more selling policies and bonds. Pensions alone accounted for sixty per cent of the division's sales by 1993. Meanwhile, the accountants have been adding up just how much it costs to send someone knocking on doors and having a chat with every other customer. The upshot is that those who want a personal cash-collection service have to pay thirteen premiums a year instead of twelve, which is effectively an eight per cent tax for those, often at the older and poorer end of the market, who like the money taken out of their hands and want the regular human contact. Terry Shrimpton, an ex-Rank Xerox executive who is director and general manager of the Home Service Division's Field Operations, explains: 'We want to do the best by our customers, but it's unlikely that the younger generation of customers are going to want the same frequency of contact that people did in the past. Often the cash collection is just an exchange of money, with no chat. Sometimes a neighbour gives the money for three or four different houses, so that it isn't even personal.'

On the other hand, as many of the former sales staff become consultants, they are trained to get to know their customers and establish a relationship with them. Every customer is 'owned' by one of the Pru's staff, which should mean fewer slip through the sales net. That is predictably popular with the field staff. Previously two Pru reps might call on the same customer on the same day, while some customers had not heard from the company for more than ten years. Now all the six million Prudential policyholders on record are supposed to have been contacted to see if they would like a visit. Particularly popular with the field staff is the notion of drawing up a contract with each customer, giving commitments on each side and crucially agreeing to a Prudential visit every so often, be it six months, a year or longer. That gives the relationship a vital continuity, and makes it easier to make the return call. Shrimpton reports: 'Market research shows that people who have dealt with us, or even have never dealt with us, are quite happy to do business with us. But we have not got in touch with them. So there will be more visits from salesmen on a cyclical basis.'

The difficult part will be for the Pru to move over to what is more like the standard notion of what an insurance salesman is and does without losing its special identity. The market is becoming crowded.

Michael George Newmarch

BORN: 19 May, 1938

EDUCATED: Tottenham County Grammar School, London University (external degree)

MARRIED: Audrey Clarke, 1959. One son, two daughters

CAREER:

1955 Prudential Corporation, Economic Intelligence Dept.
1982 Investment Manager
1982 Chief Executive, Prudential Portfolio Managers
1985 Director, Prudential Corporation
1990 Group Chief Executive

OTHER INTERESTS: Director of the Association of British Insurers, the Node and the Princess Royal Trust for Carers. Member of British Invisibles European Committee, City Research Project, Personnel Standards Led Body, J.P. Morgan Advisory Board and The Geneva Association

PRUDENTIAL CORPORATION PLC

HEAD OFFICE: 142 Holborn Bars, London EC1N 2NH
Tel: 071-405 9222

ACTIVITIES: Financial services, including pensions and life, household and accident insurance

MAIN BRAND: Prudential

'People actually welcome Industrial Branch insurance,' Newmarch concedes. 'Sir Colin Southgate at Thorn was telling me that when his people go round to collect the £14 a month from people renting televisions, they take off the box at the side and when they pour the money on the table they often find there is £50 in there. People put the money in because they can't then get it out, to make themselves save. Lots of people do think like that. So we've developed the firm proposition to look after our customers and not take advantage of them. People have always been able to rely on the fact that the Pru has handled their affairs honestly, and marrying that proposition with the professional proposition make you in my view unassailable. But we're not there yet.'

Newmarch normally talks in machine-gun bursts, but the speed goes up a notch or two when he launches into a subject which he feels strongly about, and on which he has rehearsed the arguments in his own minds. 'I do get dramatically impatient,' he has admitted. 'I am very instinctive and intuitive: I make up my mind very quickly and I get impatient if I cannot do what I want to do. And I push people to achieve the best they can. But I am not a bully.' Nevertheless he feels strongly about the growing competitive pressures of the 1990s and answers his own questions, so quickly does his mind race as he raises the tempo.

'People like us are trying very hard to modernise our businesses, without losing all of our relevant experiences and outlooks,' he states, 'and I think we're going to be very hard competition, I really do, if we get our act together. I really am open-minded about bancassurance. Just to reassure some of our people, I have promised to wear a big badge which says "Bancassurance is a serious threat"! Do I really believe that? I think the jury must be out on it. There is clearly a lot of momentum behind what the banks are presently doing, and they appear to be cannibalising their own deposit accounts. They are moving from what were relatively secure deposit accounts to long-term investments with their own life companies at high rates of interest. Are they seriously attacking the real world? Difficult to tell. We know they're creating direct sales forces, under regulation which is nowhere nearly as stringent as we face. We don't know what quality of sales forces they're creating. I assume they are using their ex-bank managers to try and sell to their existing customers. But I don't know. What do banks bring to long-term savings products? Not a great deal, in my view.

'The one quandary for me is that if I were running Barclays or NatWest Life I would clearly take advantage of whatever loyalty there is from my banking customers and try and migrate that. But would I be really committed about my ability to onsell to a Barclays customer, if I were a NatWest Life salesman? To my mind, banking brands are clearly competitive brands and people are loyal to them, whereas the Prudential brand is clearly a life brand and transcends banking. And therefore a NatWest person is quite happy to contemplate dealing with the Pru, I would have thought. Whether he's going to be happy dealing with a Barclays or Lloyds or Midland salesperson, I would have thought much less certainly.'

The thought of banks competing in the insurance market would have been dismissed as eccentric nonsense when Newmarch joined the Pru as a seventeen-year-old statistical clerk in 1955. He was brought up by his Aunt Doris in Tottenham, north London, after his mother died when he was two and a half. His father remarried seven years later and died five years after that. 'His new wife thought I would be a bit of a burden to her,' Newmarch remembers. 'I can quite understand how she felt. Money was tight, but that's just how things were. You didn't really think about it. By and large we were no different from anyone else.' However, these early setbacks taught him the value of persistence. He is the first investment manager to head the Pru and the first chief executive to oversee its expansion on a global scale.

The Pru operates in as many as forty countries, but even in the mid-1990s the overwhelming bulk of the Pru's profits still came from the UK. And that will continue to be so for the foreseeable future, because the UK is also the main engine of the Pru's growth, followed by North America. There is also a burgeoning Asia-Pacific business, in Australia, New Zealand, Malaysia, Singapore and Hong Kong. But that is a gleam in Newmarch's eye for the future. As to Europe, the Pru has dipped its toe but Newmarch is convinced that there will not be a pan-European medium and long-term savings market until the twenty-first century.

'We anticipate no advancement into other territories this century,' he maintains. 'We want to concentrate on reasserting ourselves in the UK and reorganise our direct sales force, and that is very complex. We are determined to modernise that, make it more relevant to the market place, expanding our distribution strategy to other alternatives like the Independent Financial Adviser market. We are building a franchise with that part of the market. We see the IFA as part of the market that's going to give us the opportunity to become even more important than we presently are, even though we are already the largest player. And we started much earlier than other people to do things about that. We started taking costs out when I became chief executive, and a lot of people out there don't realise that they need to do that. A lot of the products we were selling were not really in the interests of our clients. They were so expensive for them and us that they were not a good deal for anyone. If you're prepared to admit to yourselves that what you are doing is not a fair deal, you stop doing it. And you don't stop doing it in the expectation that nothing will happen, you do it with the expectation that you will increase sales.'

After Newmarch had initiated the process of giving the Pru a thorough financial and organisational spring clean, he turned his attention to the future. In 1992 he recruited Laurel Powers-Freeling, an American invest-ment banker, to be head of corporate strategy. She is the sort of powerful lady who inevitably attracts the label 'feisty'. She soon rolled up her sleeves and began a fundamental reassessment of where the Pru is going. After a hard winter's study and debate, Newmarch and Powers-Freeling agreed that the corporation should be engaged primarily in meeting people's medium to long-term savings, financial security and retirement needs. Businesses which did not clearly fit into this definition could not be core and were not therefore to be regarded as proper long-term constituents of the business.

That put a black box round Mercantile & General, the Pru's reinsurance business, which had been a repeated target for criticism from institutional shareholders. They felt it was too risky, because reinsurance is where the buck stops in insurance. Other insurance companies lay their bets off with reinsurers. The Pru did what it could to meet these gripes by angling as much as possible of M&G's business to the more predictable task of rein-suring life policies, as opposed to the notoriously volatile casualty end of the game. But the mud stuck to it as a lesser business, not worthy of a place in the Pru's magisterial Holborn castle. General insurance – household, car, accident, marine – has also been scaled down for the same reason, but Newmarch believes it serves a useful purpose of feeding customers into the core life and pensions activity.

'In all our chosen markets we anticipate substantial environmental change,' declares Newmarch. 'A general theme, but most notably in the UK, will be advancing customer awareness. We expect markets to become more critical and competitive, fanned by greater transparency and disclosure prompted by consumerists and regulators. In Prudential Portfolio Managers we have an increasingly powerful, globally equipped investment manage-ment organisation which we will continue to develop.'

He made no secret of his dislike for one aspect of the Pru he inherited – its lossmaking estate agency chain. He ordered it sold in 1990, at what many commentators regarded as near the bottom of the housing market and there-fore at a time when the business could have been reckoned to fetch its lowest price. He says: 'Our decision was based on the view that there was no valuable future for our shareholders' resources. We were relatively small scale, we were operating in a limited subset of the market place, we had been doing rather amateurishly for quite a long while, and we never really developed the mass and momentum that gave us competitive advantage. On top of all that we were at the mercy of the vagaries of the market place, and I don't like operating in those circumstances.'

In one sense, however, the Pru cannot avoid bending its knee to the verdict of the market, when the market in question is the London Stock Exchange. That is where the Pru's own shares are traded, which puts it in a slightly strange position. Not only does it have shareholders, but it is also Britain's biggest shareholder on behalf of its policyholders. That makes it vulnerable to the demand that it should do as it would be done by in its dealings with the companies in which it has holdings. Among the virtues that any active investor would wish on the companies whose shares it owns are openness and accountability, so Newmarch has built up an extensive investor relations department which organises his stately progress through the ranks of media, fund managers and securities houses to preach the gospel each year.

'We expect to see the top twenty shareholders once a year,' he explains. 'I reckon I probably spend fifteen to twenty days a year meeting investors. I'm always there if the meeting is above a certain level. If I didn't turn up, they wouldn't take it seriously. It tends to become a personality thing, but I don't run this place on my own. We try to get all the senior people in front of the shareholders, at least on an occasional basis. We can't do that for all our private shareholders, but our annual report wins awards and at other times we rely on the media to relay our messages to them. For our shareholders we intend to deliver an attractive and stably-rising flow of dividends. At the same time we organise the corporation's affairs so as to deliver business developments which offer strong prospects for dividend continuation and enhancement into the longer-term future. Our share price is something which I watch, and am interested in. But I'm not neurotic about it.'

He has been around too long to be other than philosophical, at least in the short term. When he was an investment manager, investing in other companies, Newmarch would hear chairman after chairman complaining that the market didn't understand their business and had got the share price wrong. 'Silly stuff,' he now calls it, with a dismissive wave of his hand. 'I've been around long enough to know that the market has a will and a mind of its own, and is actually quite efficient. So I ain't gonna argue with it. I will try to make sure that people understand what we are doing. In so far as I'm able to do that, they will make their own minds up and they will buy or sell the stock. If I can persuade enough to buy, simply by the Pru behaving consistently and delivering good outputs, then the price will go up. Any long-term shareholder is only interested in the share price, frankly, as a measure. Over time, the total return is delivered most accurately by revenue, not by share price. But the small shareholder and the employee who owns shares in his own corporation are interested in market value, not income. I've got to make sure they don't get confused between the two issues. But we can do nothing about the share price, other than by our efforts. The market takes its view of what the Prudential is doing. Either it will give greater or less credit for what we are doing, and investors will wish to own the shares or not.'

If supreme self-confidence and a sense of certainty that your own side is unshakably in the right were all that it took to succeed in business, Newmarch would have it made. In truth, as he is well aware, life is tougher than that because well-armed rivals possess just as much certainty and self-confidence. But Newmarch has done much to pull the Pru out of its nice but ineffectual 1950s image and convince customers and investors that it is a force to be reckoned with.

CHAPTER 14

ARCHIE NORMAN

of ASDA Group

ARCHIE NORMAN has a mission. He wants – and, more than that, needs – to create a positive culture at Asda Group, the shell-shocked Leeds-based supermarket group which he has led since the start of 1992. Asda plunged into a £365 million loss for the year ending March that year as Norman, a former finance director, cleared the decks, writing off everything in sight. In the space of sixteen months the company asked its shareholders for £704 million to shore up its rickety finances. Originally known as Associated Dairies, the Leeds-based company had got embroiled in an ill-advised merger with MFI, the flatpack furniture retailer, then paid £705 million to buy sixty-one superstores from Gateway in 1989. All the time it was being squeezed between the high-volume, sell-everything attractions of Sainsbury, Tesco and Safeway, and the no-frills price-cutting of discount chains like Kwik Save, Food Giant, Aldi and Netto. The future looked decidedly bleak.

Enter Norman. At the age of only thirty-seven he was summoned to be Asda's saviour. It was a daring choice. One of five sons of the former Physician to Great Ormond Street Hospital, he followed in his father's educational footsteps at Charterhouse and Emmanuel College, Cambridge, before collecting an MBA at Harvard Business School. That took him to McKinsey, the American management consultants, where like many of his fellow alumni he so impressed a client that the client poached him. The company in question was Kingfisher, headed by Sir Geoffrey Mulcahy, who had also been to Harvard (Chapter 13). So grateful was Sir Geoffrey at Norman's advice in helping to fend off a takeover bid from Dixons Group that he made the budding thirty-two-year-old his finance director. Though the going at

Archibald John Norman

BORN: 1 May, 1954

EDUCATED: Charterhouse School, Emmanuel College, Cambridge, Harvard Business School

MARRIED: Vanessa Peet, 1983. One daughter

CAREER:

1975	Citibank
1979	Partner, McKinsey & Co.
1986	Finance Director, Woolworth Holdings
1989	Director, Geest
1991	Chief Executive, Asda Group

OTHER INTERESTS: Director of British Rail

ASDA GROUP PLC

HEAD OFFICE: Asda House, Southbank, Great Wilson Street, Leeds LS11 5AD
Tel: 0532-435435

ACTIVITIES: Retailing of food and related non-food products

MAIN BRANDS: Asda, Dales

Kingfisher was tough at first, the Mulcahy team eventually got to grips with Kingfisher's eclectic high-street mixture of Woolworths, B&Q, Comet and Superdrug. But none of that, or anything else in Norman's previous career, had really prepared him for running Asda, so he thought long and hard about it when he was offered the job. The company was desperate, as the City's investment fund managers were proving reluctant to throw good money after bad by subscribing to a £357 million rights issue of fresh capital at the end of 1991. Norman's reputation was good enough for the City to overlook his lack of experience behind a counter. The money was raised. At thirty-five pence a share, with Norman thrown into the package at the last minute, it might turn out to be the best deal of the decade for those shareholders who were brave enough to take it up.

By the turn of the century Norman will either be one of the successes of the 1990s, possibly moving on to greater things, or will have retreated back into the consultancy world to lick his wounds. He is disarmingly frank about his initial ignorance of the business he runs: 'When you go into a business like this, people assume that you know exactly what you want to do, but in reality you never really do. When I came to Asda, I'd never met anybody from Asda – I'd never even been to Leeds before. I'd just met a couple of non-executive directors who were panicking. At first, the issue was survival. But we've done what I said we'd do and if anything, it's worked better than I had originally envisaged.'

Norman worked hard to allay the fears of investors, lenders and suppliers while he worked out a plan. Asda's place in the pecking order – below the established favourites, Sainsbury, Tesco and Safeway, but ahead of corner-shop co-operatives like Spar – ensures that his schemes will change constantly through the 1990s. But the outline of a shape emerged within a year or two.

The core will be an ever-shifting kaleidoscope of food, mixing the bread-and-baked-beans commodities with exotic high-margin fresh and convenience gems. Around that will revolve five satellite concepts that do not seem too far removed from the half-dozen departments Norman's old mentor, Sir Geoff Mulcahy, developed at Woolworths.

By 1994 the basic concepts were:

1. Gifting: cards, stationery, party stationery, flowers, pot plants, boxes of chocolates.

2. Toys and related garden toys.

3. Home care: DIY, home maintenance, kitchen and household equipment

4. Entertainment: a wide range of videos, compact discs, records, tapes and computer games.

5. Clothes: the old Asda was doing a lot of formal clothing, suits and formal shoes. Norman is concentrating on casual clothing, having done a deal with ex-Next chief George Davies to design a range under the George brand, which is Asda's property.

Norman explains: 'Those are the basic value concepts, and each one can be done with authority. It's not very far removed from the six Woolworth departments. Woolworth was about creating authority out of variety, and that's not so far from what we need to do. There's no right formula. People can make anything work if they do it well. We're not sure how big clothing should be. I think commodity grocery markets are going to be squeezed in the next three or four years. Broader markets, like clothing and toys, are going to be very important to us. By sorting the stores out into sensible, authoritative retail statements, consistent with what people would do when they are doing a weekly shop, it can be a very powerful combination.' He has the US for inspiration: the most successful American retailers are combination retailers. K-mart and Wal-mart's supercenters use the food to create the traffic, spinning it off into general merchandise.

The early Asda was just a huge discount operation, with as much as half the space devoted to non-food. Norman wants to tilt the balance seventy/thirty in favour of food.

'Our Roehampton Vale store, near Kingston in Surrey, is about 45,000 sq ft, very nearly half non-food,' Norman adds. 'I'd expect in a store of that size to find 7,000 sq ft of clothing and about 8,000 sq ft other non-food. The bigger a store you get, the more you bring in non-food. You don't need much more space for baked beans.'

Arguably, Norman was bound to look good in the first couple of years after he took over because he was starting from such a low base. Simple tidying-up had an immediate impact. By 1993 he was able to announce annual profits of £187 million and had the confidence to warn his peers: 'The halcyon days in the food industry in terms of increasing profitability are over. The industry is going into recession.' That marked him out as something of a maverick and may have been a piece of political guile, giving him the space to say 'I told you so' if things went wrong. But he had high-grade backing for his views. His former employer, McKinsey, had just published a study declaring: 'UK retailers will have to bring their costs and productivity more into line with those of their US counterparts to avoid a sharp decline in profitability. British supermarkets are particularly exposed to these trends.'

He was berated by the City for his pains. *The Investors Chronicle* warned of 'a steady, uneasy erosion of prices' that could undermine his strategy: as if on cue, Tesco announced price cuts on selected lines. Asda's share price fell. But Norman has shaped his strategy for the 1990s accordingly: no more than 200 Asda stores, and the launch of a parallel discount chain, Dales, in case the British public goes nap on the shed approach to food shopping. He states, as fact: 'Since we started, things that we talked about then have become conventional wisdom and that's always the way. The glory days are over and we're into the real world where it's very competitive, with people looking for value. The margins will come down and there will be rapid development of discounting. People now accept that discounting is going to be very big. They now accept food retailing is not recession-proof.'

That reads like a suicide note. But, like the well-trained management consultant he is, Norman has a plan. 'You've got to know exactly what you want and have a set of principles to work to,' he says.

His set of principles amounts to a four-point plan:

• The same number of stores as now, but better.

• Develop a selling culture in the company.

• Make every store a business centre containing mini profit centres.

• Offer outstanding value.

Sounds simple. The first point is easy enough, providing you have enough cash to pay for rebuilding and redecoration. And making every store a business centre requires little more than the stroke of a pen. But instilling a selling culture in employees and consistently offering better value than the competition are dreams that have crucified many a retailer before Norman. Ask Gateway. Its main success in recent years has been persuading Asda to part with £705 million for those sixty-one stores. Otherwise, it toiled through the recession along a road strewn with misery.

'Bigness isn't part of our objectives,' Norman says, 'and that's convenient because we don't have the capacity in the financial market to become a lot bigger anyway. As I see the grocery industry as becoming less profitable, it would be a great mistake to overinvest in it. We'll spend our money cannily, but at the same time we want to create a different type of superstore, one which will trade on lower margins and will be organised and managed differently from anything that happens today.'

He claims that his rivals have made the mistake of creating too much of a saving environment, from the 'money off' ads in the newspapers to the in-store banners shouting the same message. 'Sir Ian McLaurin, the chairman of Tesco, would say that you're not trying to take out the selling, you're try-ing to control the selling and achieve standards, and that's what creates the controlling approach,' Norman paraphrases. 'I don't want to overstate it, but it is a saving environment. Obviously what we want them to do is spend money on this and that, but be glad about it.'

So Norman wants to create what he calls the selling store, which gives people opportunities to buy without giving opportunities to save. It is an approach he has unashamedly poached from Ken Morrison, chairman, man-aging director and guiding light of William Morrison Supermarkets, the Bradford-based chain that, unlike Asda, has largely stuck to its West Yorkshire roots. Like Morrison, Norman believes the way to achieve that is to create a lively environment staffed by people who want to sell.

'Most retail businesses are run by people who want to administer,' Norman insists. 'That's all that's left to them. It's less true if you go into Dixons or somewhere where they're on commission, but even there it's a rudimentary thing. As a result the spiritual nature of a store is dead. Being a store manager is being a sophisticated administrator. It's a wonderful job, still, but your role in life is to keep the shelves full, get in the back and make sure you're stocked, make sure the checkouts are manned. I want a situation where every store is run by employees who want to sell. Because if you cre-ate that sense that we're all here to sell, you start to create a purpose in life. There's only one real purpose in retailing, which is selling. You can never motivate people around saving money or around keeping the shelves full, or customer service. Customer service is very, very important, but you can't motivate people around customer service. You can motivate people to sell because they want to sell what the customers want.'

He admits that it is easier to recruit the right sort of staff in some parts of the country than in others. Staff in run-down areas are more likely to be part-time, and come and go rather than building career loyalty. 'We've got to regard labour turnover as a business objective,' insists Norman. 'Each store manager has got to be planning each year's labour turnover now, because it's a huge investment for us, labour recruitment and training. And if you have high labour turnover what it is a measure of at the end of the day is how much people want to work at Asda. I'm not going to pretend that we're going to create some of the most wonderful, high-paying jobs in the world but, as we move back towards the higher employment levels in Britain, people will become more demanding about their place of work and the kind of work they do is going to become quite important. I want our stores to be the sort of places where people do stay. We have a bit of that already: families have worked for us for years and years and years and enjoyed it, and that is something we should build on.'

However, Norman would be the first to admit that some people could not sell a glass of water to someone dying of thirst. He says: 'About forty per cent of the population really never smiles, and if they never smile then forget it. They shouldn't be in our business. They shouldn't even be in the warehouse, because they'll never serve customers well, they don't like to. It's no criticism. They're brilliant at laying bricks or administering schedules or whatever it is, but they're not customer people. But if you get friendly staff then you're probably sixty per cent of the way there.'

Norman wants to channel this enthusiasm by turning each store into a number of mini profit centres. That will give, say, the bakery manager the incentive to motivate his or her staff, as well as determining the profit margin and deciding how much wastage to tolerate. He explains: 'What all the supermarkets do today is produce manuals saying this is how you make it, this is how much you make, you're not allowed more than that on the shelves der-der, dee-dum. You try and control it, you try and kill the job and for God's sake don't bake anywhere near the customers. I want the baker out here in a white hat and the ovens in there and I want him to sell and he will get, every Monday morning, his profit-and-loss account. A good food store should be a combination of craft centres, even though it may sound very old-fashioned. We have a bakery; we have a butcher who cuts meat in the store – and he can make two or three percentage points difference to your margin; we have the clothing manager, who typically runs between five and ten thousand square feet of clothing, which is like two or three Top Shops put together; we have the fishmonger; we have the deli counter. We have fruit and vegetables. The person in charge of ordering the vegetable, will say: "I'm going to sell 10,000 iceberg lettuces on Saturday, and I'm going to do a huge display of them." They are craft centres, because you have to know your fruit and vegetables. It's not thermo-nuclear physics, but the people there take pride in it. I want our stores to be a constellation of these craft centres. Then, of course, you have a commodity and grocery area as well.'

The idea is to give the staff scope to respond to local needs, wants and tastes. A store in Yorkshire will sell more bacon, cheese and sausages. One in Scotland will sell more confectionery. 'The managers will have some control over the ranges and how the stores are laid out,' says Norman, 'because they are right there with the customers and they'll have the opportunity to run local promotions and activities in the store which enable them to sell more and give them a bit of control over their own destiny. And they can ask for money to do things like installing a barbecue machine. We'll say whether we want them to do that, and if so we'll give them the money and that will create a really different type of management task that's much, much more exciting. We have a bigger range of products in our stores, with clothing and entertainment and so on. Our stores are more complex and that lends itself to a very exciting, very promotional type of trading style if you get it right.'

The final item in Norman's management shopping list, and in many ways the most difficult of all to achieve, is outstanding value. It is the hot topic of the 1990s, because many people are believed to have emerged from recession with a determination to squeeze the utmost value out of any purchase. This is, inevitably, something of a caricature. People certainly like to tell themselves that they want more value for their money, and to that extent a store that offers value is going to have a better chance of persuading them to come through the door. How many remember their zeal once they begin pushing a trolley up and down the aisles is another matter. But it is certainly a valid starting point for Norman.

'It's sort of one of those odd things,' he muses. 'In the 1980s, peculiarly, people took their eye off the ball, but now I do believe they want more value – particularly because people are aware of the huge choices. You can buy it at ten per cent cheaper or you can buy it at full price. So, I want to see a business where we really do, on the commodity lines, deliver value. And, you see, it fits together with everything else, because it's no good trying to motivate staff to sell if you are going to try and sell bad value. You won't have the staff thinking they're doing the customers a favour by selling to them – particularly in this country, they won't have any confidence about doing so. That's what I mean by a different type of store, and we are trying to set up stores that will work this way. We've got two or three experiments which we are working on.'

Norman frankly admits that he doesn't know if it is going to be feasible to run the Asda stores on lower profit margins, although he is certain that it is going to be impossible unless he can get sales up. However, given his view that the whole industry is going to suffer a severe squeeze on margins, he feels that the only recipe for survival is to get in ahead of the pack. 'Some of our stores, on that sort of economics, won't survive,' he says, 'but others will and the new ones we are building definitely will.'

The other iron Norman has in the fire is the Dales discount chain, which he launched within eight months of moving in, with the intention of catching the trend towards shopping at discount stores if it really takes off in Britain as it has in the US and in parts of the Continent. Dales has as much variety as Asda, but the stores are about three times the size of Kwik Save, with lower prices and a big fresh food rack.

'In this country we haven't had much discounting,' says Norman, 'but a primitive form of discounting is coming in and I think we have to leapfrog that. The other discounters don't go in for a lot of fresh foods, because they haven't historically had as complicated food: it's much more difficult to manage. And they don't have the integrated supply channel we've got. We can take something from the factory right through our distribution system in a controlled temperature van and put it on the shop floor in the chill cabinet, and it's much easier for us to do that than for a Kwik Save. Obviously they'll catch up on that, but we're starting from a position of having wonderful distribution where we know how to approach bakeries and a large-scale fruit and vegetable department, and that's where some of the money is. I think if you look what happens at Kwik Save and the Aldis and Nettos, they're only getting, even at their end of the demographic market, a slice of the shopping basket. If a family spends £20 a week, they're only getting £12 of it. I want to get all £20. I want to be able to cater for the whole basic shop in Dales, with good value and at low capital cost, so that we get a return on capital on the lower margins.'

If Dales and Asda are both successful then, by definition, they will in time compete with one another. Initially, of course, the Dales stores will be opened far enough away from Asdas to avoid overlap, and Norman is confident that even if they do begin to jostle one another they will have a sufficiently distinctive appeal to attract different audiences. 'Asda is a broad range superstore trading on slightly higher margins, a bigger mix and much more choice,' Norman points out, 'but it is still value for money and it will compete with Sainsbury and Savacentres and so on. Dales, on the other hand, operates in a narrow-range, low-cost but total weekly grocery shopping market. You will have a choice between the two, if we are successful. But I don't think one need crowd out the other. In the States, there are discount formats and superstore formats. They compete with each other. We've gone monolithic here and that's one of the reasons why these next few years are going to see so much change. When I first went into Asda, if I asked "Why have we got seven different types of sweetcorn and sixteen different types of canned peas?" – which we did – the answer was always, "Tesco's got eighteen, Sainsbury has nineteen so we've got seventeen." I'm sure the people in Sainsbury do exactly the same thing. In other words, it's all just copying. For Asda, that was death. We don't have the same brand image at all as Sainsbury. It's very, very important for us that we set out to be different.'

CHAPTER 15

DAVID PROSSER

of Legal & General

Tнε NORMALLY relaxed insurance world is at battle stations. Previously the undisturbed province of dedicated insurance companies, it is under an assault that will not be resolved until well into the 21st century. The attack comes from those near but, until now, unthreatening neighbours, the banks. The ground they are fighting over – and the only oddity is that it has lain undisputed for so long – is the demand for insurance policies among the millions of people who have bank accounts. The idea of banks muscling in on insurance was first shown to be a practicable proposition by the French, who called it bancassurance. This was something that one or two British banks, notably TSB, had quietly been doing for twenty years in an unaggressive way for their own customers, but now the pack is in full cry. Banks, building societies and any financial organisations with a reasonably promising customer base lurking in their computers are keen to sell insurance.

Bancassurance has been greeted by traditional insurers with a range of responses varying from insouciance to panic. At the insouciant end of the spectrum is David Prosser, the Welsh-born chief executive of Legal & General Assurance Society, which in 1993 felt its first pinch when the go-ahead Cheltenham & Gloucester building society decided not to renew its five-year contract with L&G. That contract provided for Cheltenham selling only L&G insurance policies. Instead, Cheltenham opted to concentrate on interest-only and repayment mortgages, neither of which need fancy endowment assurance escorts.

While Prosser concedes that some bancassurers will succeed, he insists that the long run favours the specialist insurance companies. 'What the average consumer wants,' he says, 'is someone to talk to about their problems

and who will be around in five years to answer their questions.' This begs the question of whether insurance salesmen will necessarily be around in five years in these competitive and unpredictable times, and touches on the central question: what does the customer want?

'Most people find life insurance savings a complicated subject,' Prosser explains, 'and we have to simplify it as far as we can and make it easy for people to meet their needs. Often, we have to identify to those people that they have those needs, because the nature of the contracts we are involved with have gratification in the future or protection for the future, and it's not like buying a consumer product. The consumer doesn't have immediate gratification, so in looking at a long-term savings contract or a life cover contract, they have to have their needs identified. I think there is a strong element in an economy such as ours for people to provide for themselves, and we try and help them do that. I think the market for life products is changing all the time. It has changed pretty significantly because of the change in the economic environment, given lower growth in the 1990s. People are orientated more towards savings products: that will probably continue. And there's a lot of cultural preference in consumers' minds. Products like endowment with-profits policies don't sell, necessarily, in other countries. That's in part cultural.'

Endowment policies are basically life insurance with a strong investment element added on. They were naturally at their most popular before tax relief was removed from life insurance in 1984. While a basic sum is promised on death or at a set date, so-called bonuses are credited to the policyholder in most years. Once highly regarded, endowment policies have come under severe criticism from commentators as an inefficient way of saving, particularly since the tax break was removed. Other forms of saving, such as investment or unit trusts, give access to the stock market without the heavy front-end loading that blights these policies. The first two years' payments can vanish in administration charges and the agent's commission. Even after ten years a policyholder may not be entitled to a full refund on instalments paid towards a twenty-five-year policy. These are seen as needless shackles, but the mild-mannered Prosser claims endowment policies reward those who stay the course.

'The returns, for people who've stayed with the with-profit endowment over the life of the contract,' he insists, 'have actually been very good: they've had excellent returns. So the people who've had policies mature, if you like, are disciples of staying with the contract and the simplicity of the product is appealing. Against that, people who took out with-profit

David John Prosser

BORN: 26 March, 1944

EDUCATED: Ogmore Grammar School, Bridgend, and University College of Wales at Aberystwyth

MARRIED: Rosemary Snuggs, 1971. Two daughters

CAREER:

1965	Sun Alliance
1969	Hoare Govett
1973	National Coal Board
1981	Managing Director, CIN Industrial Investments
1985	Managing Director, CIN Management
1988	Investment Director, Legal & General Group
1991	Chief Executive, Legal & General Group

OTHER
INTERESTS: Director of South Wales Electricity

LEGAL & GENERAL GROUP

HEAD OFFICE: Temple Court, 11 Queen Victoria Street, London EC4N 4TP
Tel: 071-528 6200

ACTIVITIES: Pension and life, household, car and accident insurance, estate agency and investment management

MAIN BRAND: Legal & General

endowments in 1988, when Mr Nigel Lawson was Chancellor of the Exchequer and told them the world was lovely, and had to surrender during the recession under his successor, Mr Norman Lamont, who said the world was ugly, have found that the surrender values in short periods are not very good. But I suppose second-hand washing machines are not worth a lot, either. And, to an extent, if people become more aware about the long-term nature of the contract, then that's probably a good thing for our part. We are working quite hard on training and improving the quality of the sales force, to ensure that there is proper understanding of the contracts, and that they put that over to the client base. Of course, that is a benefit of the Financial Services Act – that we all have to take very seriously the quality of our sales force.'

One of the points of attack by the banks has been the low reputation of British insurance sales people, often perceived as get-rich-quick merchants inclined to jam their foot in the door and hype their offerings beyond all reason to would-be consumers who are too ill-versed to argue. The law is unforgiving of such sharp practice these days, but old habits can die hard. The banks have seized on the weakness by converting some of their bank staff, including even branch managers nearing retirement, into their insurance representatives. They can capitalise on longstanding relationships and reassure wary customers with their practised bedside manner.

'During the boom period of the 1980s a lot of things went slack,' Prosser admits, 'and the decisions that were reached by the clients were on the assumption that things were going to continue. Almost certainly the salesmen would have assumed that the economic environment was going to continue as well. So everyone, if you like, succumbed to the idea of growth being the normal pattern. Consequently, everybody suffered.'

While those who were oversold might feel that that is a rather kind interpretation of the conduct of the sales reps they were subjected to, the Financial Services Act ushered in a system of regulation, including minimum training and standards of competence. These oblige the seller to accumulate hard evidence that he or she has identified a genuine need and recommended the most appropriate policies to meet that need.

'That is a major step forward,' Prosser admits, implicitly accepting that the law has stepped in where insurance companies too often turned a blind eye. 'In terms of running a life insurance business,' he adds, 'we must see the excellence in our sales force: properly trained, well-qualified, competent people. We must seek excellence in our after-sale service to the customer, and that's particularly where our quality programme has come in. It has made us a more efficient business. We have improved our operating ratios by about ten per cent during the period that our quality programme has been in place.'

Bar-room wisdom has it that life policies are not bought – they are sold, suggesting that demand for them is at best watery. But Prosser insists that, underneath those layers of reticence, people really do want to commit themselves to long-term and relatively inflexible forms of savings. 'I think generally people like the idea of saving a bit for the future,' he argues. 'It's a human characteristic. I think that is endorsed by the great success of personal pensions: they like to know that they've got some control of their lives, and they recognise that to put money away for the future is a sensible thing to do. The lesson to be learned is try not to overcommit, that is, take on commitments that are greater than you can afford – and watch out for the government making a mess of it.'

Prosser is attuned to the impact of government economic decisions; he spent most of his career as an investment analyst or fund manager. That was the key to his arrival at Legal & General in 1988 as group investment director after three years as chief executive of CIN, the British Coal pension fund.

Numbers have always been in his blood. His father was the first of a family of hill farmers to move up the social scale, becoming a maths teacher. David got a place at Ogmore grammar school in Bridgend, Mid Glamorgan, going on to a first-class degree in mathematics at Aberystwyth University and then qualifying as an actuary while he was with his first employer, Sun Alliance and London Assurance. However, Prosser is more than a swot: his other passion was rugby union, in the 1960s and 1970s when Wales ruled that game. Tall and square-shouldered, he played in the pack at number eight for Glamorgan and the Welsh B team. The fire still lurks close to the surface. 'I don't lose my temper that often,' he says, 'but if something has gone wrong through human error, I do get very annoyed. I explode. I have been known to swear occasionally, but then I'm a South Wales rugby forward, so what do you expect?'

He soon decided that the life of an actuary was not enough for him, so he left Sun Alliance and joined the research department of the stockbrokers Hoare Govett. That paved the way for him to move into fund management at the miners' pension fund, including four years running its venture capital operations. After three years in charge of Legal & General's billions he was promoted to deputy chief executive, succeeding to the top job in September 1991. Not surprisingly, in view of Prosser's background, he sees better and consistent investment performance as the key to L&G's prosperity.

He recalls: 'My first period here was spent getting the investment operation into the shape I wanted it, and its performance has been consistently above average. We must seek excellence in our investment area, providing very good returns for people who trust us with their money. We've done that. We've produced above-median returns on our free-managed funds against our peer groups over a five-year period. We have a strong desire to be consistently above average in every area of our business and being consistently above average provides, over the long term, the highest standards of excellence.'

Prosser's plan was to use that performance as a rallying cry to galvanise the rest of the company's 5,000 employees, some of whom he had perceived as more than a little set in their ways. Hence the company-wide quality programme.

'I wanted to take that through the rest of the business and give greater focus on looking after our customers,' he explains. 'When I took over as chief executive, there was a question mark over the need for change, because people who'd grown up with Legal & General had seen the company prosper over long periods, and after all we'd only just come through the boom period of the 1980s. That's where our quality programme came in: in improving a staff of 5,000 people, many of whom have been with the company for a long period of time, you need an initiative and a positive and rigorous programme to change the culture of the organisation. I identified that the 1990s would be a period of much slower growth, and therefore the organisation had to change culturally. Then I had to implicate a period of cultural change within the company to make the company realise that changes did take place on a regular basis, and that there was nothing to be afraid of in change.'

Prosser is able to claim that the benefits from the quality programme have begun to come through. Stick-in-the-muds who previously shied away from any form of targeting are now, he reports, asking to be given targets. 'One shouldn't underestimate those boom years of the 1980s and the way people reacted during those years to a long period of growth,' he adds. 'If you have a long period of growth like that, it is not conducive to a lean machine. It was very important for us to change to a leaner, higher-quality structure for the 1990s, and we've been doing that.'

As part of that plan, Prosser split the sales force into three divisions – direct sales to the public, sales to independent financial advisers and sales to tied agents such as building societies or firms of solicitors. Each was given its own management structure, organisation and focus so that they could respond more quickly and flexibly to changes in their own corner of the market. There is a clearly defensive aspect to this reorganisation. It is as much an attempt to protect L&G against harsh weather and competitive attacks as with any notion of expansion in mind. And if the going is going to be rough for a company the size of L&G, second only to the Prudential in the UK, then lesser fry are going to sweat.

'I think, in the 1990s anyway, the economic climate is going to be tougher,' Prosser says. 'There is going to be room for L&G in the market place, but a lot of smaller brethren are going to come under significant pressure. The combination of lower levels of business, weaker balance sheets in terms of free asset ratios, lower investment returns, is going to put a bit of a squeeze on the middle area of the market. Niche players are going to be OK, they are going to retain their niche by being focused. But there are too many middle-sized, broadly-based players, all trying to do the same thing. So I see rationalisation in life business coming through during the 1990s, probably in the same way it has been coming through among the building societies. I see rationalisation coming through on the composite insurers – those like L&G offering general life insurance – because of the need to remain world players.'

But there are several obstacles in the way of an outright wave of mergers in the industry. Outsiders have traditionally fought shy of buying their way in, because of regulatory problems which among other things force owners to insulate life funds from other parts of the business. And that also makes it harder for life companies to extract worthwhile juice from merging with one another. One of the differences between life businesses and other businesses is that the benefits of synergy are more elusive. Even if two banks merge, they can close one product range very quickly, and develop a single range across both companies. The two businesses can operate almost as cheaply as one. But with a life company, the products are very long-term and so they cannot be closed easily. That means running the administration and the systems for the products already sold for the remaining life of those products – which can be twenty-five years, or the whole of the policyholders' lives!

Says Prosser: 'I rather think companies will tend to focus on niche areas. Businesses that might be spread across the whole product range will decide that they want to support and develop new systems, to upgrade a product range and focus and become much narrower. To a certain extent one might have already seen some of this, with companies dropping endowment with-profit, coming out of final salary schemes, and turning off unitised, with-profits contracts and certain types of personal pension plans. So companies are beginning to focus and not offer the wide product range. New companies in the life business, like NatWest, are very focused.'

Up to 1994, Legal & General had opted out of this game because, Prosser claims, it had critical mass in its chosen product areas. 'If we ceased to have critical mass,' he explains, 'then we would do the same. But I think, for the company with a broad product range, the answer is either to limit the range or your business structure must create niche businesses within it. But you've got to monitor them, and have accountability and structure. That is pretty heavy in terms of analysis, and would certainly be a change in thinking for life companies. At the moment they tend to think of the life fund as being one entity, rather than a series of entities. Certainly, we're focusing on greater analysis of product range, and the profit contribution of the various products. As margins become tighter, you need to do that more. I think this may bring about a change in the nature of the market.'

Just as the banks have been moving into assurance to make better use of their customer lists, so Prosser believes that the mainstream insurers, true to their cautious, conservative roots, have been slow to use their customer bases to cross-sell. But, as others have found before him, those who patronise financial service providers can be remarkably easy to take offence if they feel they are being pushed into something they don't want, or that they think is not quite right.

'People who have bought Legal & General products know the brand, know the service, know the company and therefore should be amenable to knowing about more Legal & General products,' Prosser maintains. 'What we have to be very careful to do is to ensure that we do not allow our sales force to become jacks of all trades. They are specialists in their area, and the nature of the regulatory framework means that they have to be very specialised and very precise in the life area. I don't think there's enormous mileage in regarding those very skilled people as being general insurance salesmen. So, you musn't put down the composite sales structure, but I think it's entirely sensible if we make our clients more aware of Legal & General products.'

Pensions and other forms of savings are obvious areas for the life companies to capitalise on, especially as the demographic time bomb is producing a financial fallout which is gradually transferring wealth from grandparents to children and grandchildren. As that capital cascades down the generations it will be looking for a home. Some will go into housing, but that circle is already showing signs of being completed, in that many of the potential property inheritors have inherited. Prosser naturally hopes that a proportion will be translated into long-term savings schemes.

'I'd like us to be the best provider of investment products in the UK market,' he declares, 'continuing with a wide range of products and more than ever good investment performance so that we can be represented in an area of the market where we haven't probably been represented in the past, the market for independent financial advisers. If we concentrate on being the best provider then there is plenty of opportunity for us. We have been in the forefront of improving products in the investment area, with capital guaranteed products and guaranteed equity funds. I think people will always like downside protection, and as far as Legal & General is concerned as an insurance company, you can see that those are natural products for us. The strength of a lot of our products is regular saving through the economic cycle of boom-recession-boom. The strength of with-profits policies is that people commit to paying annual premiums when markets are cheap as well as through the up cycles, and that has an element of pound-cost averaging about it which brings about the good returns.'

This very much chimes in with Prosser's investment background, and he has contained the risks associated with general insurance by entering co-insurance and re-insurance deals. That leaves him free to concentrate on what he regards as the core of the business: UK life and pensions. That means the rest of Europe is on the back burner. Indeed, Prosser is more concerned that Continental insurers will take advantage of European Union rules to cross the English Channel in worrying numbers.

'I see the UK general insurance industry as being weakened,' he admits. 'We've not had the ability to reserve sufficiently, as our European counterparts certainly have. They've been able to build up tax-free reserves over a period of time, and these reserves help them through difficult circumstances. I've got a concern that the European companies are going to be in a much stronger position than the UK companies. Although UK in general insurance is a world player as a country, none of the companies are really world players. L&G is very much a domestic market, and oriented into the residential market and personal area. Sun Alliance and Royal are not world players compared with the Europeans, Americans and Japanese. Even Lloyd's is not really a world player in terms of total premium income compared with these other companies, although a lot of its business is international.'

So Prosser is busily trying to make the most of what he sees as the jewel in L&G's crown, the fund management operation. He has already instructed that department to treat the company's life and pension funds as no more than a client, and to build up a portfolio of other clients outside the group.

That suggests that L&G will enter the next century as a more broadly-based investment house, in which life and pensions will be only one arrow in the quiver. But, in going down that route, Prosser is all too well aware that he will encounter many more competitors in what is becoming an increasingly acrimonious battle for the saver's mite.

'I would want to focus management resource and capital in my core activities,' he insists. 'That's where I want to be best, and that's what will provide the best payback for shareholders.'

CHAPTER 16

IAN PROSSER

of Bass

BASS IS THE international hotelier that wants to become a global brewer. Its success in buying and absorbing Holiday Inns has given its chairman and chief executive, Ian Prosser, a taste for the international stage. He is too wary of the competition to try his luck with a worldwide eating chain. Instead, he hopes that he can establish Bass as a global brand, supported by Carling Black Label and Tennent's, before his rivals get their act together. The biggest of these are American, and it is the US which may turn out to be the battle ground. The odds look daunting.

Prosser seemed destined for a life of checking the books for Midlands' audit clients when, like many an accountant before and since, he decided it would be more fun to work for an industrial company. He is the fourth child and only son of a former tobacco salesman, and was brought up in Bath and Watford. His sojourn in the Midlands began with a degree in commerce at Birmingham University, where he met his wife, Liz, in the coffee bar.

His first employer was the Birmingham branch of the accountants Cooper Brothers, now Coopers & Lybrand Deloitte. Although Bass is based in London these days, its cradle is Burton-on-Trent, so it was almost a local firm for Prosser and thus a pretty natural choice of employer for him to move to. Within a few years he had come up with a proposal for Bass to install its first financial planning and control system. That was instrumental in getting him the job of finance director at the age of only thirty-three. More importantly, he had caught the eye of the group's chairman, the formidable Sir Derek Palmar. Six years later Prosser became vice chairman and group managing director, and he was only forty-three when he succeeded Sir Derek as chairman.

'I think that Bass, like any other major brewer, has been through an

Ian Maurice Gray Prosser

BORN:	5 July, 1943
EDUCATED:	King Edward's School, Bath, Watford Grammar School and Birmingham University
MARRIED:	Elizabeth Herman 1975. Two daughters

CAREER:

1964	Cooper Brothers, accountants
1967	Qualified Chartered Accountant
1969	Bass Charrington
1978	Director of Bass
1984	Vice Chairman and Group Managing Director
1987	Chairman and Chief Executive

OTHER INTERESTS: Non-executive Director of The Boots Company and Lloyds Bank. Chairman of the Brewers' Society. Chairman of the Stock Exchange Listed Companies Advisory Committee. Governor of the Berkhampsted Schools

BASS PLC

HEAD OFFICE: 20 North Audley Street, London W1Y 1WE
Tel: 071-409 1919

ACTIVITIES: Brewing, soft drinks, pubs, leisure, hotels

MAIN BRANDS: Bass, Carling Black Label, Tennent's and Worthington beers, Britvic and Tango soft drinks, Bass Tavern pubs, Coral betting shops, Hollywood Bowl bowling alleys, Gala bingo clubs and Holiday Inn hotels

enormous period of change,' Prosser explained. 'We've probably con-
certinaed into the first three years of the 1990s the amount of change that
any normal business would expect it might have to face over five to ten
years. It has been pretty pressurised in terms of the people who work in the
business. But the experience has probably been very good for the company
in the long term, working under pressure and a change in the environment
that, to put it positively, very few businesses have the opportunity to cope
with! But we will, I believe, see much more change in the 1990s than in the
1980s in our market places, and in the movement within product groups
within our market places.' He points to the need for management to be able
to cope with fast-changing products and market places. 'I think, looking
across all our businesses, without any doubt the area that I see changing
most is going to be the area of management structures,' he says, 'and it will
be the application of information technology, not just to broad businesses
but to consumer services as well.'

What Prosser has in mind is the way that the hotel industry has been transformed by computers' ability to organise reservation systems, co-ordinate
them across the world to generate additional business for franchisees in
Bass' Holiday Inn chain and so throw off more profit for Bass. Add to that
the increasing convenience of video conferencing, satellites to move data
around international businesses, and to show live horse racing in its Coral
betting shops.

'All this is bound to impact on our organisation,' says Prosser, 'because
you look at new ways of running the organisation – not necessarily just on a
cost-effective basis, although patently it has an effect on that – it also affects
the way you organise data flows within the business. Very crudely, instead
of looking at data flowing vertically up and down the finance, sales and marketing lines, we're looking at it flowing horizontally across the business.
Data is tending to follow the flow of the business rather than the old-fashioned division into functions. I think a lot of this is in the development stage,
for industry and for the world in general. It is moving at such a pace that
people are having to cope with changes in everything they used to take to be
standard. It's very exciting.'

Even the fruit machine in a pub is micro-processor driven these days, and
it is hard to avoid the impression that these technological miracles excite
Prosser considerably more than the prospect of developing a delicious new
drink, or finding a way of guaranteeing the perfect omelette every time a
chef cracks an egg into a pan.

'I think that there is a major convergence of technology going on,' he enthuses, 'which we used to talk about in the 1970s. We used to say that all the data would be in one pot and we'd dip in and pluck it out because we'd got it all. And of course we hadn't, but that was twenty years ago: we're virtually there now, and therefore we are capable of achieving enormously powerful benefits. Electronic Point of Sale machinery is having a huge effect in our pubs. We're using the latest forms of retail technology and systems, and that can benefit the customer enormously in terms of being able to deliver what the customer wants. It's bound to affect restaurant technology. We're finding both of those are coming together.'

The immediate impact of this progress has been a huge cut in Bass' wages bill. The number of full-time employed and their equivalent, in the UK alone, came down from 98,345 to 84,095 between 1990 and 1992. While a pub still needs bar staff and restaurants need waiters, pen-pushing and stock control are cut to a minimum. In clubs and ten-pin bowling alleys, it is possible to run a far bigger operation with the same number of people as, or fewer than, before. While, Prosser hopes, most of that is now out of the way, he and his top team are only starting to come to grips with what the convergence of the group's pubs, restaurants, bingo clubs and ten-pin bowling could mean for the future of Bass.

'Our existing businesses offer us a lot of opportunities,' he says. 'I think the pubs, clubs, bowling and bingo are possibly exportable. You don't export anything until you are extremely good at it in your own environment, but I think that we are becoming extremely good at hotels. And we already have a thirty-six-lane bowling alley on the way in from the airport at Beijing, the capital of China. The great thing about Bass is that all our businesses are businesses that everybody you know partakes of. They have a drink or eat in a pub, or sleep in a hotel, have a beer or a Britvic soft drink at home. And therefore it is a business in which you are constantly in contact with your customers – and therefore your critics, which is great fun, and I think keeps everybody in the business very alive to what is going on.'

Quite where this will take Bass, Prosser is not sure. He is mixing the cocktail labelled convergence, confident in the belief that somehow it will produce a winning formula flexible enough to respond to rapidly evolving consumer tastes. Bass has to venture into the unknown because it no longer has the relative position in brewing that it had a few years ago, before the Courage and Allied mergers, with Fosters and Carlsberg respectively.

According to Prosser, 'as the vertical integration of the old system disappears, scale and size will be very important in terms of capturing benefits. I think there will be fewer pubs, and fewer brands of beer in the year 2000, with some much bigger brands than there are at the moment. Although I'm delighted to say that Carling Black Label and the Tennent's umbrella are the two biggest beer brands in the UK. We haven't got a stout, and in premium lagers we have launched Tennent's Gold and a German-brewed beer, Tag. We will be strong in those areas of the market that offer high profit growth.' Lesser brews seem doomed to go the way of mild, milk stout and barley wine in the race for volume and standardisation.

So, although Bass has naturally joined in the brewers' chorus of derision at Lord Young's Beer Orders (see page 109), those edicts have at least given Prosser the excuse to trim the group's pub estate and diversify into potentially more lucrative areas, whilst blaming the transformation on nasty politicians and Whitehall bureaucrats.

'Interestingly, the British pub consumer is very different from anywhere else in the world,' says Prosser, 'because of the history of the pub and its place in the community. Every community tends to have its own pub. One of the defining factors of a pub is its name, and the fact that its name is different from the pub in the community over the hill, in the next village or wherever it is. So there's a great sense of belonging. I believe that that is endangered by the Beer Orders, because the only place that really had vertical integration in the world was Britain, and the only place that had local pubs was Britain. I know coincidences exist, but . . .' and he shrugs expressively.

It is a dire threat, which Prosser is happy to wash his hands of. Yet it is also hard to avoid the impression that he is quite glad to reduce Bass' exposure to the perennial pub-goer's grumble about the price of a pint. He, along with his rivals in the trade, have long tried to wriggle off this – to them – tiresome hook, for which they feel they have been unfairly singled out by the dogged British tippler. But it seems that it will never go away until pubs become places where much more value is added than merely pouring a pint and handing it across the counter. Something, in fact, not unlike a club or an eatery.

'Other products don't attract the same level of criticism over price increases,' Prosser claims, 'for a very simple reason: that the price that you pay for a beer in a pub reflects the cost of running the whole pub. When you go into a hotel and you pay the price for a room, you've got exactly the same issue. You're not just paying for the bed in the room you're in, you're paying for the receptionist, the boy, and for this and that. In the mind of somebody objectively, it's quite hard to drag in all of these things, put them on the price of a pint, and then say the price of that pint compares sensibly with the one you pay much less for in a supermarket, where you don't have that bundle of amenities.

'I think that, as an industry, one of the problems with the Monopolies Commission investigation, and indeed the reasons for the investigation, was the lack of understanding of the industry. I mean, do you expect to pay the same for your steak in one of Bass' Toby restaurants as in the Savoy? The Savoy seems to have no problem in getting across to you that you should expect to pay more. We seem to have a great deal of problem getting across to the customer objectively that the beer in supermarkets is bound to be cheaper than the beer in a pub. But he still goes to the pub and has his pint of bitter, thank goodness. So he's got to find something attractive in the pub, and subjectively there is no doubt that he does. I don't know how we can uncouple this: we work very hard at trying to do it. The boiled egg does seem to be more distinctive in the mind of the consumer than the pint. The Continentals, of course, accept vastly different price ratios and they don't bat an eyelid.'

Meanwhile, Bass is gearing up production to collar as large a share of the UK beer market as it can. John Spicer of Warburg Securities observes: 'Bass would appear to be aggressively chasing market share. Its strong financial position has allowed it to increase its number of free-trade loans and be in a position to offer discounts if necessary.'

During the 1980s, Bass was able to package its beer and produce new products that drove its profit margins up. The big question is whether it will be able to continue to do that through the 1990s as well. 'There are natural trends in the market that I think help us,' says Prosser. 'There is no doubt that the sales of draught Bass and draught Stones, our premium cask ales, have been growing very fast, even in the recession. The premium lager area is very important. It's our job to produce the innovation, both in new-product development and in marketing, to produce the best return for our shareholders. I think Guinness actually took over a business that had a lot of potential to do that. I think that we've got a lot that we can still learn in the brewing industry.'

That is giving Bass the platform from which to see what it can do in the international beer market, which no one has really cracked because of beer-drinkers' innate resistance to change. The monster in the melting pot is America's Annheuser Busch which, if it started to motor, could become the beer trade's equivalent of Pepsi and Coke rolled into one. But, while the giant slumbers, there is a chink of light which could allow a group like Bass to set itself up on a global scale.

'It's early days yet,' declares Prosser. 'I guess that the Holiday Inn business is helping us substantially in that context, because Holiday Inn is operating in fifty countries. We have learned to manage a very international business, and we have in place management which has knowledge across a very wide number of countries. And they will have contacts and under-standing of industries such as brewing, because patently they recognise Bass' interest in that area. So I think that we will find synergies from the Holiday Inn business, in terms of development opportunities in internation-al brewing. We will either brew or distribute, or both.'

Bass is also gathering experience from its soft drinks operation. It has the distributorship of Pepsi in the UK, through Britvic, the second largest pro-ducer in the UK after Coca-Cola and Schweppes Beverages, the venture owned jointly by Coke and Cadbury Schweppes. The present-day Britvic results from a merger with Canada Dry, Beechams and Whites in the mid-1980s. Apart from Pepsi, Britvic makes Tango, the market leader among Britain's carbonated orange drinks. As it hopes to do in brewing, Bass' expansion in soft drinks has meant that it has been able to drive costs down and show reasonable returns on capital, despite the real price of carbonated soft drinks falling. And, because Bass has given up any hopes of making a mark in the rarified world of wine and spirits business, it can concentrate its international firepower on trying to establish global beer brands. Bass Ale is already one of the top ten imported beers into the US, and Prosser claims that it is the largest imported draught beer into the US. But, beer being the bulky stuff it is, there is a limit to how much a brewer can export if it has ambitions in that direction. Sooner or later, it has to get its hands on foreign breweries, in the way that Allied did in Europe in the 1960s.

'There are a few beer brands that are known at a very high level,' Prosser points out, 'but they flatter to deceive because if you look at the amount of beer that crosses national boundaries it is infinitesimally small. What you actually have is a series of national market places with very little relative movement between them. I think it will be a long time before there is an internationalisation in the sense that there has been with soft drinks and spir-its. What will happen, I think, is that more companies will become players in more national markets. But that's different from global branding. Beers are very much within their community and it will take a long time to change. You have the Germans looking for a different sort of beer in the south to the north, you have the French buying different sorts of beers to the Italians or the Americans. In Britain we even have ale, lager and Scottish ales against southern ales. They're very different and distinctive tastes.'

While lagers could well become the cola of the beer market, the problem for the likes of Bass is that there is a phenomenal difference in taste between a French, German and American lager. Drinkers perceive those tastes as very different, and are not easily persuaded to change.

Intriguingly, Prosser rates Holiday Inns as closer to brewing than to retailing, because he sees it as being about a brand, a reservation system and driving forward a major branded business. 'Within that,' he points out, 'we have the opportunity to own the property and to manage the hotel. So we have a mixture, giving us a series of business opportunities, all within the Holiday Inn business. But it is brand and marketing driven, which distinguishes it from the retail pub business, where the consumer generally at the moment wants to go to the Dog and Duck rather than to some generic brand name that covers a thousand pubs. We think of Holiday Inn as a retail business, but in terms of retailing through the pubs I think we would be looking at expanding our brewing business first. Hotels are more internationally homogeneous than any other form of retailing, and they are becoming highly branded – which was again why we wanted to buy Holiday Inn. We believe that the American experience of development of hotels as members of chains with high advertising power and big reservation systems, would work on a global basis, as indeed they have. As many as two-thirds of American hotels are members of branded chains. Globally we are seeing the same trend.'

Prosser's world is marketing-led and profit-driven. Nothing wrong with either of those, from the point of view of running a public company with shareholders as widely varied as dedicated pub customers and huge investment institutions hungry for money to pay their pension and insurance policyholders. But it is still an open question whether Bass can break out of its national confines in drinks. The group has a global flagwaver in the Holiday Inns chain, and it has the UK licence to make Pepsi Cola. It is a moot point whether that will be enough of a springboard to establish beachheads around the world in a fight that, when it really gets going, will be one of the fiercest seen in the commercial arena for many years.

CHAPTER **17**

GERRY ROBINSON

of Granada Group

GERRY ROBINSON is a catalogue of contrasts. He delights in keeping people off-balance, yet prefers to run businesses that are repetitive. He likes to be the bean-counter with a human face, a humorous and charming Irishman who can wield the knife with deadly speed, a cautious strategist who suddenly strikes out in unexpected directions. He is a man to watch.

He will always be remembered as the upstart who sacked David Plowright, a doyen of Granada Television, within three months of becoming the TV rental, leisure and catering group's chief executive at the age of forty-three. Sixteen months later Robinson set the rest of the British television industry on its heels when he secretly paid City institutions a third over the market price to buy a fifteen per cent stake in LWT (Holdings), holder of the London weekend franchise. That turned out to be the platform for a fullscale takeover. It was only the latest move in a complicated sequence of chase-my-tail through which Carlton and Granada have positioned themselves to dominate the industry and withstand a possible takeover onslaught by foreign invaders, as well as British companies with no previous TV interests.

Robinson describes the Plowright episode as 'a terrible pain in the backside from every point of view. We could have handled it a bit more cleverly from a PR point of view but we'd have still done the same thing. Essentially, I don't really regret the changes that we've made because we've now got a company that works very well. We have a good feel about Granada Television. You know what it's doing and there's an openness about what's going on. In a funny sort of way it's not a difficult thing to get right, the balance between commercial input and an artistic input. It's not that difficult if you have a reasonable cooperation on both sides – a will to make the thing work.'

That was, of course, the trouble. Plowright, brother of the actress Joan Plowright, had been widely credited with establishing *Coronation Street* as the country's leading soap opera back in the 1960s and producing award-winners such as *World in Action* while Robinson was still being beaten by the priests at his Catholic boarding school in Lancashire. After the retirement of Sidney Bernstein, Granada's founder, Plowright was gradually allowed to turn the television operation into his own fief. He was a ripe target for Robinson, appointed chief executive in November 1991, to show the rest of the group's management just who was boss. When Plowright fairly predictably failed to come to heel and produce the requested budgets and business plans, Robinson fired him. The furore from the artistic community was even more predictable, although it is a measure of Robinson's lack of experience in show business that the backlash took him by surprise. Most visible among the critics was the former clown turned millionaire management guru, John Cleese, who sent Robinson a fax to let him know that in Cleese's opinion he was 'an upstart caterer'. This, although he may not have realised it at first blush, was Robinson's lucky break. It pulled a wavering financial community over onto his side and enabled him to don the martyr's robes.

'I'm not saying you don't get the odd clash,' Robinson concedes magnanimously, 'you should, but it does require a bit of goodwill on both sides. If it's not been that way then it's going to be difficult to accept the changes, if you've been running it. Having said that, Granada has benefited enormously from a commercial point of view. We're selling more programmes than we ever had, we're selling more to ITV than we ever had, we've got the biggest audiences that we've ever had, so something must be right. The chap in charge of making programmes and the chap in charge of actually broadcasting are deeply television people, they're both from Granada's long TV history and they've both been here for a very long time. There's the commercial input to the thing which rests quite comfortably with those guys. By definition, what you're aiming to do to Granada Television as a whole is likely to have quite high degrees of flexibility to it. Television is the simplest of the businesses that we have – extraordinarily simple in a commercial sense. Clearly there is complexity in programme-making, but there's half a dozen key issues that you've got to get right and there are many businesses that are far more complex than that.'

Like its main rivals, Granada Television is a two-part business in which making programmes is separate from broadcasting them – the regional franchises. Granada's national reputation has been built on its tradition of

Gerald Jude Robinson

BORN: 23 October, 1948

EDUCATED: St Mary's College, Castlehead

MARRIED: Heather Leaman, 1990. One son, two daughters

CAREER:

1965 Cost office, Lesney Products

1974 Chief Management Accountant, Lesney Products

1974 Management Accountant for Volvo network of Lex Service

1980 Financial Controller and Finance Director, Lex Industrial Distribution and Hire

1980 Finance Director, Coca-cola division of Grand Metropolitan

1983 Managing Director, Grand Metropolitan's International Services division

1987 Led management buyout of Compass Group from Grand Metropolitan

1991 Chief Executive, Granada Group

OTHER INTERESTS: Director of Caradon, trustee of Common Purpose

GRANADA GROUP

HEAD OFFICE: 36 Golden Square, London W1R 4AH
Tel: 071-734 8080

ACTIVITIES: Broadcasting, television production, television rentals, motorway services, computer maintenance, catering, bingo, bowling centres

MAIN BRANDS: Granada, GX Superbowl, Visionhire

making high-quality programmes which earned brownie points for the whole ITV network. The likes of *Maigret, Prime Suspect* and the classic *Brideshead Revisited* enabled the commercial stations to hold their head up in the one-upmanship battle with the BBC. Such praised output also helped Granada to retain its north-west franchise in the periodic reviews over the years. But the advent of more competition, particularly from satellite channels, has sharpened the distinction between programme making and broadcasting.

'We are fairly tightly tied into the ITV system,' Robinson points out, 'but we have a minority stake in BSkyB, and you will see that growing as a buyer of programmes. Clearly the BBC, Channel Four and the cable companies are going to be opportunities for programme sales. We certainly sell more programmes than anyone else in the UK, by a long way. We have the highest-rated programmes in the UK, obviously helped immensely by *Coronation Street*, but that's a business which, if you do it effectively, you can make a reasonable return on and we intend to do that as well as we can.'

Robinson admits that, unlike the BBC, Granada has done very little to sell programmes overseas, aside from a modest venture with LWT in which they put their programme catalogues together.

'We do do some joint programming,' he says. 'We did one on the Middle East hostages which cost something like £1.25 million, co-financed with Home Box Office in America. Quite sensible stuff that, because we won't get the price from ITV but if you manage to do a joint venture, then if it's good quality you can offer it to ITV and HBO can use it in its home market. But the idea of going into programme-making on spec or film-making on spec, I hate, because it's such a difficult business unless you're a big American operator making twenty or thirty films a year where you hope five of them work and four are OK. But it's not for me.'

In UK broadcasting, Robinson and his counterparts elsewhere in the network have to operate under the occupational hazard that the rules change every few years – and Margaret Thatcher's 1990 Act was particularly byzantine. Any one company was allowed to operate one franchise and have a percentage in others. But under European Union rules companies from other member states could from January 1994 come in and take over UK franchise-holders. Hence the precautionary stakebuilding merry-go-round.

'I think that'll change,' argues Robinson. 'It's inevitable. I think it'll be very difficult to see that there'll be more than five or six companies holding franchises by the turn of the century. I'll be very surprised if there are more.'

As Granada and Carlton were easily the two largest operators to emerge from the 1991 franchise round, they had the most financial muscle to make serious acquisitions. All the others were essentially in television only, and comparatively small, with the exception of Meridian, backed by the financial services group MAI.

'I don't think you are going to be able to own more than two, maybe three at a stretch,' claims Robinson, 'so there's plenty of scope for ourselves, Carlton and probably one other. Having contiguous territories really isn't that important because you can broadcast to any part of the UK from one location: technically it's very easy to do that. You only ever make programmes in one location, and you have a sales operation in London. No matter where you come from, most companies' sales are based in London. So it wouldn't matter which other station you picked up really, you'd make most of the savings associated with having just one as opposed to two. You'd certainly have some geographical ties if you put Yorkshire and Granada together. That would be a patch that it would be difficult for an advertiser to ignore. But, again, LWT and Granada is difficult to ignore, too: two big patches with one sales force.

While Granada flirted with potentially enormous losses in satellite before Rupert Murdoch came along and banged heads together, cable remains the enigma in UK television. The big companies have largely stayed out of it, leaving the field clear for a raft of US telephone companies and a few hardy local independents. But, now that British viewers are getting used to the idea of dozens of channels after decades of a heavily regulated handful, the commercial prospects for cable are looking up.

'We are looking at cable from the point of view of trying to get a really good feel of how it's going to turn out,' Robinson explains. 'I think it'll be hugely successful for someone in the UK, but along that road I think someone will have lost a hell of a lot of money – as has already been demonstrated by a number of operators who have not stayed the course. I think it's more than unlikely that we would want to play a risk-laden game in a cable company in terms of setting up the infrastructure and waiting for the payoff to come a long way down the road. We've done that once with BSkyB and we were very lucky that it paid off, but I don't think that it's in the nature of Granada to be risk-positioned in that way again. Whether or not there are opportunities in cable once things are established, or when companies lose their commitment to it and there might be opportunities to pick things up at a reasonable value along the way, maybe, maybe. Maybe the timing on that could be right in one or two areas and certainly, there should be a market place for that in terms of installing, in terms of our TV rental business and selling programmes. So it's very interesting, and we are keeping the right kind of relationships with cable companies like Videotron. We are interested, but not if it costs half a billion pounds over the next eight years before it starts paying off.'

Although he is not worth anything like half a billion, Robinson became independently wealthy when he organised a £168 million management buy-out of Compass Group, the contract caterer, from Grand Metropolitan. It was then the biggest UK buyout, and it netted him an estimated £5 million, but in characteristically Irish style he finds a way of looking on the black side: 'I did a lot of sorting out and made it profitable again. Then we did the really smart thing. Having sorted it out we bought it, rather than the other way around. I won't make that mistake again.'

He is the ninth child of a Donegal carpenter, but he has lived in England since he won a scholarship to St Mary's College, Castlehead, a robust boarding school run by missionaries on the Lancashire coast. Whilst he was there his family emigrated to Essex and he began work in that area, as a cost clerk with Lesney, the Matchbox toy makers. He went to night school to qualify as an accountant, moving on to a car dealer called Lex Service Group before landing at Grand Metropolitan. He admits he took on the Granada job because it was 'a prestigious-sounding company and it was capable of getting back into shape.' So he has been a pragmatic careerist rather than having a vocation for one industry. It was that pragmatism more than anything that stung the canteen divas at Granada Television: he was most definitely not one of them. And, for all his bonhomie, it is still the bottom line that interests Robinson most.

'We're much more inclined to the services, repetitive-contractual side than towards retail and risky and capital-intensive businesses,' he asserts. 'It happens that, quite contrary to the way Granada has been viewed in the past, it is very heavily contractual. The TV rental part is the largest part – that's totally contracted – most of what we've got in catering is contracted. Certainly, the computer maintenance business is contracted. Motorway services ain't contracted, but by Christ it doesn't move by much from week to week. I could almost guarantee to give you within two to three per cent what the volumes and profits will be next week.'

Granada is the second largest player in UK TV rental after Thorn, so the opportunity to expand in that business is limited. There is a distant prospect of merging these two competitors, but the circumstances would have to be right to escape the censure of the Monopolies and Mergers Commission. 'That's unlikely in the short term,' says Robinson, 'and therefore we have taken the view that we have to run that business sensibly for profit. It clearly produces a lot of cash, but it is a slowly declining industry, therefore within it we've concentrated on the non-rental bits for growth, like phones. We operate with both BT and Mercury, running help desks where we do the service back-up and actually service some of the phone systems. We're very involved with the cable companies and the satellite companies. We retail TVs and videos, we really push quite hard the non-rental side of the business. We think there'll be a big opportunity in personal telephones as a potential rental product, but maybe just as a servicer to that product. The real key for that business is to run it very tightly, very effectively. We probably produce more cash from it than profit. We will get a bit of profit growth but a very strong cash growth to the end of the century.'

After television and TV rental, Granada is plugged into communications in a third way: computer maintenance, which brings with it some big customers. Like TV rental, it involves lots of engineers going out to sites, repairing electronic equipment, and surprisingly often the equipment is the same because of the tie-up between televisions and VDUs. Robinson admits: 'That's the business we've really made the biggest balls-up of in the past. It took us a year to get it into profit. It's now beginning to not just make some money, but show signs of growing and we're winning new contracts in a serious way. I think that's one that, down the road, we'll be saying to ourselves we need to make an acquisition for. We're already the largest in Europe by quite a long way, of the third-party maintenance operators. I think that the marketplace is growing, it's one place where service really matters and therefore you can get price to follow service and that's really quite an interesting area for us. I really believe you've got to be absolutely sharp and slick. We've just won a contract from BAe, to go in and maintain all their kit on a given site. If you pick up a contract like that for £3 million or £4 million a year, you don't have to go out and buy masses of stock: you've actually got it. The wider you can spread that, the more cost-effective you can be and the more you can close other players out of the operation.'

The other division Robinson inherited at Granada was leisure, which is eighty per cent motorway service stations plus theme parks, ten-pin bowling and holidays. Like TV rental, motorway services are low-growth but high profit, hemmed in by planning restrictions and the belief of every farmer in Britain that the station operators are an easy touch for buying otherwise unusable plots of land.

'They are a super business from the point of view of being predictable,' Robinson enthuses, 'having the potential to continue to grow and to add new sites as and when they become available, but it is a very slow process in the nature of finding the site and getting planning permission. There are unlikely to be acquisition opportunities in motorways because there's only us and Forte and Brightreasons, the company that controls the Pavilion chain. But there's tremendous profit growth to come out of that semi-monopolistic business in a highly predictable way.'

Robinson dismisses the rest of Granada's leisure businesses as too unpredictable for comfort, too small to make much impact, giving the distinct impression that he would sell them as and when opportunity arose.

Significantly, the first sizable acquisition Robinson made at Granada was the purchase of Sutcliffe, a catering and linen services company, from P&O for £360 million in 1993. It is a direct competitor of Compass, so he was getting back into a business he knew.

'There are catering opportunities and there are services opportunities in Sutcliffe,' he says, 'perhaps the latter is more important than the former because that's an industry that has yet to settle down. In contract catering there are three players in the UK, it might come down to two, it might not, but that's it. Whereas in the services, there are eight or nine players around and that'll probably end up as two or three also, so there's quite a lot more room for manoeuvre there. Compass makes a ten per cent margin on its business, which has grown very nicely. Sutcliffe made four per cent when we bought it, and clearly there was a good opportunity there. I think we'll continue to share the growth that's coming out of institutional catering, which is the prison service, military, police force, schools, hospitals – there are terrific opportunities there for contracting out and that's where the business comes from. You'd be amazed at how few contracts actually shift from one contract caterer to another, very small. The net shift is negligible. The real growth comes out of people saying that it's better to go to a contractor rather than do the catering themselves.'

Because of the way in which its businesses throw off cash, Robinson sees regular acquisitions as part of Granada's long-term pattern. While this opens the way to nigh-automatic growth, it also carries the danger of getting sucked into diversifications that seem superficially logical but in practice don't work or take up too much management time. Robinson is of course properly cautious and determined to be dispassionate.

'In the nature of Granada, we produce very large chunks of cash,' he confirms. 'If we hadn't acquired Sutcliffe our gearing would have fallen from 100 per cent to about twenty per cent in 1993, which shows how cash-generative we are. But I don't think you can acquire lots of companies and manage them well. I expect Granada to make a major acquisition and get that onto a good operating schedule in the following two or three years. Some cash rolls in in that time and then you are in a position to look again at what you might go for. If somewhere down that path it was suddenly possible to acquire Yorkshire Television, clearly we would go for it but that's a different proposition altogether. But to acquire something significant – I think you'd be kidding yourself, because it takes time. It's got to be integrated within the system, you've got to learn how things work. The only reason you buy something is because you think you can do more with it than the person who had it, so there's a lot of work to be done in terms of getting the management right, getting the processes right. If there are opportunities in either the catering or the services side, it would be hard not to take advantage of those along the way. Clearly you wouldn't say, "Sorry, it's not three years yet." We must be fairly pragmatic in that sense.'

Before long, however, Robinson's pragmatism and his dislike of risk will be tested to the full. He recognises that, as most of Granada's present operations are already market leaders or nearly so, he will have to start looking overseas for takeover possibilities.

He admits: 'Our view is that in the next three to five years we need to start looking at overseas opportunities in a serious way, but at the moment that is very secondary to making sure that everything we've got in the UK works very well. I'm doubly nervous: an acquisition in its own right is quite risky, but an acquisition outside your own geography is even more risky. I am actually quite risk-averse, and I think that someone risk-averse in Granada is a bloody good thing! Certainly at least for a while.'

CHAPTER 18

JAMES ROSS

of Cable & Wireless

JAMES ROSS, ex-public school, Royal Navy and British Petroleum, has always had a hankering to be master of his own ship. Tall, angular, Oxford-educated, in 1992 he got most of his wish when he became chief executive of Cable & Wireless, the nineteenth-century cable-laying company that is snapping at the heels of British Telecom in the global battle over phone networks. Ross did not get the whole territory all at once because that wily politician, former trade secretary Lord Young, remained executive chairman over Ross' head and retained responsibility for strategy and contacts with Whitehall. Nevertheless Ross stepped behind the chief executive's desk at a delicate time for C&W, when it was in danger of getting left behind in the race to find an international partner with which to fight the global fight. His task is to secure it a defendable position in that struggle.

Most telecoms companies started off with a base of a national or local monopoly, but C&W has always had to exist on its wits. Its founder, a Manchester textile merchant called Sir John Pender, laid the first transatlantic telegraph cable in 1866 and soon linked the main land masses of Asia and Australasia with one another, and with the UK. After Marconi discovered and developed radio telegraphy his business was merged with Pender's legacy to form what became known as Cable & Wireless in 1934. It was nationalised in 1947, and unavoidably became encrusted with the usual quota of civil servants and hangers-on.

So the company was left standing when telephone began to make great strides forward in the 1970s, once satellite links were established. It had neither a statutory monopoly nor the freedom to roam. But it found a role when Margaret Thatcher's government chose the company to challenge British

Telecom and gave it a chairman, Lord Sharp, who knew the corridors of Whitehall as well as the jungle warfare of private industry. C&W was privatised in 1981 and in the same year formed Mercury Communications, a consortium with British Petroleum and Barclays which had been given a licence to compete with BT. Mercury became wholly owned by C&W in 1984 and remained so until 1993.

Enter James Ross, lean, mean and unencumbered with the culture of bygone days. After thirty-three years at BP, he was said to have a safe pair of hands, a statesman rather than a streetfighter who would not rush to challenge Lord Young's coveted figurehead status. Ross had been with BP since 1959, working in France, Africa, the UK and the US. He started off selling aviation fuel, became the group's chief planner and head of BP Oil International, the worldwide refining and marketing business, before switching to America where he became chairman and chief executive of BP America. Significantly Lord Young welcomed him aboard with the remark that it was 'more important to get a good international manager than someone who knows telecommunications'. In other words, a dealmaker.

He went for the simple notion that it is better to make money than not. So he concentrated his efforts on possibilities which offered the chance of higher profits than in the past, whilst tightening productivity and cash management.

'We just don't have the people to do everything that presents itself, so we have to be selective,' Ross declares. 'We are operating in the most sophisticated ends of the market, using mobile phone expertise as an enabling technology for us to access new countries or new markets, or get access to the local loop.' After more than ten years in Britain, in 1993 Mercury launched its mobile Personal Communications Network, One-2-One. That was initially confined to the area bounded by the M25 motorway, but would gradually fan out to cover the whole country.

The key for C&W is winning telecoms licences round the world. But to do that, it had to have muscle – or get into bed with muscle. Almost as soon as Ross arrived at C&W's monolithic office in London's Theobalds Road, he started talking with BCE of Canada, a conglomerate which operates the Bell Canada telecommunications interest and is Canada's largest company. Within nine months BCE had paid £480 million for a twenty per cent stake in Mercury. C&W was on the dance floor in earnest, and beginning to tango. Like US West, BCE has London cable TV franchises, which are attractive to C&W because Mercury can push its phone lines down the cables into homes which might otherwise be committed to BT. But as people sign up for

James Hood Ross

BORN:	13 September, 1938
EDUCATED:	Sherbourne, Oxford University, Manchester Business School
MARRIED:	Sara Purcell, 1964. One son, two daughters

CAREER:

1957	Royal Navy
1959	Aviation sales, British Petroleum
1964	BP France
1967	BP London marketing department
1969	General Manager, BP Zaire, Burundi and Rwanda
1972	BP UK
1976	Assistant General Manager (Commercial), BP Tanker Company
1977	Deputy Chairman, Stolt Tankers and Terminals
1979	Regional Coordinator, Western Hemisphere, BP
1981	General Manager, BP Group Corporate Planning
1986	Chief Executive, BP Oil International
1988	President and Chief Executive, BP America
1992	Chief Executive, Cable & Wireless

CABLE & WIRELESS PLC

HEAD OFFICE:	124 Theobalds Road, London WC1X 8RX Tel: 071-315 4000
ACTIVITIES:	International telecommunication services
MAIN BRANDS:	Mercury Communications, Mercury Personal Communications, Mercury Paging, Cable & Wireless (Marine), Northern Ocean Services, Worldwide Ocean Surveying

cable TV they are also offered cut-price phone services if they will make the switch. Thousands do. On top of that, the BCE tie-up gives Mercury access to the Canadians' telecommunications technology. But Ross admits that this technology is changing the way people work – and no one has got to grips with the social implications of that.

'I think this will probably be the pattern of telephony round the world,' says Ross. 'The market is only gradually realising the scope that telecommunications can offer. Fax is the most obvious example and many people feel, in this country, that video telephones and video conferencing will be another example. We're in the middle of the revolution that has enabled companies to take out large numbers of layers of management who were there to escalate and de-escalate information, which computers have been promising to do for twenty years plus and have never done it. We're in a fundamental generational shift, and the people who are being made unemployed because we're finding new ways of doing business are not going to come back into those same jobs when the cycle turns up. I think that will be followed by another fundamental change – over what time period, I don't know, but foreseeable – in which the ability to handle information will free up organisations to manage themselves in quite different ways. That will liberate companies from the traditional hierarchical organisation with many, many layers. It will liberate them from being tied by location to great concentrations of people in relatively few locations. It's going to allow the dispersion of people, whether it's relatively large numbers of people working in remote locations or working from home, or whether globally, so that a company like C&W with many centres around the world can link itself together. That will give a whole new twist to the way in which international companies organise globally. People will still probably need to get together for a long time to come, but if you look at how video conferencing and body travel goes, one does not substitute for the other: they reinforce each other. The more you use video conferencing, the more you think "I really need to meet that guy face to face" – and vice versa. I think it will enable us to do things in a very different light.'

Ross is shrewd enough to see that this revolution has to begin at home. C&W is experimenting with concepts like having a more federal structure and setting up centres of excellence in different aspects of the business that can be dispersed around the world so they do not have to be duplicated in every centre. That inevitably involves continuous, high-quality communication.

He explains: 'Our management has been fairly conventionally organised up until now, primarily on a geographic basis, and what we're looking at is ways in which we can, not walk away from that geographical base because that's still the heart of our particular strength as operating units, but make sure that those same managers at the same time can wear group hats and have a group responsibility for different aspects of the business. It may be a technological aspect, it may be accountability for regulatory affairs and making sure that we can have an overview of how regulation operates in different parts of the world.'

C&W is often consulted by countries in the process of privatising their monopolies or setting up second forces like Mercury, who want to learn from the group's experience in the 1980s of privatisation and competition in the UK. To discuss such issues sensibly, C&W's top people need to be able to understand the interaction of Washington's Federal Communications Commission and the European Commission in Brussels. The idea is to give a senior manager accountability for that aspect of the business, even if he has totally unrelated accountability for particular geographic operations.

'It's a much more fluid organisation,' Ross claims, 'one that can evolve, than a very rigid box-like hierarchical structure. I think it's fairly typical of our high-technology industry that it tends to be a much younger industry with younger attitudes in it and much less formality, and they are used to living with a greater pace of change. The shorthand always is that no one likes change, but I don't actually believe that: a lot of people thrive on change. People who don't want change feel threatened by it because they're not in control of it – change happens to them and they're not shaping it. That's incredibly important in terms of maintaining morale within a company during a period of continuous change. I think we're within that period, and I don't see us coming out of it in the next five or ten years.'

But, armed with his BCE tie-up, Ross sees C&W making its money in the next forty years from plugging into the global village that half of the population of this world who still don't have a telephone or aren't within reach of one. 'The pace is accelerating,' he reports. 'Look at the rate at which we're putting in lines to a country like Jamaica, which you would say is not in the forefront of economic development in the world, but we're putting modern technology and digital phones in, and we'll probably have half a million lines there in the next few years, mainly so that Jamaicans who have emigrated to other parts of the world can call back in to their families. Look at the patterns of emigration all over the world and you can imagine an enormous explosion. One of the fastest-growing routes in the world is Hong Kong to Canada. Why? Because many Hong Kong Chinese have emigrated to Canada, and to Australia, America and the UK. Multiply that all over the world, plus the fact that China is now opening up, which has meant that the growth of our business through China and Hong Kong is more than forty per cent a year. It is staggering. So you don't have to go into flights of fancy about the technological developments of this industry to imagine the enormous growth we've got ahead of us, just on simple, basic telecommunications. If I had to pick one single theme for Cable & Wireless, what I'd see is that process continuing, probably accelerating at least over the next decade and probably over the next three or four decades, and that's where a lot of our bread and butter is going to be.'

Ross bases C&W's global strategy on three hubs: Hong Kong, the Caribbean and London. Hong Kong will, political upheavals and 1997 permitting, be the door through which the group taps the potentially huge Chinese market. Guangdong province, adjacent to Hong Kong, has sixty million people and is growing very fast indeed, so that will give the group enough to be going on with, and other Asian countries beckon. London will be the base for expansion into continental western Europe where, there is considerable pent-up demand thanks to the persistence of state monopolies. Hub number three is the Caribbean, where C&W has been historically strong. That will take the group into central America and parts of South America.

'We will then look at one or two other areas,' explains Ross, 'again very selectively, in an attempt to gain, over the years, a fourth hub. Now, where that is depends on what the opportunities are and what our assessment is. But we're clearly present in the former Soviet Union and Eastern Europe, and we've got lots of opportunities in the Middle East. We'll probably concentrate on those and one or two other possibilities. But our attempt is not to proliferate all our ventures, it's very much to concentrate on the three hubs and then to search for a fourth hub. I shall be surprised if we've satisfied that strategy and need to move on to something really radically very different within the next five to ten years. We don't have a management yet that is anywhere approaching the diversity of countries that we're in and the global interests that we have. I think you can expect to see that change, too, over the next five to ten years.'

The riskiest of C&W's three hubs is undoubtedly Hong Kong. Ross is sanguine about the group's exposure to events there, but has high hopes that those risks are worth taking.

He says: 'Hong Kong is high-risk, but it's also high reward and very important to our future. I would like our stake in Hong Kong and China to be a smaller proportion of our total activity and our total profit, but the best way to do that is to grow other parts of it faster and not walk away from Hong Kong. The trouble is, that is extremely difficult given the pace at which things are growing in China. But after 1997 we will be the majority shareholder in a very large company that will be part of the People's Republic of China. I think, obviously, there are political risks as far as Hong Kong is concerned and when there's a lot of uncertainty people tend to emphasise disproportionately the risk. All I would say is that were we to walk away from it now in any way, then we would be held accountable by future generations for doing so at the very moment when we had more than just a toehold in mainland China. We'd be walking away from the most enormous opportunity, but we're going to have to work very hard to prise it open.'

Eastern Europe is more problematical, so Ross' approach is to build relationships and opportunities without exposing enormous amounts of money. The group has activities in Moscow and St Petersburg, with a project to link the large towns in that part of Russia, and is also operating in Sakhalin and Nakhodka on the Pacific coast.

'If you look at it,' Ross points out, 'that is the shortest route between two of the fastest growing telecommunications areas in the world, Asia and Europe. If we could complete that somehow over time, there may be political stability and less concern about security if they allow us to do that, and then that could be a very viable route. And right in the middle of it, Tyumen and a lot of the oilfield development areas. So we're being very selective about where we place our bets in terms of being there for the long term and building a traffic route that will be viable for many, many years. A lot of the traffic will come out of the western part of the territory by satellite into Mercury. From the east it'll come out into Hong Kong, but in the long term with cable technology improving the whole time, it will probably be a combination of the cheapest and the best.'

Then there is the US, characterised by regulatory turmoil in the midst of which the authorities are trying not to leave any accidental loopholes for foreign companies. C&W has a small operation there, which is both tied to offering long-distance calls and restricted in its ability to go international. Ross is optimistic that the logjam will eventually disentangle, allowing C&W to exploit its position. Meanwhile, he plays a waiting game.

'Our attitude to the US is that it's somewhere that we have to be for two reasons,' he argues. 'One is that the US is where most applications of new technology are being implemented in the market place first. That doesn't mean it's being invented there first, but usually that's where the new applications are being tested out. Then it's only a matter of time before they're introduced into other parts of the world. So, if we don't want our competitors to leapfrog us in the world we need a window on the US. Secondly, because we have a pretty unique spread of assets and activities in the three main trading blocks – Europe, the western hemisphere and the east – international traffic and business with multinational companies is very important to us. A disproportionate number of those companies are American-based, so we have to have access to them. The only question is how best to do that. If you asked me, "it's such a big market, why don't you expand there?" I would point out that it's also the least profitable market because it is highly competitive. We make an adequate, but only barely adequate, return in the US. We make a far better return here in the UK and certainly a far better return in Hong Kong and the Far East. So if you look at the marginal dollar of investment, is it going to go to the US as our first choice? No, because we can earn more on that dollar somewhere else, but we can't afford not to do that so it's a question of positioning. How do we do that? Do we do that as we are doing it at the moment? Do we grow slowly and open up as the regulation changes? Do we make a number of acquisitions and try to grow more rapidly? Do we look for alliances with other people? The answer to that is we don't know. We're churning all those options. It's almost the cost of doing business elsewhere in the world. As long as that cost isn't very high and we're actually making a profit, then we're getting the experience out of the US and transferring it elsewhere. That's fine.'

So Ross comes back, rightly, to the bottom line. As a late recruit to the telecoms industry, he is perhaps less dazzled by the gadgetry and more focused on the money to be made. And, as other industries from tobacco to electronics have found, there are rich pickings to be had from selling the basic product to poor countries.

CHAPTER 19

DAVID SAINSBURY

of J. Sainsbury

'CONSTANT IMPROVEMENT and continuous change are the hallmarks of our business,' says David Sainsbury. 'Any change will be evolutionary rather than revolutionary.' If you are at the top of your industry, the range of strategic options narrows ruthlessly. You must try to maintain your lead over the opposition by going onwards and upwards. That is very much the Sainsbury approach, made the more acute by the fact that this huge supermarket group is still family-run despite having gone public in 1973. The family ethos, dating from a now-defunct Victorian grocery in London's Drury Lane, continues to pervade the group, giving it a sense of continuity, of direction, even of moral purpose. As Anita Roddick has discovered with her Body Shop International group, the moral high ground can be a powerful position to capture – all the more so for retailers, who must employ and deal directly with the public yet cannot have quite so many trade secrets as manufacturers. Although there is a massive behind-the-scenes logistical operation in moving and storing the smallest possible amount of stock consistent with keeping the shelves full, what the customers see is broadly what they get. Yet, like many of the world's best retailers, Sainsbury sails forth with a self-assurance that would be the envy of the most daring tightrope walker. That millions of people will flock to its temples of consumerism is not in doubt; nowadays, the concerns are to do with fine tuning, making subtle adjustments in the mix of goods on offer to ensure that they leave behind as much of their cash as possible.

Since November 1992 the group has been run by David Sainsbury, the quiet intellectual of the family. He studied at Eton and King's College, Cambridge, where he read history and psychology, and joined the family

David John Sainsbury

BORN: 24 October, 1940

EDUCATED: Eton, King's College, Cambridge, and Columbia University, New York

MARRIED: Susan Reid, 1973. Three daughters

CAREER:

1963 Personnel dept., J. Sainsbury
1973 Finance Director
1988 Deputy Chairman
1992 Chairman and Chief Executive

OTHER INTERESTS: Governor of London Business School, Visiting Fellow, Nuffield College, Oxford

J. SAINSBURY PLC

HEAD OFFICE: Stamford House, Stamford Street, London SE1 9LL
Tel: 071-921 6000

ACTIVITIES: Food retailing

MAIN BRANDS: Sainsbury, Homebase, Savacentre, Bulksava

firm in 1963. Much of his £2 billion personal fortune is diverted into charitable projects, to do with mental health and social policy, but also helping young unemployed and young entrepreneurs. He is forward-looking without being a radical. Sainsbury supermarkets will still be selling bread and baked beans in the 21st century – but so much else as well.

'I still think that most of the trends that we saw in the 1980s, which are the underlying trends of what consumers wanted due to their changing lifestyles, are likely to continue in the 1990s,' he intones. 'As a whole, I still believe you'll see more people going on holiday abroad, you'll see more women working, you'll see more people with microwave ovens, more people with two cars or one car. So the thing that those trends lead to will continue: there'll be a continuing emphasis on convenience, a continuing desire to shop by car and a continuing emphasis in the quality of food along a number of dimensions, such as healthy eating, which I think will become much stronger. People will continue to be interested in health issues and how that relates to sport and activity, and of course you get diet in that. They'll be concerned about variety of food and the authenticity of the foods, so that they represent the taste of the countries they're supposed to represent – authentic Indian, authentic French and so on. The trends all point to wider product ranges, more perishable goods and bigger overseas interests.'

Sainsbury accepts that price will continue to be extremely important, as a major component of the drive for value for money to an audience that will predominantly be carrying around the memory of the early 1990s recession. But that will not stop them demanding higher standards at the same time, particularly higher standards of service. Sainsbury sees the vogue for foreign holidays as the key.

'At the beginning of the 1980s,' he points out, 'you had twelve million people taking foreign holidays a year. By the end of the 1980s, twenty million were going abroad. I believe that those consumers were affected seeing a greater variety of food and coming back and saying "we want to be able to buy pasta" or "we want to buy Greek yoghurt" or "we want to buy Indian food, we are no longer satisfied with bacon and eggs, or fish and chips". Everything tells me that more people will go on holidays abroad as their income rises. They become more interested in foreign travel, they become more interested in variety. Then they become more interested in quality of food, because you start saying that you'll pay more for food which hasn't got additives, or food which is of a higher quality.'

In the face of such change supermarkets, like other retailers, have realised that they cannot afford to sit back passively and wait for suppliers to offer them additive-free taramasalata or sag alloo. As J. Sainsbury and the other leading supermarket groups have acquired a bigger and bigger share of the market, they have annexed the power to take a leaf out of Marks & Spencer's book and act more like manufacturers without factories. Before customers have a chance to defect to a rival, the supermarketeers are telling suppliers what they want. Response times are shrinking.

'I think there's going to be more emphasis on working with suppliers for innovation and quality,' Sainsbury confirms. 'To get the kind of quality that we're looking for, you have to have very good relations with the suppliers and with the primary producers of products, because it's all about us talking to them about what our needs are in terms of quality and value for money. You only get that when you feed back to suppliers what the market is looking for in terms of quality and work with them to achieve that quality and innovation.'

You might assume that this is all about inventing fancier sauces, but even humble slabs of meat and fish are getting the treatment. The Sainsbury group has worked closely with butchers to give meat greater maturation. That makes it tenderer and, naturally, justifies higher prices because of the longer time it takes to reach the desired level of maturity. Fish, meanwhile, is becoming fresher – and, of course, the customer will be expected to pay more for that, too.

Commentators readily dismiss the local competition Sainsbury and its ilk encounter whenever they land in a new territory. The standard view is that corner shops are simply steamrollered out of existence as the mighty machine clanks into action. However, David Sainsbury sees it differently. 'I think it's very difficult,' he says, 'because retailing depends so much on local knowledge that it takes time to get to know that well. To start with at least, you don't have a great technological advantage over the local chains. It takes time to have a feel for how that market works, to have a feel for the geography, to know the different areas well. After maybe ten years you have a feel for it. That's how we started off, just in London. I think very bold moves are a mistake in retailing because it is very difficult to build up that knowledge.'

Nevertheless, Sainsbury's technological lead over 'mom'n'pop' stores is massive and becoming greater all the time. Once they have built local tastes into the system, sheer scale begins to tell. Much of this is to do with the 'just in time' supply chain. 'Just in time' is usually associated with the Japanese assault on the car industry, where parts-makers are dragooned into making daily or even hourly deliveries to keep the production lines rolling without the car manufacturer having to hold large stocks. But American supermarkets hit on the idea first, ordering only as shelves emptied.

'We don't want to hold baked beans in the supply chain longer than we have to,' Sainsbury explains, 'and we have been helped by developments like electronic scanning. The quicker you can get scanning information to suppliers, the quicker they can adjust the supplies and the less stock we have to have in the system. I don't think this will make a huge difference to the size of supermarkets, though I think there will be a bit because the range and variety of goods will both increase. But I don't think it will change as much as it has done in the recent past. I think there will be a few additional departments, and that will make the stores slightly bigger. Every two or three years, we find a new department. In the recent past, it's been newspapers and flowers. I can't help feeling that there will be a few more departments like that.' And, in a wonderfully virtuous circle, the bigger the supermarkets become, the higher their sales per square foot, the lower the labour cost per pound of sales, and therefore the higher the profit margin.

Newspapers, flowers and other specialities are turning into the big supermarket groups' main defence against the invasion of the discount stores, both the home-grown Kwik Save and the likes of Aldi and Netto from abroad. Surprisingly, Sainsbury is more prepared than some of his peers to concede ground to the newcomers – before dismissing them as no more than a little local difficulty.

'It's clear that the discounters will take a higher proportion of the market,' he accepts, 'and that's very much about the discounters becoming the local stores. There's a bit of a market which will become the discount market, where price is the major consideration, and discounters will take a large chunk of that market. But that's never been our market anyway. I think that many people go to the local Kwik Save for stuff like bread and milk, where they would've gone to the local pop-in shop before.'

As the propaganda battle with the discounters warms up, Sainsbury and other market leaders are choosing to compare unlike with unlike, pointing out that in 1993 Sainsbury own labels were an average of twenty-three per cent cheaper than a similar basket of goods at Kwik Save. But Kwik Save does not sell on its own label: it and the other discounters stock only a few well-known brands across a narrow range of goods.

Says David Sainsbury: 'I don't think you're going to see in this country the level of acceptance discounters have had on the Continent, because the British consumer is already demanding and expecting a higher level of service. You've only got one kind of cornflake there, one kind of peas, no chilled food, no perishables. Consumers require variety way beyond what you can get in a Kwik Save. There is a bit of a market for that and if you're rushing home and you want some peas and there's only one kind of peas then you're happy with that, and if there aren't any cornflakes in the house but Kelloggs cornflakes, all right, but people usually want to choose cinnamon toasties or whatever selection they want. I think British consumers have already gone beyond that in their demands for value for money. If there were sites available, there would be a big gap in the market for us in Germany.'

Although Sainsbury, like other supermarket leaders, insists that there is still plenty of room for expansion in Britain, increasingly his eyes are turning abroad. Whether or not there is unexplored territory at home, the fact is that the Monopolies and Mergers Commission would almost certainly frown on any attempt to speed up the process through takeovers. However, no such inhibition applies beyond these shores. Sainsbury already owns Shaw's Supermarkets, which has more than seventy outlets in the north-eastern corner of the United States. It would be surprising if the group stopped there.

'There's quite a lot of people having operations in more than one country and I would have thought that's a trend that's likely to continue,' observes Sainsbury. 'The interesting thing is that Northern European retailers – like ourselves, Delhaize, Tengelmann and Ahold – have tended to go to America when they've expanded and Southern European retailers have tended to expand into other Southern European countries. The likelihood is that there'll be more international retailing than there has been in the past and with modern communications, it's very much easier to buy products from all over the world. Within that, we as British food retailers have a responsibility to work with British suppliers so that wherever possible we get supplies in this country. That's something we take very seriously and that's going to remain important throughout this decade. We're never going to buy what isn't best for our customers, but we'll always make an extra effort to use British suppliers. There is a very good economic reason to have your suppliers close at hand and that is so that you get a faster reaction time but partly, because we are a large British company, we have a social responsibility to work closely with British suppliers and I think we do that.'

Sainsbury says he has no plans to follow Argyll and Tesco into Europe, but that is more a matter of opportunity than any deep-rooted opposition. Indeed, the logic points inexorably in that direction with improved motorways, the opening of the Channel Tunnel and the prospect of a second tunnel being dug before Eurotunnel's option runs out in 2020. 'I can't help feeling we're going to become a more international company in ten years' time than we are today,' says Sainsbury. 'Things are likely to converge because you're more likely to have more international food manufacturers who are likely to seize the opportunity to sell the same product in different countries. What makes it more homogenous is the better transport which makes it much easier to shift things around the world and we may be buying the same fruit and vegetables as French people, simply because we're buying them in some foreign country and you get a world market that everyone buys from. If people from this country can go to France and buy cheese cheaper then they'll buy some English cheeses and some French cheeses and it'll be a challenge for food retailers here that when French people come across here then we've got to do a better job of selling them English cheese. If that happens, the end result will be French people eating a wider range of cheese that includes Cheddar and Stilton, and English people eating a wider range which includes French cheese. In that sense, what we eat and what French people eat will become more similar. It won't mean there is a Euro product which everyone eats; people will be eating a wider range of products with a higher proportion of foreign food in it.' This will be music at the tills, for shoppers are notoriously less price-fussy about exotic food and drink. While that differential can be expected to narrow, for a long time to come, people will be happy to pay a premium for what they regard as something special. In the jargon, supermarkets will be adding value in bringing such delicacies within reach, instead of simply offering a plain local commodity.

As the range of goods widens, along with the network of suppliers, so trust will become an increasingly important weapon in the successful food retailer's armoury – the trust of suppliers that they will be paid on time, customers that they will get a good deal, and employees that their loyalty will be rewarded.

Says Sainsbury: 'In our business, the biggest asset is the loyalty of our customers and their trust in us. Trust within the company is very important, trust from customers is very important to companies and when you get to supplier relationships, equally, I don't think you can run it without some level of trust and commitment. If you're asking people to innovate and change and so on, you can't pin that down in a contract, it has to be on the basis of understanding and commitment on both sides, and that's all part of the same thing, really. All the emphasis was on mobility, individual incentives: I think there is a move towards more sense of team work and group incentives, and the importance of relationships and commitment. I think that on the whole is healthy. Most people don't want to spend all their time worrying about whether the product they're buying is of high quality and will do what it's supposed to do, and the bottle won't break, and so on. What they want is trust and confidence in that company, that that company will always deliver. If anything, that will become more important as people's expectations become higher. It's vital that they are confident that we will look at product quality, that what we sell our customers is in every way right, whether it's in terms of taste and packaging or health issues and diet issues. In all those, people want to have confidence. If all you want is price then you shop around to go to where the price is cheapest, but if you're interested in quality and value for money then you want to make a decision and say: "That is where I have confidence."'

CHAPTER **20**

SIR ALLEN SHEPPARD

of Grand Metropolitan

GRAND METROPOLITAN, once a force in the hotel trade, is at a crossroads: already the world's No. 1 drinks group, it wants to establish itself as a world-class food provider and retailer. But it entered the mid-1990s only twelfth in the international food league and its retailing hopes were being increasingly pinned on Burger King as it sold or cut back other high-street brands.

In its present form GrandMet is very much the creation of Sir Allen Sheppard, the son of an Ilford train driver who went to the London School of Economics and spent the first half of his career in the motor trade, starting with ten years at Ford. But in 1975 he tumbled out of the then British Leyland – the rump of which was subsequently renamed Rover, taken over by British Aerospace and sold in 1994 to BMW. Sheppard was recruited by GrandMet to run Watney's, the brewery and pub chain. 'I thought it was a joke that I should spend eighteen years in the motor industry in order to take over a series of breweries,' he recalls with his oblique sense of humour, 'but there was a lot to do: GrandMet was a successful company, but it had a blurred portfolio.'

Despite his efforts, which brought him a knighthood in 1990, the signs are that the group is again proving hard to tidy up. GrandMet was a postwar property vehicle for the late Sir Maxwell Joseph, a former estate agent. At the same time as the legendary Sir Charles Clore was exploiting the property potential of shoe shops, Joseph was doing the same with hotels. From that base he gradually bought his way into pubs, brewing, dairies and dance halls. Sir Max died in 1982. By the time Sir Allen became chairman in 1986 it had become a sprawling group that was in danger of losing its way. He

says: 'We had to answer a number of questions. Did GrandMet add any value, and how did we add value? What should we be focusing on, with an eye on what may happen over the next couple of decades?'

Whereas Joseph's starting point had been what he called kickable assets, Sir Allen concentrated on what those businesses could earn. For a generation of managers, the property crash of the mid-1970s had demolished the myth that property was an invincible investment: overload it with too much debt and it can – and did – come crashing down. So in 1989 Sir Allen took GrandMet out of hotels. It seemed a cataclysmic decision at the time, almost like Sainsbury getting out of supermarkets. But his timing was superb. He sold the Inter-Continental chain for £1.35 billion, a price that probably would not have been attainable again until the next century as the 1990s recession cast its long shadow over the industry. 'It was an emotional decision to get out of hotels,' Sir Allen admits, 'but it was very easy commercially. Staying in was for the birds.' Four years later, Sir Allen completed the clear-out by persuading the brewers Scottish & Newcastle to pay £620 million for its Chef and Brewer pub-restaurants and sold 235 pubs owned by Inntrepreneur, its joint venture with Courage.

To replace all that activity, Sir Allen lit on a jewel that had originally been hidden away in Watney when GrandMet bought it in 1972 after what was then one of the biggest and most bitterly fought takeover battles the City had ever seen. The gem was International Distillers and Vintners, a wines and spirits distribution business that owned Gilbey's gin, Croft Original port and J&B Rare whisky. Since then it has added such labels as Piat D'Or, Popov, Metaxa, Cinzano and Malibu. But IDV's master stroke so far has been the invention of Baileys Original Irish Cream, the milky, coffee-coloured concoction based on Irish whiskey. It was developed in conjunction with another part of GrandMet, Express Dairies. 'Nobody actually asked for Baileys,' Sir Allen points out, 'but the world was sitting there unaware that it was their great desire. Somebody – it was a combination of Express and IDV – anticipated that if they could solve the technical problem of blending cream and spirit they would have a product which the consumer would want. To some extent it wasn't finding what the consumers wanted, it was finding what the consumers would want. So new product development is a fundamental part of our business, as are acquisitions.'

IDV's record on new products is impressive. It is hard to break into the world's 100 top drinks brands: their average age is a hundred years. Since the beginning of the 1970s, only seven have made it. Of those seven, four are national products and three are international, all of which were developed by

Sir Allen John George Sheppard

BORN:	25 December, 1932
EDUCATED:	Ilford County School and London School of Economics
MARRIED:	Peggy Jones 1959, Mary Stewart 1980. No children

CAREER:

1956	College lecturer
1958	Junior Financial Analyst, Ford Motor Company
1968	Export Manager Rootes/Chrysler
1971	Marketing Director, British Leyland international division
1975	Grand Metropolitan: Head of Watneys
1982	Group Managing Director
1986–1993	Chief Executive
1987	Chairman

OTHER INTERESTS: Director of UBM Group, Mallinson-Denny Group, Business in the Community, Board of Trustees – Prince's Youth Business Trust, Advisory Board, British-American Chamber of Commerce

GRAND METROPOLITAN

HEAD OFFICE: 20 St James's Square, London SW1Y 4RR
Tel: 071-321 6000

ACTIVITIES: Distilling, drinks distribution, food retailing

MAIN BRANDS: J&B whisky, Gilbey's gin, Smirnoff vodka, Croft Original port, Cinzano vermouth, Malibu and Baileys Irish Cream liqueurs, Piat d'Or wine, Pillsbury dough, Green Giant processed vegetables, Häagen-Dazs ice cream, Alpo petfood, Burger King restaurants, Pearle opticians and Inntrepreneur pubs.

IDV: Baileys, Malibu and Absolut vodka. IDV has also exploited new trends, marketing ready-mixed drinks in the US, and producing an upmarket health drink, Aqua Libra. By 1994 IDV owned eleven of the world's top hundred brands. Some of those, like the biggest-selling vodka, Smirnoff, have been acquired. Smirnoff came with the US distributor Heublein in 1987, which gave IDV an entré into the world's most lucrative drinks market. With the help of such add-ons, by the mid-1990s IDV had graduated to generating more than half GrandMet's operating profit. It was still relatively weak in Asia Pacific but it was moving into China. Although IDV was campaigning in that region without a cognac or a champagne, particularly a cognac, it was developing J&B variants and had the licence for Dunhill whisky in Japan.

Says Sir Allen: 'We are number one in wines and spirits which, if you take it negatively, means that there is only downwards to go but you could also look at it as having plenty of opportunity for the industry to rationalise and for us to keep ahead. There is still a lot of scope, because although Allied-Domecq, Seagrams, Guinness and ourselves are way ahead of anybody else, we still take a relatively small part of the world's wine and spirits market between us. So I think there will be greater globalisation. I see the big four rising from about thirty-five per cent of the market in 1993 to about fifty per cent in 2010. That will be partly by organic growth, because the top 100 brands are growing faster than the total market, but it will be partly also by acquisitions. I think the tendency towards people drinking less and drinking better will continue. I think drinking will get better in terms of quality of product, and premiumisation will continue. There's no sign of that having been blunted by the recession. I see the trends of the last twenty-five years continuing at least for the next ten or twenty.'

That makes the sizzle, in the form of brand marketing, at least as important as the sausage of the underlying potions. And that is the main reason why Sir Allen rejected his longstanding heir apparent, Ian Martin, in 1993 and instead promoted to chief executive George Bull, who had been widely credited with the success of IDV. His task was to maintain that impetus and impart some of it to the food and retailing businesses. 'It is my intention to position GrandMet very firmly as a market-oriented company,' says Bull. 'I am not a bean counter. I am a sales and marketing man, and have been all my life.'

Although the group's food operations are well behind IDV in international status, the rules of the game are the same: bigger suppliers, greater globalisation, more emphasis on brands. The difference lies in the way the two industries are structured. Drinks are dominated by the four giants, who are harried by hundreds of national and local brewers, distillers and vintners. But in food the Swiss-based Nestlé and America's Philip Morris are well ahead of an international pack of about a dozen pursuers, including the Anglo-Dutch Unilever, BSN in France, Kelloggs, Quaker, Mars and Hershey in the US and GrandMet. But they are all so big that alliances and trading links seemed more likely than outright mergers, coupled with brand swaps.

'Food is entirely different from drink because the world is our oyster or the oyster is our world, whichever way you want to put it,' quips Sir Allen. 'I think the industry will fragment between commodity-driven businesses and the more brand-dominated businesses such as ourselves, Nestlé, Unilever, Kelloggs and Quaker. I think tastes are going to become more homogenous. You're not going to get people moving away from being rice eaters to becoming wheat eaters, but they will gather around the profitable, branded end of the business, like Häagen-Dazs, which we sell around the world. You're already beginning to get the situation where you get brands that do well in both America and Japan. You've got this huge two-way pull of the person wanting to be an individual and at the same time, through television, seeing certain things that we should associate with an international way of life to some extent. It's a bit schizophrenic, I guess. They've got to be distinct products that actually meets people's local pattern. And each brand must cover the same product: I don't think you can have a brand name which covers fifteen different products in different parts of the world but are called the same. The other thing is that for an international product, you've got to be willing to consistently support it with marketing and new product innovation. The revitalisation of Häagen-Dazs was to do with the Exträas product, which made it even more premium. We don't see it as just an ice cream: it's partly a dessert business, it's partly a snack business, and a lot of our new products have been designed particularly for that customer.'

In 1993 Häagen-Dazs was the market leader among premium ice creams in Japan and it was doing so well in Europe that GrandMet had to build a new plant in France instead of importing from America. But North America was the only place where GrandMet had what it regarded as critical mass in foods, accounting for eighty per cent of its food business with brands like Green Giant vegetables and Pillsbury dough, pizzas and desserts. Green Giant has also been available in Europe for more than a decade, and it was even being advertised on Japanese television. Pillsbury dough was spreading from the UK across Europe. However, development, promotional and marketing costs are so high in what is an enormously competitive market that all these brands – including Häagen-Dazs – were still making losses into the mid-1990s.

'It costs an arm and a leg,' Sir Allen admits, 'but we do all of that because, in the long term, we believe they have got huge potential. Pillsbury is slightly better on course than we'd anticipated, but they're going to make no money for five years and then for the next five years you make a bit of money, and after ten years-plus you have a winner on your hands. Other brands we have tend to be local regional brands rather than international, like Ski yoghurt and Express dairy brands, and Alpo cat food in America. They are very strong in their own markets, but not internationally. So, in terms of food, we've got to decide if we're going to be a North American food company with some international brands, or a world food company. It's too early to call that yet.'

Although retailing ranks as GrandMet's third arm, it was significant that David Nash was promoted in December 1993 to be head of the food and international retailing operations combined. That suggested the high-street businesses were not making the breakthrough Sir Allen had hoped for them. Apart from the main flagwaver, Burger King, which was standing up to the mighty McDonalds around the world, the group's only other large-scale name was Pearle, the US optician chain. Many others had been tried with varying degrees of success, including Pizzaland, Perfect Pizza, Pastificio, Spaghetti Factory and Wienerwald – which sold spit-roasted chicken to German snackers.

'Our retail business is less mature and less advanced than food,' Sir Allen concedes, 'in the same way that food is less advanced than drinks. There aren't that many multinational retail brands around, so we have been carefully searching for something to go alongside Burger King and Pearle. But up to 1993 we had not found anything that had come to the management committee, let alone the board.'

The attraction of retailing is that, however big or small a chain, it needs similar skills in property management, information systems, people handling and merchandising. The more outlets a company has, the more thinly those overheads can be spread, bringing trading margins through to the bottom line with the minimum possible dilution. But, as the 1990s progressed, it looked an even bet whether Sir Allen would stick with what was increasingly looking like a business that would never match the international reach of McDonald's or Body Shop. Indeed, Sir Allen accepts that consumers are becoming more demanding - which may imply that it makes better sense for all but the retail specialists to stay in the back room of the supply process.

'Consumer democracy will become even more of a reality than it is in the 1990s, which is more than it has ever been historically,' he predicts. 'Increasingly, consumers look through the statements and products of businesses and services which supply them and advertise to them and so on, and will be determining what they think of those businesses in terms of social responsibility and the environment and so on, as well as looking at the product and deciding whether it genuinely has added-value. So, generally, I think there will be more pressure from the consumer and it will become even more sophisticated and democratic, with housewives getting a vote every day and every week. I think they'll still be complex, saying one thing and doing another. Saying that they want bland food with no additives and for the most part, eating it, but then going outside and treating themselves. Certainly, value for money will continue strongly. I don't think that undermines the brand. I think it means that if you don't have robust brands, if you have brands that are not properly supported to marketing quality standards, then you're in for death row. If you've got genuinely premium or value-for-money brands, that will actually favour you.'

That is partly – only partly – why Sir Allen works so assiduously on community projects and has been such a tireless supporter of the charity Business in the Community. He believes that companies must embrace customers, employees, shareholders and everyone they come into contact with in a caring and responsible manner. The rewards are intangible and long-term, but they do make a slight but important difference in people's day-to-day decisions and attitudes. But it is more than a sales aid: if that was all there was to it, the sham would be spotted and the public would soon turn its back on GrandMet. No one who has met Sir Allen is in any doubt of his pride in his working-class origins, and his desire to see the workers get their fair share.

'People will look at the firms in terms of social responsibility,' he claims 'and decide whether they want to work for the company or not. That particularly applies to graduates where, ignoring the recent recession, they'll have more choice. Volunteerism will become much more marked. I think staff will be looking for much more time to be involved with community projects. At the less qualified end there will be real problems of how a job in society works, and how we avoid there being two societies: the mainstream and a massive dropout society which we've almost had already, but more extreme. I think we've got to think through what we mean by a welfare society. Is it daft to have a state which makes a lot of money from people to give a lot of it back to the same people? There must be an easier way of cooking an egg.

Therefore, I think one will have to be a lot more selective about what one means by a welfare state, and that gets you back to means testing and what is means testing. I don't know the answer to that.'

In September 1993 Sir Allen's sense of social responsibility did not stop him sacking 3,000 GrandMet staff, about three per cent of the workforce, mainly at Green Giant and Pearle in the US. But he is still dedicated to improving the quality of the jobs he has on offer.

'It's about how you employ under-qualified people and expect them to have initiative and be self-starters,' he explains. 'For management, therefore, it's not a case of dampening down initiatives, it's a matter of trying to ride whilst keeping control and sticking to a strategy and some basic ethical rules. How do you get the workers not to say no, but get them to take the work out of it and leave them with a much more thinking job, so that the supervision is much more efficient? Management should be much more to do with harnessing a skilled labour force which is self-thinking and not willing to be ordered around and treated like a robot. I think there needs to be different types of training, some of which will be edging towards volunteerism just to give them something to do.'

And where will that leave GrandMet's management? Sir Allen is sardonic.

'I guess management will be more complex and pressurising,' he says, 'because of the employee and consumer reaction. But the basics of it won't change, in the sense that there will always be some kind of lunatic fringe which will pick up some of the management responsibilities.'

CHAPTER **21**

LIAM STRONG

of Sears

ANYONE WHO can compare Reckitt & Colman mustard with Sears, the British-based retailing group that owns Selfridges, Richards, Wallis, Dolcis, Saxone, Olympus and Adams must either have bizarre tastes – or be a dedicated marketeer. Liam Strong is definitely the latter.

'Sears is much more like the maturer consumer goods market I had operated in at Reckitt,' he says. 'There is not going to be a lot of inherent growth and we are really going to have to work hard to get the products right and make sure we make as much money as we possibly can on them. Obviously the best way to do that is through quality. In general, I find in any business that if you analyse your business through its key processes, you'll find that the areas where you're spending more costs than you should are also probably the areas where you're not producing as much quality. The replenishment system in British Shoe is a good point, where it was costing us more money to bring shoes into the warehouse and decide which sizes to go in which shop, moving shoes from one shop to another in a very cumbersome way. That wasn't just costing us more money: because it was an inefficient system, it was logistically contributing to having the wrong shoes in the wrong place. So quite often you find that if you can get people to think that way, improving efficiency and improving service can go hand in hand.'

Eyebrows were raised when Strong stepped into the chief executive's shoes at Sears in February 1992, after seventeen years at Reckitt, and a briefer and more controversial spell as marketing director of British Airways. Born in Northern Ireland the son of a cattle-trading garage owner, he graduated in philosophy from Trinity College, Dublin, and learned his marketing at that other university, Procter & Gamble. He was brought into

Liam Gerald Strong

BORN: 6 January, 1945

EDUCATED: Portora school and Trinity College, Dublin

MARRIED: Jacqueline Gray, 1970. One son, one daughter

CAREER:

1967	Graduate Trainee, Procter & Gamble
1971	Reckitt & Colman
1980	Sunset Designs
1982	Reckitt & Colman
1984	President, Durkee French Foods
1989	Director of Marketing and Operations, British Airways
1991	Chief Executive, Sears

OTHER INTERESTS: Director of Inchcape

SEARS PLC

HEAD OFFICE: 40 Duke Street, London W1A 2HP
Tel: 071-408 1180

ACTIVITIES: Retailing

MAIN BRANDS: Selfridges, Miss Selfridge, Olympus Sports, Wallis, Dolcis, Adams, Fosters, Warehouse

Sears by the chairman, Geoffrey Maitland Smith, to shake up the organisation and kick it forward after a period of tidying-up under Strong's predecessor, Michael Pickard. That had become long overdue in the wake of the corporate hotch-potch left by the group's modern-day founder, Sir Charles Clore, who had bought control of what had mainly been a shoemaker and took it into retailing to exploit the property potential on Britain's high street.

'Success in the 1990s will depend on how radical you are prepared to be,' Strong declares. 'People compare the early 1990s recession to the 1930s, but if you look at the 1930s who would have forecast in 1932 the boom in consumer electronics – Bakelite radios, vacuum cleaners, irons, synthetic fibres? This time, the whole issue of telecommunications and the interaction between all aspects of the media are going to be very important. By the end of the century, that will affect the way people shop. Home shopping is something that people have been talking about for the last ten years, but as you get a PC in your home which has got a high-definition screen with good visuals, you can plug that into entertainment, information, personal services, that becomes a proper network. And by the turn of the century we will be dealing with people who understand this stuff. My son understands it intuitively in a way I never will. The computer is becoming the pencil of the late 20th century, and it's a generational thing. The impact of all that technology on what are pretty non-technological businesses like ours is going to be very profound, particularly in the use of data.'

This will mark a dramatic watershed for the traditional retailer, who has by and large been relatively passive, opening the store each morning and waiting for people to come in. But Strong is one of the growing number of retail industry chiefs who have been recruited from other industries, giving him the perspective to see that what will matter is the extent to which they can reach out and positively identify the people they want to do business with, knowing they have the wherewithal to talk to them directly about why they should shop at that outlet or that group of stores.

'I think we will be constantly searching to become more focused,' says Strong, who early in his reign decided to get Sears out of property and menswear and concentrate on women's wear, shoes, children's wear, and sports and leisure. 'We are building up, within the people in the business, skills in key areas in which we wish to be superior, skills that can be applied across all our businesses. The more commonality we can build up between our businesses, and the more focused we can become, the more effective we can become. So the issue is building up our retailing skills and constantly challenging our retail companies to ensure that they are as close to the line as they can be. That's the concept we will apply in terms of the portfolio of businesses we have at the moment. We are looking to develop a smaller number of bigger businesses to really dominate and get on top of things. We will look carefully at Europe, simply because we already have 500 outlets there. Otherwise we are almost totally exposed to one economy, the UK economy.'

Like any good manager appointed to a top job in a different industry from his previous experience, Strong has studied the best overseas retail operations to see what he might aspire to. The one that attracts his warmest praise is Nordstrom, the American department store chain. It could be a trailer for what the Sears shops – including, of course, Selfridges – are destined to become under Strong's leadership.

'Nordstrom probably have the best reputation in retail for service,' he says. 'Their people get paid high commission but they work within a structure whereby, if they were just chasing sales and alienating customers, that would be picked up on very quickly. The whole basis of it is repeat business: they build relationships and want people to come back. They are the neighbourhood store, so every sales representative is trying to get a name and telephone number so they can call you for the next sale. They are trained to think of not just one sale, and they are trained to think service. So it's not just getting the sale – it's how far you can go. It's the whole ethos and the stories in Nordstrom are about how much further they went with a customer. That is completely against the concept of "here's an easy mark, we'll just fill him up and get rid of him". They are always thinking about how people are going to feel when they leave a store – what are they going to say about us, when are they going to come back, when am I going to see them again? Handing over telephone numbers and addresses requires a huge amount of trust on the part of the customer, but if you talk to a Nordstrom sales representative, you'd be surprised how easy it can feel at the end of it to do that. They really are very good. It's not so much training: it's developing a culture in the company. If you're in a church or a disco you know what's expected of you. I want to create a company where people know what's expected of them, and the sense of alignment, so that what the people are saying at the top of the organisation is the same as what people are saying at the front of the organisation, and what employees read about the company in the press is broadly in line with what they think of it themselves. Employees are always prepared to believe the newspapers before the management!'

Given that he was in charge of operations as well as marketing at British

Airways, it is not surprising that Strong sees the staff as the key to success – nor that his favourite reading is military history. 'I have been interested in military history since I was a kid and I would love to be running an army in battle,' he says. It may be significant that he first came to public attention when he was given the credit for inventing the World's Biggest Offer, a global airline ticket lottery that had a military resonance because it was a response to the collapse in business following the 1991 Gulf War. But Strong recognises that, unlike his predecessors of a generation ago, he cannot get results by barking the orders of the parade ground.

He recalls: 'In the British corporate life one went into in the late 1960s, early 1970s, many of the senior people you were working for had been in the Second World War. So they had a military background and were certainly much more formal, and the baby boomers who are now in quite senior positions see themselves quite differently. Without wishing to generalise, I think they see themselves in a much more egalitarian way – although I'm quite senior and have a lot of authority it's as much responsibility as authority, and the fact that I've got that really doesn't make me any different when I step outside those trappings, compared with someone who does not have that. In many cases it's been a choice by those people not to. Regardless of that, in the grand scheme of things if you genuinely start to believe that you're significantly more important or more significant than anybody else, that's pretty disruptive in terms of running an organisation where everybody's contribution is important. And I think there is an element of utilitarianism in that. It's a sensible way to act. But it may again be a generational thing.

'I think people in businesses have always wanted to identify with the people running the organisation and understand how they think, but it's more important than ever today. At one time you could get away with saying: "I'm in charge and I'm different, and it's OK for me to do these different things, because they're all so different for me than they are for you." I think for organisations in the 1990s people have to understand that broadly speaking the same rules apply to everyone. The issue of scale is different, and if the senior people get treated differently there have to be good reasons for it. You travel in a certain way because you are expected to get off the plane at eight o'clock in the morning and work. And if you have a driver, it's because you spend your time working when you're on the road. You do 50,000 miles a year, and if you drove that it would be bad for the shareholders. So anything you do, and any way you're treated, can be justified in terms that are right for the business and understandable to shareholders and employees. I think that concept of accountability and being prepared to discuss these things are examples of how organisations have become different. I think that work-forces are going to continue to become more challenging. I think that's quite right, because if you're asking people to contribute, then once you open the box they will want to talk about everything, and you have to be prepared to deal with that. I think the organisations that do deal with that will get much more out of their workforce.'

What does Strong want in return for such an open organisation? Enthusiasm, which he sees as the difference between people just standing around a shop and actively selling, avoiding customers and moving towards them with a smile and offering to help, knowing what sort of service the customer wants, and the best way to provide it. This has indeed been the Holy Grail for British retailers, frustrated by the 'Sharon 'n' Tracy' attitude that delights in telling customers there's no call for the item they want, or that the till is closed because they have to take a lunch break. Some might argue that such mulish mentality is so deeply ingrained in the culture of certain parts of Britain that no amount of exhortation will erase it. But Strong is determined to try. This is no mere idealism, for he has a fear at the back of his mind that the worm in the standard British customer is beginning to turn. 'I'm beginning to see British customers take a much stronger line on this, because they're in a buyers' market,' he reports. 'So I think, combined with getting your product absolutely right, clearly differentiated, there has to be very good service. It's not beyond the wit and wisdom of mankind to get decent service in the UK. In Selfridges we've been investing in service now for a few years. As we measure it, we see palpable gains. And if you can get your people to give decent service, life is much more fun for them because customers become much nicer to them. You get real positive feedback from it, once you break through.'

The twin keys to persuading 'Sharon 'n' Tracy' to stop painting their nails and pay attention to the customer are, according to Strong, alignment and learning.

'Alignment,' he explains, 'is simply from the top to the bottom of the business, from the back to the front, ensuring that everybody's moving in a straight line, everybody's on the same line, the line is pointed where you want to go and finally, hopefully, there's a satisfied customer at the end of it. If you can get that line working, then you're going to be very powerful. That covers everything from communications to an understanding of the market you're in, an understanding of the challenges you have, an understanding of what everybody is doing to contribute from the idea through to the satisfied customer, that you have as clear and as straight a linkage as you possibly can. Because basically, if you think about it, the issue in a large organisation is actually bringing everybody to bear on the final interaction with the customer. And so the more you can get them all aligned, knowing what their job and the overall plan is, and understanding how well they're doing – feedback is very important – the better you will do. So that's one idea that I think you'll hear more and more of because it's a more demanding market. There is less room for error and you really have to make sure you're getting the best out of it.

'The second concept is a real cliché, and I make no excuses for that. It's being a learning organisation. You really are trying – particularly if you're looking at the balance between improving productivity and improving service and quality at the same time – to unlock the potential right the way down the organisation. In tough times, quite often, top management has to become more directing, saying: "We haven't got time to argue, this is serious, we really have to get these things done and we have to get them done right." Now that was fine for a time, but after a while everybody in the organisation says, "Well, those guys are going to do it, and even if we think of something they're going to do what they want anyway, so we'll just sit and wait." And if you've got a large organisation of 20,000 or 30,000 people, and two-thirds of them are just sitting and waiting, you're missing out on a lot. So you have to try and get, not so much the feeling, but the genuine belief down the organisation that everybody is important: I'm important, he's important, she's important. He may have more responsibility than I do, but in my area I'm very important, and I can have ideas. And, most importantly, if they're good ideas, they'll be listened to, and I'll see them put into practice pretty quickly. And to get people to feel a sense of their worth and the contribution they can make to the organisation, that that's valued and put into practice. It's very powerful.'

Powerful it may be, but the test for staff wages and shareholder dividends is how far it transforms Sears and whether it translates into value for customers' money. It is clear that, for some time to come, Strong's views are going to be coloured by the dead hand of the early 1990s recession and the accompanying assumption that consumers are going to be watching the pennies.

He says: 'The challenge, I think, for any business is going to be giving people a better reason to buy, because everyone shopped till they dropped in the 1980s, and they still have a lot of those goods in the cupboards or around the place. You're not talking about basic, first-time acquisitions: you're talking in most cases now about replacements. But there will be growth to be had for people who find ways of presenting products that are quite different. IKEA, for example, in the furniture area is a very good case in point of somebody who has reconfigured the market in a way that makes people say "yes, I'll have some of that." The fact that Sainsbury continues to do well in the mature grocery market is in no small way due to the fact that they've continued a very aggressive programme of new-product introduction over the period of the recession, whereas a lot of other people have not. You look at the number of new tags on a Sainsbury shelf as you go through.'

But Strong has had the courage to turn some assumptions on their heads, particularly that people will always want to trade down. The Wallis chain has introduced a range called W, which is deliberately pitched slightly dearer than normal. 'It's very good fabrics, it's classic tailoring, and it's designed to pull down the customers who shop in a department store for brands like Nicole Farhi, and give them those products at a much better price,' Strong points out. 'People usually think of value products as going downmarket, whereas these are value products that go upmarket, giving value to people who are hurting. Because a lady who used to be prepared to spend £200 on a jacket may well be thinking twice about that now, so we're giving them the same jacket at £130. So people who reconfigure are going to have to offer real difference. The challenge in the 1990s is going to be how much you can differentiate yourself and have a very clear position in the market, and a position that takes account of the fact that your customers are sophisticated but they already have most of the things they want, and they have money to spend, if you give them a good reason and hit the button on exactly what their needs are. That, I think, is the biggest challenge from our point of view: how we get our merchandise right, and how we get the service proposition installed.'

Knocking seventy pounds off Wallis jackets is a start, but Strong will have to do a lot more than that to keep his flock of retail brands flying in an increasingly cut-throat market. Economic recovery and the next big women's fashion may solve his problems for him, but he has a major task that will take at least until the turn of the century to sort out. By then he will either be an acknowledged retail success, or he will have moved on to other pastures in the marketing landscape.

CHAPTER 22

MARTIN TAYLOR

of Barclays

HIS FAIR HAIR, wide mouth and large eyes give him an angelic aura. Although he is over forty, Martin Taylor has kept the boyish looks that deceived many a company chairman into a sense of false security at the press conferences he attended when he worked for the *Financial Times*. A few unusually penetrating questions soon had an enematic effect. About half-way through a press conference, after the routine points had been covered, Taylor would deferentially raise his hand to ask a question. That would often be the cue for a one-man cross-examination that would leave the hapless chairman groping for answers, and Taylor's fellow journalists thanking their lucky stars that someone was asking the telling questions. Not that he hogged the floor. It was just that he usually had a line of inquiry which he wanted to pursue, and he would patiently do just that until he had reached the logical conclusion. As often as not, though, a desperate public relations officer would interrupt Taylor before he had got to the payoff line and invite him to have a private chat with the chairman later. That suited Taylor, because it meant that he could keep his own thinking and the chairman's replies to himself. It also suited the PRO, for any shortcomings would not be broadcast across the whole of the financial press the next morning. Instead, they would be confined to the pages of the *FT* and hopefully be lost in the rush of other company results reports in that distinguished journal.

Now, though, Taylor is on the other side of the rostrum as chief executive of Barclays, having been in the same role at Courtaulds Textiles since the age of thirty-eight. That made him one of the youngest heads of a major company. So far he has glided through every test with apparent ease, without ever seeming to be anchored to any fixed point. But the examination is

becoming harder as he lays down the strategy for one of the country's two leading banks, at a time when banks are at their lowest in public esteem. They were not much higher in Taylor's as he strode from the rag-trade ghetto off London's Oxford Street to the heart of the City.

'The banks' public relations has been atrocious,' he claims. 'It's absurd that they take all this stick for doing business that costs them money. I'm very suspicious of the view that all banks seem to hold, that lending money to companies inclines them to do all sorts of other business with you. I think companies see the provision of borrowed funds as a semi-commodity thing you just buy in the cheapest market. There are some things, if you do them really well, will make people inclined to do more business with you. Businesses do want corporate relationships with organisations that understand them. But I'm just suspicious of the idea that lending is the key that opens the door.'

Suspicion was bred in Taylor during his time on the *FT*'s Lex company analysis column. Lex can make and break reputations, so the *FT* reserves it for its brightest talents. It was during the thousand company analyses Taylor performed during his four years at the *FT* that he found himself becoming fascinated by the workings of large companies. It is no coincidence that this was between 1978 and 1982, a period which spanned the main recession of the Thatcher era. That was nowhere near as severe as the recession of the early 1990s, but it gave the perceptive and highly intelligent Taylor a foretaste of the sort of problem he would face as chief executive of Courtaulds Textiles. He has since claimed that he always wanted to go into industry as opposed to the less intellectually satisfying money culture of the City of London, but this may have been a convenient rationalisation of hindsight while he was at Courtaulds. 'I came to Barclays as a manager. This is not an "industry versus the City" thing. I didn't come here to be a banker – we've got lots of those. Barclays needed an outsider: I'm more and more clear about that, the more time I spend here. I think it was going through a very introspective stage, and an outsider can help catalyse.' No, it's not a tremendously convincing argument, but few in his position could have resisted such a job offer in what has already been a glittering career.

Taylor's predominant thought as he left Oxford seems to have been, reasonably enough, that he wanted a job that would enable him to use his second-class degree in Chinese. That suggested travel, which led him to Reuters, the international news agency. But he got little further east than Paris, where he was plonked on the economics desk – quite a shock for someone whose first love was the classics, who took A Levels in maths,

John Martin Taylor

BORN:	June 8, 1952
EDUCATED:	Eton and Balliol College, Oxford
MARRIED:	Janet Davey, 1976. Two daughters

CAREER:

1974	Graduate trainee at Reuters news agency
1978	Writer on Lex column for *Financial Times*
1982	Courtaulds
1987	Managing Director, Courtaulds Textiles
1994	Chief Executive of Barclays

OTHER INTERESTS: Director of W.H. Smith Group

BARCLAYS PLC

HEAD OFFICE: 54 Lombard Street, London EC3P 3AH
Tel: 071-626 1567

ACTIVITIES: Banking, insurance, mortgages, credit cards, stockbroking, merchant banking

MAIN BRANDS: Barclays Bank, Barclaycard, Barclays Stockbrokers, Barclays de Zoete Wedd, Mercantile Credit

physics and chemistry and won a place at Oxford to read English! News agencies are debilitating places to work unless a journalist gets some extra kick out of it, like travel, so after a while Taylor began to look around for a more satisfying billet. The *FT* suited nicely.

It was in some ways the final piece of an educational jigsaw which had begun when his stepfather sent him to a Yorkshire preparatory school, and then to Eton. He was born in Burnley, Lancashire in 1952, the son of an accountant who died when Taylor was a child. The pursuits he learned were intellectual, not trivial, and he exhibits an intellectual's enthusiasm for more than one subject at a time.

'I've always been interested in ideas and language,' he says. 'I'm hopelessly unmechanical, but I took science A Levels because I just felt desperately ill-educated in that area and felt a need to inform myself about those matters.' That is an indulgence only the brightest can allow themselves. Most kids are glad just to get the grades in their best subject to take them to the next stage. In Taylor's case that was Oxford, and inevitably to Balliol, one of the university's most formidable colleges in those days. But, having switched to English, he spent a year teaching in a school in Karachi before he went up. The East wove its spell, and he saw the possible advantages of knowing Chinese. It is the most widespread language of the East, and when China finally opens its doors to the West there are going to be unimaginable commercial opportunities. And Taylor decided he wanted to read ancient Chinese verse in the original. So he arrived in Oxford and almost immediately requested a move from the English school to the Chinese. 'I was awfully frivolous at Oxford,' he recalls with a grin. 'I spent more time reading other people's subjects than my own.' Balliol was not amused. He had to wait a year, leaving him only two years to work for his degree. The delay confined him to a second, rather than the first that someone of his intelligence might have expected.

But that was no obstacle to a job in journalism. Indeed, a first-class degree might have been a handicap in a business that still distrusts intellectuals and prides itself on the virtues of instinct and experience. Reuters did not send him to the Orient, but it did give him a grounding in economics and financial analysis. That was enough to get him on the *Financial Times* after four years, where Taylor gravitated naturally to the Lex desk, turning out pithy comments on company results and economic news. A new enthusiasm took over. 'I became fascinated by the workings of big companies. It was the 1980-1 recession, they were in trouble, I was curious, and through Lex I had access to every public company in the land.'

He already had access to Courtaulds at the highest level, because of a chance social contact. The wife of Sir Christopher Hogg, then chairman and chief executive of Courtaulds, taught at Oxford. One of her pupils was a friend of Janet Davey, who became Taylor's wife. So when, in 1982, Taylor began to feel that he had done all he wanted to do in journalism, Hogg was one of the first people he turned to for advice. 'I was getting extraordinarily interested in the companies that I was writing about, and Chris offered me a way into it,' he explains. 'I chose industry over the City because industry always seemed more socially useful. There were tons and tons of talented people in the City and, on the whole, jobs were quite well done; I couldn't see myself making a significant contribution, really. But I did feel that industry was far more in need of people than the City was, and there was this enormous disparity of skills. I was concerned about the way the City was sponging up so much of the available talent. I just didn't feel terribly turned on by that kind of work.' What's more, despite several offers of high-powered jobs in stockbroking and the like, in the wake of a recession Courtaulds was the only industrial company willing to employ Taylor. That doubtless says more about industry and its low opinion of journalists than it does about either Hogg or Taylor. After about a year as Hogg's personal assistant, working on endless projects that never seemed to come to anything, Taylor was packed off to the clothing side of Courtaulds.

'I thought they were crazy to send me to the clothing business,' says Taylor. 'I thought I had none of the qualities required to succeed in it and I thought I had too much to learn. I couldn't have been more wrong about it as a place to train. The process is very simple – buy the cloth, cut it up and stick it back together again – so you don't have to spend a long time learning what goes on in the processing. The process by which clothes are designed and sold and engineered to a price is quite complex, but at least the process is straightforward and secondly, it's very fast-moving. It's one of the businesses where innumerable small decisions have to be taken and you get feedback on decisions very fast. If it's a good one and things seem good then things get better, but if it's a bad one things get worse, so you are rewarded and penalised very quickly. If you get the price wrong then either you lose the business or you make a loss next month. In some industries, you can make a mistake and not be aware of it for years, if you miscalculate a range, if you quote a price wrong, if you make a wrong tactical decision in relation to your customer. So you learn the business quickly, and it's extremely people-intensive, and I just found that fascinating.'

Taylor became wrapped up in what was then Courtaulds' big secret project: the plan to divide itself in two. It was a chemicals company that had gone into textiles as a way of guaranteeing an outlet for its fibres business, best known for its Courtelle and rayon fabrics as well as cellophane wrapping for perfume and champagne bottles. While textiles had remained consumer-led, labour-intensive and using fairly basic manufacturing technology, the chemicals side had become quite the opposite – hi-tech, capital-intensive, making paint, toothpaste tubes and sealant for jumbo jets. So Hogg increasingly thought of them as two distinct enterprises under one roof, and he turned Courtaulds Textiles into a separate company in 1985.

The demerger took place in 1990, just as the recession was gathering momentum. Rather to his surprise, Hogg picked Taylor to be chief executive of the new company. 'I was too young for the job at the time,' he recalls, 'and I was absolutely amazed to be given it, I wasn't expecting that at all. I thought they'd move me on somewhere else. What helped me a great deal was that Chris himself was viewed in Courtaulds in general as having awesome powers of judgement, so if you were one of the things he judged good then you had a following wind. I've been surrounded, on the whole, by decent and generous people who have given me terrific help.'

For much of his reign, Taylor was concerned with tidying up Courtaulds Textiles, selling off more than a dozen operations and following many other companies in trimming fat, generating cash, ensuring survival. But he inevitably began to think about the future, beyond recession and into the next century.

'In ten years Courtaulds Textiles will be a different shape,' he asserts confidently. 'But if the present management knew which shape, they'd go there tomorrow. I think most chief executives, if they're honest, have to believe that. Not that they will do things to it: the world will do things to it. I mean, look at what's happened to Courtaulds in the last ten years – it's unrecognisable. It lost a third of its workforce, had two huge arms lopped off it, and it's got much more self-confident.'

Most entities, corporate or personal, do not tend to gain in self-confidence when they have had two arms cut off, but Taylor is a great theoriser about companies and their optimum sizes. Wherever possible, he believes that small is beautiful.

'I just can't stand corporate dinosaurs, really,' he explains. 'I don't know whether I'd like to work in them. I think one of the reasons is that business is very risky, and large organisations give one the illusion of safety. They're not very safe at all, as we have seen. Business requires determination and aggression and confidence, in sensible amounts. Large companies can just be stupendously inefficient organisations, and when their individual operations come under competitive pressure they haven't been so quick to see the global organisation as being a source of competitive disadvantage. Which it so easily can be, because they're not taught to think that way. Large companies are supposed to confer benefits in some automatic way. Our experience has been that that's not the case. One thing that people found in the 1980s was that they didn't have enhanced job security in a large corporation – quite the opposite. In order to take certain sorts of risk, a company has to be big enough. But if you take it too far, what you are really saying is that a company has to be big enough to have a licence to make a number of very bad mistakes.'

And in the past, at least, Taylor argues that the banks were among the most notorious holders of that particular licence.

He explains: 'I think that big organisations just make big mistakes and a big mess – look at the banks. If they had been rather smaller, some would presumably have made bad mistakes and gone under, but small organisations couldn't have made mistakes on the epic scale that large banks have managed to. Not only does market dominance attract the unwelcome notice of anti-trust authorities, but to a large extent theories of dominance have been swept away by market fragmentation, which is extreme in the textile and clothing industries, where success is just as likely to go to the nimble as to the powerful. So the powerful have to learn how to be nimble: the elephant must go to ballet school.' The challenge for Taylor is to see if he can take Barclays to ballet school. That will involve a massive cultural revolution, but in characteristic style Taylor is confident that he can persuade the upper echelons of Barclays' top management to don their tutus.

'I think the secret is to run a large company as if it's a group of small companies,' he says. 'Barclays has a better chance than any of the other banks of doing this because it's kept its regional structure: it was originally an alliance of regional banks, so it's slightly less centralised. I think that's an advantage: it means you have more senior people on the ground. I'd like to think over time that we can increase their authority.'

But, even with enhanced authority, these small local groups will still need a leader at head office to orchestrate their efforts – a manager, whose practical experience of the industry may be limited, but who can apply the strategic vision: someone, in fact, not unlike Martin Taylor. This view of his own role, and the fear of being typecast, led him to ask if he could become chairman of Courtaulds Textiles at the same time as being chief executive of Barclays. To his temporary frustration, neither board was keen on this dual arrangement. It would, however, have been a fascinating experiment.

'I'm interested in the whole question of the social purpose of these organisations,' he says, 'and in their complexity – the number of choices and the huge difference in outcome between getting it right and getting it wrong for the company. I think companies are very complex organisations. By their nature, their nature's changing all the time. It's really a question of understanding where strength lies. We've been through a period where the growth of large companies was all to do with scale. In some industries and in some areas scale becomes disadvantageous from time to time.'

One reason for his mistrust of size is that Taylor is also extremely wary of the way in which many men in authority use companies as playthings for their own personal peccadilloes. He believes that anthropology has more to teach us than many a business school about the behaviour of corporate gorillas and other mammals more normally associated with jungle or zoo.

'There's a huge amount of childishness among people who run large companies which has always seemed to me distressing,' Taylor says. 'You really come down to the role of the ego in business, and people's desire to ride big bicycles. The masculine ego and territoriality has been responsible for most of the wrong and unpleasant things that have happened in history. When the ego rules the brain, you better watch it. If you see a company where the ego rules the brain you'd better sell the shares. It's a good general rule. I'm afraid you've just got to avoid people whose ego is very much bigger than their brains. An awful lot of the ego drive is less helpful than it is generally supposed to be, in that organisations that are driven like that are not very good, not very durable. A lot just pander to the chief executive's ego in such a way as to make him feel good. The pretext for that is to make him more effective because he's working in a calm environment and so on. It's very flattering, and even the strongest people are very vulnerable to flattery. It's very dangerous. A lot of assumptions run from that which just don't make very good organisations. If you have a whole class of people being more interested in status than the job, then you have trouble. You have to go back to zoology for the explanation of how these people gather disciples who egg them on. This is an inevitable concomitant of human nature, it's just that small companies are less likely to fall for it as badly as big ones. There is a certainly a cycle of manager, in recession as incompetent, in boom as genius, then as crook.'

Taylor claims that the future lies with a different type of corporate formula, a different model of vehicle to carry the collection of qualities that an industrial organisation needs if it is to be effective.

'The world of the future organisation is not complicated but clear, simple but ambiguous,' he insists. 'For philosophical and cultural reasons, the Japanese are much more at home in this world than we are: too many Europeans and Americans seem to me to miss the point of the Cartesian legacy, and to mistake tidy-mindedness for rationality. People are very tidy-minded, and human beings find it very difficult to cope with tremendous ambiguity. They like to know where they are. They can't carry uncertainty in their minds, and that means that they try to set up organisations which give them an illusion of certainty, and it makes them feel comfortable. That's a very dangerous feeling: animals in the wild who have an illusion of comfort get eaten. Animals have to have their ears pricked up and looking around them, and going around trees and down little holes, or they get preyed on. And the large corporation, set up on the military organisation model, deals with certainties. And, just as the large armies in the first world war have given way to the SAS and guerrilla armies, so companies have to as well. There's no point in having your field marshal on a white horse and your armies arrayed. There's no strength in that, because the weapons that are ranged against you are unpredictable and deadly. Companies had better be simple, because they're just easier to manage, but people have to learn to tolerate ambiguity and uncertainty. People can't tolerate ambiguity on too many axes simultaneously. They can tolerate it on one thing, but they want to know where they are on other things. So if you have an organisation whose task is quite simple, then you get people in it to deal with all sorts of uncertainty which they can manage. That's what companies should be doing. But pretending the present resembles the past, and the future will resemble the present, which large companies are extremely prone to do, seems to me to be one of the most certain ways to ensure extinction. And there's a great yearning for things to stop and slow down, and for things to fall back to where they were. This is something that business can't afford to tolerate. It's a form of indulgence that it can't grant itself.'

One of the first priorities on Taylor's desk when he became chief executive of Barclays in January 1994 was to resolve the internal tension between the group's clearing bank and its City merchant bank, Barclays de Zoete Wedd. This has been a long-running sore, ever since BZW was formed before Big Bang, the London Stock Exchange's 1986 deregulatory explosion. In the early years the fledgling bled money, to the undisguised ire of Barclays' branch managers up and down the country. It certainly did not help in the process of developing a stockbroking service for the bank's high street customers.

'Barclays has a rather paradoxical sort of cultural tension inside it,' Taylor points out, 'which comes from being the only clearing bank to create a successful investment bank. Barclays and BZW have become very different sorts of organisations, and the relationship between them in recognition of that seems to me essential for the future health of the group. It's an opportunity, not a threat, but it's going to be much easier for someone from outside to help them in that, than someone who comes from one side or the other. I think it has something to do with the type of activity and the time horizons. The trading mentality is very different from the lending relationship, very different. BZW is a trading house. The people there are brought face-to-face daily with the horrible things the market drops on them. If you make a mistake, the market tells you and it can be cruel. In a lending bank, it's much easier to evade responsibility for mistakes, distance yourself from the consequences of the market. One would hope they would grow up with an understanding of the business cycle, and a certain amount of mutual respect.'

This is not an uncommon problem at Barclays, whose activities are much wider than the other main clearers'. It has a much higher proportion of its assets and lending powers outside the UK than any other bank, and for many years the overseas operation was a separate company with its own board and share quote. Inevitably, at any one time different parts of the group are going to doing better or worse than others, prompting questions over strategy. Taylor takes a radical approach to such difficulties – lending to companies, for instance.

'The principal problem for Barclays and the other banks is that one of their core businesses, corporate lending, is a deeply unattractive business,' he declares. 'And it's largely because of the crazy way they do their accounts. They make provisions only when people cannot pay, as opposed to taking the risk when the loan is taken. When you make a loan you are taking risk, but the accounts don't tell you that. You make a loan and take the full income from it, right away, and then if it goes wrong you write it off. That means your profits are very cyclical. We have been going through a period when we hoped bad debt provisions would fall and profits look better: they weren't better, fundamentally, it's just the way they were presented. They were good enough to make people feel that they've cracked it. Well, they haven't. Banks always want to impress people with their financial strength. The trouble is that can actually fool the staff, because banks are very risky, highly geared businesses. Some people in Barclays talk a lot about risk management in the sense of managing their portfolio, but they don't talk enough in my opinion about pricing risk. I think if you don't focus on that, you won't get it right. But banks have tended not to distinguish between the pricing of different types of risk.'

Taylor robustly believes that banks shouldn't put up with being criticised for charging small businesses higher interest than large companies pay, even though small-firm loans are riskier. And, despite customers being used over many years to free banking if their accounts are in credit, Taylor is sure that they are prepared to pay when they feel they are receiving a service. 'I think the banks, not particularly Barclays, have done themselves a lot of harm in being seen to be sneaky about charges,' he says. 'That's not an original thing to say, but the reputation of a bank is important, and you don't want your customers to think you're the person that picks their pocket when they're not looking. Maybe banks are just one of those classes of organisation that people just love to misunderstand. They think you're obscenely greedy when things are going well and you're making good profits. And when you're not making a good return they think you're incompetent. And, because of the inbuilt leverage, you tend to flip from one to the next. On the one hand people say you mustn't charge us for running our account, and on the other they say you mustn't close our branches. They want it both ways.'

Such are the trials of running a business that deals directly with the public instead of nice, sensible, rational business customers – let alone one that gets heavily leant on by governments at times of crisis. It looks as though he will be talking to himself increasingly frequently in the next few years. Although Taylor is happily married with two daughters, many of his relaxations are solitary. He likes long walks in remote spots where he can talk to himself out loud, then coming home to play the piano or read one of the several books in different languages he has on the go at any one time.

'I'm not a masochist, not at all,' he declares. 'I like peculiar challenges, but I'm frightened of feeling fifty before my time. I grow restless, and I dread getting bored. So I don't get bored. I think restlessness is quite a good thing. If people don't move on they just repeat themselves and they get stale. I left the *FT*, although I loved it, because I just had a sense that I'd done what I was doing for long enough. When that happens here I shall leave here, too. It's part of a management's job to replace itself. You just hope you will do it at a time when people will still say "Gosh, we're sorry to lose him, we'll miss him terribly." It's vanity to think you're irreplaceable.'

At the age he took it on, forty-one, the Barclays job was critical to Taylor's career. He had shown his paces and come out with flying colours at Courtaulds Textiles, even though he left it on a downturn. If he transforms

Barclays, his reputation will be made and he will be able to contemplate doing something of national importance in his fifties. Should he fail, he may seek something smaller but absorbing. Or, who knows, he could return to writing with a book telling us how to do it – in Mandarin, of course.

CHAPTER 23

SIR IAIN VALLANCE

of British Telecommunications

IN A WAY, it's reassuring that a company with as dynamic a future as British Telecom's should have such a stolid chairman as Sir Iain Vallance. Son of a former head of the Scottish Post Office, he sauntered through the Anglo-Scottish educational establishment via Glasgow and Edinburgh Academies to an Oxford degree in English Literature. After an MSc at the London Graduate School of Business Studies he dutifully followed in his parents' footsteps by joining the Post Office, which in those days was also responsible for the telephone service. He met his wife, Elizabeth, when they were teenagers and she is a professor of politics.

That background does not suggest someone who gets overexcited too easily, tempted to give away a free fax machine to every tenth subscriber or blow billions on the latest gadget brought to him by some breathless boffin. No, Vallance is used to committee grind, schooled for fourteen years in the nationalised industry way of doing things before BT was privatised in 1984. Yet he has hidden shallows. When I met him his eyes were gleaming like the proverbial kid with a new toy, the toy in this case being one of the first video telephones to roll off the production line. Like the early televisions, the picture was a bit jerky and if you moved your head too much it took a while for your lips to catch up with what you had just said, but it was still pretty impressive. Naturally you need two to play, one at either end, and as the boss Sir Iain could send the other set to anyone in the country he chose, from the Prime Minister to Cilla Black. Did he? No chance. 'I've been given this one to try out,' he told me proudly, 'and I've sent one to my parents in Edinburgh.' Can you see me, mother?

That boyish enthusiasm has also revealed itself the odd flash of yearning

Sir Iain David Thomas Vallance

BORN: 20 May, 1943

EDUCATED: Edinburgh Academy, Dulwich College, Glasgow Academy, Brasenose College, Oxford, and London Graduate School of Business Studies

MARRIED: Elizabeth McGonnigill, 1967. One son, one daughter

CAREER:

1966	Post Office
1976	Director of Central Finance, Post Office
1978	Director of Telecommunications Finance, Post Office
1979	Director of Materials Department, Post Office
1981	Board member for organisation and business systems, British Telecommunications
1983	Managing Director, local communications services
1985	Chief of Operations, BT
1986	Chief Executive, BT
1987	Chairman, BT

OTHER INTERESTS: Chairman, Princess Royal Trust for Carers. Trustee of Police Foundation. Member of President's Committee, CBI, President's Committee and Advisory Council, Business in the Community, Advisory Board of British-American Chamber of Commerce. Fellow of London Business School

BRITISH TELECOMMUNICATIONS PLC

HEAD OFFICE: 81 Newgate Street, London EC1A 7AJ
Tel: 071-356 5000

ACTIVITIES: Telecommunications

MAIN BRAND: BT

for the bright lights in Sir Iain's otherwise granite-like career, which brought him the chairmanship of BT, one of the world's biggest companies, at the relatively tender age of forty-four. He dabbled with journalism at an early age, and considered the glamorous life of a television reporter - not on some out-of-the-way station in the Outer Hebrides, but in Michigan, USA. 'I never thought I was going to be there for long,' he insists, 'but they kept giving me jobs that were fun.' The fun came to an abrupt end when it was borne in on Vallance that the longer he lingered the greater the chance of his being called up for service with the US forces in Vietnam. He was soon touching down at Heathrow, having already characteristically passed the British civil service entry exams before flirting with fame in a far-off land.

In the first few years of BT's life in the private sector it was treated as just another utility, like British Gas or the electricity companies. Its first regulator, Sir Bryan Carsberg, (Chapter 2) set about curbing its monopolistic tendencies and making it more responsive to customers. At first that manifested itself in such humble forms as Mickey Mouse telephones, but then a succession of developments from mobile phones to cheaper transatlantic calls encouraged a rush of competitors: Mercury, AT&T, Hutchison Cellular, Vodaphone and the US phone companies that bought their way into UK cable TV franchises. Most began as mere fleabites, but all had the potential to sting, and Sir Iain was increasingly irked that their path was being smoothed whilst BT's was strewn with the bureaucratic equivalent of broken bottles. If there is one subject guaranteed to get the ultra-soft-spoken Vallance to raise his voice half a decibel, it is the regulatory machinations of Oftel.

He says: 'There is no doubt that the UK's regulated, but largely competitive, telecommunications market structure has produced services of a range, quality and price generally unmatched in the rest of Europe. But I think that what the regulator should be doing is working himself out of a job so there is sufficient competition in place to mean that we can be regulated along with everyone else. There is a rather extraordinary concentration of power on one man who is accountable to parliament, which isn't a very taut accountability to say the least. If one were to apply the Cadbury report on corporate governance to the regulators, then they would go down with all hands because there's not even the equivalent of the odd non-executive or two around the place, which might be sensible. Given that they have immense industrial and commercial power, they are able to take decisions without explaining why. In fact there's an arrangement *not* to explain why. If they do then they find themselves open to some kind of judicial review.'

All of which shows that although Sir Iain presides over an empire of more than 200,000 employees, he is acutely conscious that he is not master in his own house. No wonder, then, that he spends much of his energy wishing the regulator into oblivion.

'I think the regulation we have now will change a lot through time,' he says. 'Water and electricity will be regulated forever. They are genuine bottleneck monopolies, and there is no way people are going to compete with each other to put electricity cables into houses, let alone water or sewage. Telecommunications is more interesting, in that you have cable television as well as telecommunications and if you have radio means in the home, then that monopoly will be eroded over time to get away from special regulations. In telecommunications, what you want is a regulatory measure which is a bit like scaffolding – it's there for a while, but you can take it down with the minimum of hassle when competition takes over. If the monopoly is there for good, then the regulation is a buttress rather than a scaffold and is there permanently.'

As if that were not enough to frighten the rest of us into calling for the consumers' main champion to be banished, Sir Iain paints what he sees as an even more horrifying picture in which the industry comes back under state control.

'The doomsday scenario,' he intones solemnly, 'is that the regulator finds it impossible to regulate – we're almost at that stage now – and then frankly you're tinkering – you don't know what you're doing. You get a chaotic development of different players and networks, convergence of this and that, and then with some left-wing government in the year 2109, it'll all be re-nationalised because it's such a mess.'

Meanwhile, and for some time to come, Britain's national communication regulations will be overlaid by the pronouncements of the European Union, in which consultation and memorandum intertwine around one another in a multilingual gavotte designed to exhaust all but the most intrepid explorer.

The European Commission in Brussels has two arms that affect BT: DG13 on information technology and DG4 for competition. Much of the 1990s will be taken up with discussions by these bodies over whether public subscription voice and infrastructure should be liberalised. According to Vallance, they have four options: do nothing; regulate to get rid of high prices, particularly of the international services; complete liberalisation; or merely to liberalise trans-border communications, which might bring prices down but would be very difficult to define.

'I think Brussels will play a significant but slow role,' Sir Iain concedes.

'We take the view that they should liberalise the lot by the beginning of 1995 and issue a Directive along those lines. But the chances of them doing that are relatively slim because, apart from the UK and to a lesser extent the Dutch and the Danes, if you ask most of the countries they'll want liberalisation but not in their time. I think that'll be difficult for the Commission to deal with. It'll happen: I've noticed over the last few years that the main telecommunications operators in Europe have moved from a belief that what has happened in the UK and the USA is an aberration that will go away, into an acceptance that it's coming, probably with privatisation as well, and it's only a matter of time. Of course what they'd like is privatisation and to still keep their monopolies.'

Once the barriers are lifted, BT and the Americans will be first over the fence to claim these new territories. Vallance's goal is nothing less than global coverage, as and when markets and local vested interests permit.

'The ability to go global is dependent on what's happening on the regulatory scene around the world,' he points out, 'and it's all very different. The liberalised world – the UK, the US, Japan – all have different forms of liberalisation and the rest of the world has different forms of illiberalisation. I think that the international services may become like the high seas with opportunities for piracy. The current tariffing and settlement arrangements lead to very high rates of return that I don't think are sustainable. Reciprocal charging rates and correspondent relations between international players will go. If you add that to the convergence of computing, which is not regulated into telecommunications and some of the entertainment networks which are not regulated then you'll probably get a morass which will be impossible to regulate, not too deep into the twenty-first century.'

It is hard to avoid the impression that Sir Iain relishes the prospect of these morasses as cocktails of chaos out of which he expects BT to pull winners. And indeed, the signs are that the technology will in the end defeat the efforts of the pen-pushers to legislate against what is becoming as all-pervading as the printing press, without providing the same degree of physical presence at which to point accusing fingers.

'Satellite communications make a mockery of national monopolies,' says Sir Iain contentedly. 'With satellites, you get into a position where you cannot regulate, like citizens' band radio: it was illegal and then it had to be made legal because it was there. At the moment there are national rules around Europe that make it difficult for satellites, allowing downlinks but not uplinks. But that's due to be liberalised.' The prospect of unfettered telecoms markets is what is making the big groups jockey for position, striking alliances, trying to forge mergers, taking stakes here and there, in anticipation of the day when the only rule is that there are no rules other than the basic legal framework. That is why BT paid nearly £1 billion in 1989 for seventeen per cent of McCaw Cellular Communications, then America's largest mobile-phone operator, but sold the stake to AT&T in 1993 for £1.2 billion after conceding that it could not overcome US regulatory hurdles. However, the money was immediately put towards a £3.8 billion deal in which BT bought twenty per cent of MCI, America's second biggest long-distance telecoms carrier and a research hotbed, and set up a joint venture with the US group to provide voice, data and video to multinational corporations and manage their internal telecoms networks. Just as there were high hopes when the deal was struck with McCaw, so when the MCI agreement was signed Vallance insisted: 'This is the single most important step we have taken in our development outside Britain, and probably the most important development in world telecommunications over the last few years.' Bert Roberts, MCI's chairman, took a cooler line, describing it as merely 'the deal of the century'. Only time would tell whether it would turn into a long-term relationship, or be just another of the many brief romances which fluttered across the industry in the early 1990s.

The mighty engine behind all this activity is the continual advance in telephone-related gadgets, of which Sir Iain's videophone is only one of the more trivial examples. The upcoming wonders of virtual reality may make it possible for groups of people not only to see and hear one another, but by wearing data suits to interact with one another in what appears to each of them to be the same room – even though they are thousands of miles apart. In that sense, radio and fibre links are doing a considerable amount to abolish distance and bring us the nearest thing to instant travel, short of the 'beam me up, Scotty' fantasies of *Star Trek*. The big money is still going to be made on providing long-distance calls, even though their price will come down. Along with that will come the ability to compress the amount of data that is sent down a line, in ways that will make today's faxes seem achingly slow. Faster datacoms, as it is known, will revolutionise business traffic and pave the way for films to be digitalised and sent direct to home computers – or computers hidden in our televisions.

'I think we're on the edge of quite fantastic developments in services across the network,' Sir Iain declares. 'You will see multimedia communications, any time any place, at an economical price. There will be further convergence between telecommunications and computers at the customer interface. And you're seeing convergence of some of the entertainment industries and communication, cable television being the obvious case. Dixons and other electrical retailers are almost bound to be selling more gadgets that will plug into phone lines. If you look at what's happened over the last few years, we've moved away from the fairly standard dial phone into a whole range of types of phones, with more or less intelligence in them – at the simplest level, things like clocks and memories, moving up to fac-simile and video. It's only the imagination that will put limits on what you can do with these phones.'

The other offshoot of the convergence of computing and telecommunica-tions will be more and more intelligence in the network itself, which tele-phone users will have access to – especially call forwarding and messaging systems, which will eventually put the answerphone facility in the network itself, rather than sitting next to your phone amidst a nest of wires.

'I think you'll see radio coming into use for two reasons,' Vallance pre-dicts. 'One is straight mobility, whether you call it cellular or PCN doesn't matter too much. There'll always be some kind of constraint on that, because the radio spectrum is finite, as opposed to the fibre network which is virtu-ally infinite in what it can carry. But more and more ingenious engineers will find more and more ways of using such radio spectrum as there is. Apart from mobility, the second thing you'll see radio spectrum being used for will be as a cheap and easy way to terminate the fixed network, possibly with mobility in and around the home. Like the cordless phone, but there will be lots of different ways of attacking it, many of which we don't even know yet.

'The dependence of society on telecommunications is going to grow. Bank cash machines depend on telecommunications, although you don't think of it. Smart cards to buy things in supermarkets or petrol stations are becoming communications-related. The emergency services and more and more med-ical facilities like remote diagnostics require telecommunications. More and more of our learning and training will be telecommunications-related, for things like distance learning. You'll find that in the information-based sec-tors of industry, more and more work will be moved to people rather than people coming to work. You may even find the terminal decline of the big cities. Most of them were brought about by a combination of access to com-munication routes like sea routes and smokestack industries which required goods to be carried by sea or rail. But in the information industry, you aren't carrying goods, you're actually playing with information.'

A pride and joy of BT is its directory enquiry service, a large chunk of which has been devolved to a series of operators sitting at terminals in their homes in northern Scotland. They have access to what is the biggest database in the UK, and can see colleagues and supervisors through a split screen, so that they can see other people at the same time. They work whatever shifts suit them. 'That work is in a rural setting,' says Sir Iain, 'when not so long ago it would have been in the City of London. A lot of these things are irreversible and many of those information-based industries could be scattered around the place. And they don't even have to be in one country. It's quite possible to export the work to the places where you've got the most value for money in terms of the skills of people.'

BT exports some of its software development to India, where the programmers are in contact with their employers in Britain through a network. 'Heaven knows what the social consequences of all that will be once you get well into the twenty-first century,' Vallance ponders. 'You could have cottage industries in village halls. The main point is that companies can put that work where they get value for money for the skills, rather than shoving it naturally into the centre of the big city. I think the impact of that on BT is very difficult to predict.'

The charging mechanisms for this plethora of gee-whizzery are going to be correspondingly complicated, with add-ons for this and that and discounts for the other. Which suggests that some kind of regulator, if only the backstop of the Office of Fair Trading, will have to keep an eye on the telecoms titans to ensure that they do not rip off customers.

Sir Iain forecasts: 'At the turn of the century I see BT being one of only a handful of major telecommunications global players, with networks across the world. I think with two or three big firms in each market, it's shaping up to being a battle of the global giants. I'd have thought there'll be one or two from North America, one or two from Europe. Japan hasn't started yet, but no doubt when it does start it'll be interesting and they'll be players in a genuinely global sense with others becoming more national. There are a lot of Americans here in a big way but the Japanese stopped themselves entering here because their own circumstances are not very cleverly arranged, with the complete separation of the long distance and the national. The Americans can get in here now with the regional Bell operating companies and most of the cable television companies.

'We could have a substantial interest in Europe, there's no doubt about that, having moved across, in part, into the computing services business. We could offer pan-European services of one type or another, probably have quite a significant interest in North America and to a lesser extent in the Pacific Rim. Here in the UK we could by that point be providing the full gamut of services, including a combination of multi-media cable television.'

CHAPTER **24**

DEREK WANLESS

of National Westminster Bank

DEREK WANLESS is, to say the least of it, unusual among the close-knit and often secretive fraternity of banking's elite. A Geordie who rightly makes no effort to hide his origins, he stepped into the top executive job at National Westminster Bank at the age of forty-four – an age when most of his contemporaries would have been grateful just to creep in the back door of head office. Wanless, by contrast, had been familiar with NatWest's imposing headquarters behind the Bank of England for a good six years before that, first as director of personal banking services, then successively general manager of UK branch business, and chief executive of UK financial services. He was not only the bank's youngest chief executive, but the first to boast a degree: first-class honours in maths at King's College, Cambridge, where he was senior wrangler.

This is the sort of apparently effortless success which is not exactly designed to endear anyone to older colleagues who have been passed over, dashing long-cherished family ambitions of careers that might have been crowned with the supreme accolade. So, on the face of it, Wanless should have been prepared for hostility lurking in the thick-pile carpeting. He brushed off the danger as if it were a spot of dust on a lapel. 'Oh, I've been used to dealing with older people for a long time,' he ripostes. 'When I went to Newcastle in 1982 as area director, I didn't have a branch manager who was younger than me. Some were twenty-five years older than me, and I did that all right. My approach was always to be quite hard on the facts of any case, but sympathetic about the people, providing they were doing their best. It was never a ruthless style, though it could have been. I'm not like that, unless people were sloppy or not trying to perform, in which case I have

237

no problem about dealing with people who are freewheeling along.'

In other words, I'll have a pint if you're buying, thanks, but don't take liberties. It is only to be expected that there should be a streak of hard steel running through the man brought in to restore NatWest's fortunes after the disastrous Blue Arrow affair. Blue Arrow was a temporary employment group that launched an £837 million rights issue of new shares just before the 1987 stock market crash. Blue Arrow's price collapsed in line with the market, and few wanted the new shares. That left half of them with the underwriters, including County NatWest, the bank's merchant banking arm. County disguised its holding in the hope that the Blue Arrow price might recover. Department of Trade and Industry inspectors investigated County's role and decided that the stock market was misled, provisions of the Companies Act were not complied with and there was no justification for what happened. The upshot was an almighty upheaval in the top management of NatWest, which finally resulted in Wanless's predecessor, Tom Frost, relinquishing the group chief executive's seat and becoming deputy chairman as a further DTI inquiry began hearing evidence. Frost was totally exonerated, but by then Wanless was in command.

Wanless was thus given a possible sixteen-year tenure on one of banking's top jobs, if he stays up to the normal retirement age of sixty. That is an ample span in which to bend even a change-resistant organisation like a UK clearing bank to a leader's vision. Wanless's task up to and into the early years of the next century is to come up with a vision that will give NatWest the ability to maintain its position against increasingly fierce competition.

'Banking was one of the industries in the 1980s that in some senses didn't feel it had to make choices,' Wanless points out. 'It had or could get all the capital it needed, and therefore had freedom to pursue whatever strategies it liked. One of the things we see very clearly now is that the business is constrained. We do have to make choices. Even the fact that we're making them is a startling change.'

The Wanless tale begins on the terraces of St James's Park, home of Newcastle United Football Club. That is where his father, a cement storeman for Blue Circle, used to take his only child on Saturday afternoons. Derek craved the thrill of pulling on United's distinctive black-and-white striped shirt, in the days before they went on sale to any fan willing to pay their inflated price. Instead, he is to be glimpsed on the pavilion balcony at Lord's cricket ground each September, helping to distribute the prizes to the finalist of the annual NatWest Bank Trophy.

He won a scholarship to Newcastle Royal Grammar School, and thence

Derek Wanless

BORN: 29 September, 1947

EDUCATED: Royal Grammar School, Newcastle-upon-Tyne, and King's College, Cambridge

MARRIED: Vera West, 1971. One son, four daughters

CAREER:

1970	National Westminster Bank
1982	Area Director, North East Area
1985	Area Director, West Yorkshire
1986	Director of Personal Banking
1989	General Manager, UK branch business
1990	Chief Executive, UK Financial Services
1991	Director of National Westminster Bank
1992	Group Chief Executive

OTHER INTERESTS: Chairman of Financial Sector of Advisory committee for Business and the Environment

NATIONAL WESTMINSTER BANK PLC

HEAD OFFICE: 41 Lothbury, London EC2P 2BP
Tel: 071-726 1000

ACTIVITIES: Banking, insurance, mortgages, credit cards, stockbroking, corporate finance

MAIN BRANDS: National Westminster, Access, NatWest Stockbrokers, NatWest Capital Markets

to Cambridge. But in between school playground and ivy-clad quadrangle he got a job as a junior at the then Westminster Bank's Darlington branch. Wanless recalls: 'I did all the jobs, from making the tea to fetching the ledgers from the safe.' He so impressed the manager that he won one of only two university scholarships awarded by the bank each year. That secured his finances and, although no strings were attached, gave him an automatic employment opportunity. 'I wanted to get out into the commercial world,' he explains. 'I had become more and more interested in business through going back to work at the bank in Newcastle during my vacations.'

From his panelled chief executive's cockpit, he sees NatWest in terms of four clear business sectors: UK branches (biggest), NatWest Markets (wholesale activities worldwide), NatWest Bancorp (US retail) and International Business – Lombard North Central, Ulster Bank, Coutts & Co., international private banking and the European retail arms.

County NatWest has been sorted out in rapid order after the Blue Arrow fiasco, with merchant banking, treasury, capital markets and corporate finance all packed into NatWest Markets. There is less chance of the different parts competing with one another that way, and head office can keep a closer eye on what is a very different animal from a high street bank branch.

Otherwise, Wanless has been concentrating on repositioning the group for the challenges of the 1990s. He says: 'During the recession, bankers kept their long-held position, and a pretty unpopular one it is, too! I don't think the recession changed it: there is a lot of anecdotal stuff about individual cases where one side of the story is reported, and some newspapers seemed out to get us. In terms of the broader research, I think it's fair to say that customers say the service is getting better, with remote banking, Automated Teller Machines and other things. But it's probably not getting better as fast as customer expectations are getting higher. There is an increasing demand for a 100 per cent error-free service, more and more rapid response to enquiries. But if you ask people to relate it back to the actual service they got five, ten, fifteen years ago, there are many services in which the service is better, but the expectation has got greater and greater. We're continually trying to catch up with the expectation.'

So Wanless is trying to re-humanise NatWest. In 1987 he introduced the idea of personal account executives to NatWest, playing to customer demand to build relationships with banks rather than be treated as a mere number. The typical NatWest personal account executive probably has about 400 customers, depending on where they are and the nature of the customer.

'There has been a benign neglect of the personal customer base in banking,' says Wanless. 'But it's a question of getting into place a lot of building blocks, to enable us to move forward strongly in the personal banking side. When I was director of personal banking services, we put resources back into the system and got the technology in place to do it. Looking back, we've changed a hell of a lot. As you go through it, it's like watching something in slow motion, but we've now got over 400 personal account executives in place, plus the back-up teams behind them. But it's a big exercise. It's moving faster now, because we've proved it works and we know how to do it, how to train people to do it, how to keep them up to date, how to give them the technology to help them to do it better.'

The technology enables the personal bankers to stay personal. No one in practice can keep the details of 400 customers in his or her head. So Wanless ordered a massive computer system containing all relevant details of all customers. It took four years to assemble. Now, if anybody in any branch or remote location needs to look up a customer's records, they can see everything in one file. Wanless claims that it is possibly the biggest relational database in the world – as opposed to British Telecom's directory inquiries database, which is bigger but simpler.

'It's about as attractive as building the foundations of a house,' Wanless adds. 'In itself it's not terribly exciting. But when you think what we can do with that in the future, in terms of operational efficiency in the branch network, in terms of service to you from a remote location twenty-four hours a day, seven days a week, 365 days a year, it opens up tremendous possibilities for customer service. It opens up possibilities for us looking at you, in total, all the things you've got, what your personal financial services requirements are going to be in the future. Can we afford to give you a personal bank manager, a personal account executive, who can develop our relationship with you, and make sure you know about all the savings, insurance and investment products we've got, mortgages and so on? That way we can make much better decisions about who we can afford to give that level of service to.'

That is being supported by telephone banking, which every bank is quietly moving into after the success of Midland Bank's First Direct service. NatWest has its Action Line, but like some other banks and unlike Midland, NatWest reckons customers want both an orthodox current account and a twenty-four-hours-a-day telephone service on top.

'People want aspects of remote service as part of their current account,' Wanless insists. 'I think everybody in the market will be driven towards that, where people have a current account and the possibility of a relationship on a local basis, but also the benefits of all those cash dispensers, and Switch or Visa/Delta at point of sale, so that they don't have cheque books, they don't have paper in the way that they used to. The Association of Payment and Clearing Systems sees a very sharp decline in the number of cheques, the number of pieces of paper that will be around the banking system in the next decade. That has implications for what work is done on the high street or in processing centres. There should be less of it about, and that will change the nature of the branch network that we need to serve customers. There will be no paper passing from the "shop" to anywhere else. There is potential for smart cards like Mondex developing as well. It's another way in which work will be taken out of the branch network and done automatically. They can be programmed to say how many units a card has got left, in the style of Phonecards, and reloaded down the phone line. It's all part of the communications revolution.'

But plugging the latest gadgetry into the system is relatively straightforward. If it makes financial sense, do it. However, life in the banking parlours is not so simple. Wanless has been confronting the more perplexing transition from the affluent eighties to the nervous nineties, when nothing is quite as clear as it seems and tough decisions have to be made if NatWest is to remain competitive. Assumptions are being challenged, shibboleths overturned.

'One of the things that banks and companies generally have done wrong has been to plan as if there is one view of the future,' Wanless points out. 'It was at its worst in the late 1980s, when people had this over-optimism, which NatWest suffered from as much as anyone. Now I think it's important to have the ability to sit back and say "What if the world's a different place? How does our business look? What risks can I really take? How can I have contingency plans ready if one of those particularly gloomy pictures looks like it's the one that's going to come about?" There's a lot of detailed thinking which needs to be done, thinking which banks generally tended not to do in the second half of the 1980s, but instead tried to push along a central path.'

Understandably, Wanless has looked closely at NatWest's retail operations. It is where he came from, and the focus has switched there from the previously pre-eminent corporate end of the business as profit margins on corporate lending have been squeezed. Hole-in-the-wall cash machines and a move towards more postal and telephone banking have challenged the wisdom of having vast branch estates. NatWest alone is expected to close more than 500 of the 2,600 branches it had in 1993.

'The retail end is very competitive,' Wanless explained. 'Take new entrants to current accounts like building societies: there was a thinking that if building societies have a cost-income ratio of only forty-something per cent, and banks have a cost-income ratio of sixty-something per cent, building societies can come in and do current account business more cheaply than the banks. It just didn't stand up to analysis, because our mortgage and savings business has a cost-income ratio very similar to that of a building society. But we can't do current account business with the same cost-income ratio, and nor can building societies. So there are a lot of fairly superficial bits of thinking going round about that. Inevitably, the number of building societies has changed dramatically over the last two decades, and will continue to change, possibly sharply. Exactly how much, is going to depend on the UK housing market to a considerable degree. But, when we look at the personal market, too much of the high street is taken up with financial services. Given the way technology is changing the business, there are too many people occupied in retail banking right across the whole market place. Technology is having a massive effect.

'The number of branches on the high street is changing as that happens. We've been reducing them by over a hundred a year since 1990. If anything, that rate'll increase. How quickly it'll increase will depend on how successful we are at building relationships with customers. The better we are at it, the more evidence there is that customers welcome the chance to pop into a physical location and talk about financial affairs, the more branches we'll have. The more customers who say "we'd like somebody visiting us in our homes," the more of a dilemma there will be between investing in branches and in peripatetic staff. At the end of the day customer requirements will dictate what we do.'

One customer requirement that banks found increasingly difficult to meet in the early 1990s was that there should be no charges for personal accounts that were in credit. Although a generation of customers had grown up with the notion that this was how it always was, free-if-in-credit dated only from the early 1980s.

'To a degree,' he argues, 'the future of free-if-in-credit banking depends on what happens to the cost structure of the business, the extent to which we can get costs down. If interest rates are low and if technology doesn't make massive changes to the cost base, then we will have a lot of unprofitable personal customers, even more than there are now. Then it depends on how well we sell other services. You can have a loss leader if it leads to a profitable growing customer base, doing a lot of mortgage, savings, insurance and investment business. If in fact we're not doing as much of that as we'd like although we'll be fighting for it, we can't put up with a loss on a substantial customer base. We'll have charges under review right through the 1990s. There's no business that doesn't have its charges under review. In some ways it's easier to run a business if you've got income and costs falling in more or less the same place, and having less cross-subsidisation than we've got. We'll never get rid of it all, but we've got to get rid of some of it in the 1990s. Either that, or certain types of customer will just become so unprofitable to the banks that nobody will want to do business with them – though I think it's more likely that the solution will be to increase prices.'

A burden shared by building societies and banks is that people find it hard to see the value of the service that they get. Indeed, that is a problem with services as a whole, compared with selling goods you can pick up and peer at. But the banks suffer most of all because they do not have the goodwill attached to building societies and people have a simple but understandable belief if they put a tenner in they are entitled to get a tenner out again. Banks on the other hand, in common with virtually every other financial organisation, exist on skimming a little of the torrents of cash that pass through their hands. Never mind that there is hardly another country in the world that has free banking in the way it took root in the UK.

'It is anomalous,' Wanless agrees, 'but we certainly wouldn't understate customer attitudes to it. Unless customers actually value the service they're getting, then people aren't going to pay for it. You've got to give people perceived value. Because it's an intangible service, that's not a particularly easy matter for us to do.'

The other hot topic in retail financial services in the 1990s is bancassurance, the banks' move into offering life insurance to their chequing customers and the public at large. The potential they have for converting their huge customer lists into buying insurance policies have certainly worried the traditional insurance companies, who thought they had their patch to themselves. NatWest Life certainly made early inroads into the market, suggesting that they were going to offer strong competition.

'By 1993 we had a team of 1,400 insurance advisers, which we built up in a couple of years from nothing and are talking to customers about life assurance and pensions,' says Wanless. 'They've got desks in branches, but they spend most of their time out visiting customers. They've got laptop computers they can plug in wherever they go to get quotes up on the screen. Technology is having a massive effect in a way which people really haven't quite caught on to what's happening and what's possible, because there isn't enough of it yet. The people who are going to find life very difficult are the small operators, who don't have a warm customer base in the way that a bank or a big building society does. How well the building societies can do depends on the extent to which they grow from their natural core business of mortgage and basic savings.'

However, it is still a massive cultural change for banks' senior managements to be giving top priority to such matters as life insurance and keeping personal customers sweet, after decades in which the high-rolling, big borrowing company client was the apple of their eyes. It is so much more flattering to be talking deep strategy and high finance with a captain of industry than to ponder how to keep the rank and file in order.

Two main factors have prompted the change. One is the impact of bad debts and the banks' painfully-learned understanding of risk in markets, like property and the Third World, that were thought to be pretty well risk-free. Secondly, the fact that banks now have to keep a minimum amount of capital in relation to their lending.

Wanless confirms: 'That's had a tremendous effect on the way people perceive businesses like large corporate lending. Banks used to feel they could afford to do business at the margin. They weren't making an adequate return, but if they had surplus capital it didn't matter. Whereas people now are looking much more closely at the total capital position in every bank and saying it really doesn't make much sense to do business if they don't get good returns. Banks are much, much keener now on looking at how much capital they've got tied up in each of their businesses. They are looking at major corporate lending and saying "do we really want to be in that?" Increasingly, as we've seen in London, Japanese and American banks have taken a view that they didn't want to be part of that any more in the same way they had been. So the margins certainly improved in that sort of market.'

The question is, what will happen as the economic climate improves? The so-called capital adequacy rules aren't going to change back, so in the major corporate market the banks have less and less chance to lend a lot of money very cheaply. But banks will always look at their total relationship with a customer and stretch a point if a good payer wants a bit extra.

'It's a change in attitude towards the customer and customer relationship,' Wanless admits. 'What we've got to do is to build up the other services which the corporate might come to us for, the value-added, fee-based service that doesn't take a lot of capital. We're doing that increasingly. The trick's going to be to get the right balance of advisory services, where we're earning fees, and putting our balance sheet behind a company to lend large amounts of money when the need arises. In other words, the customer's going to have to want some sort of partnership with us because we're attractive and strong, we've got the relationship, we're there if they want it. At the same time we're getting the other bits of business because we're good enough to do it. So, from our point of view, we've got to build good corporate finance, capital markets, equities operations. There's not going to be any room for second-rate operations. Nobody's going to do business in most of the markets just because they think, "Oh, they're good, we might need them one day." We've got to be up with the market in all those areas, to get the business.'

That very different view of how to handle corporate customers is just part of the overall no-holds-barred re-examination of banking practice that has been going on in the 1990s, according to Wanless. He sees one of the fundamental issues of the next few years as being to what degree banking as most people think of it – processing payments and transactions – is just a special case of something else. Are there real skills in financial services and banking? Or are the banks just in the game of processing confidential information?

'That is what some of it starts to become through the 1990s,' Wanless believes. 'I think there are still resource management skills, lending skills, savings and investment skills, distribution skills, that will enable us to preserve financial services institutions. I think the way the whole industry is regulated will probably help ensure that happens. Because the regulators are faced with regulating something that isn't just a bank but a conglomerate of other types of institution. Apart from anything else, that will help preserve the present institutions that we call banks. In the personal sector, if you look at how people actually manage their finances, there's not a whole mass of sophisticated personal finance managers out there. By and large, people don't know what's available because they've got better things to do with their time than find out. They actually just want to know who they can trust, and we've got the opportunity to be part of that. I think the customer need is going to be there for that personal service and personalisation of financial services.'